THE NILE TO THE NETHERLANDS

The Nile to the Netherlands

Our Faith Journey

BRIAN LEA

THANKFUL BOOKS

Published by Thankful Books
70 Milton Road, Eastbourne, East Sussex BN21 1SS, England.

ISBN 13:   978 1 905084 06 7
ISBN 10:   1 905084 06 4

Book design and production for the publisher by
Bookprint Creative Services, P.O. Box 827, BN21 3YJ, England.
Printed in Great Britain.

For our grandchildren

Ulysse, Timothy, Demi, Benjamin,
Declan and Ivan

CONTENTS

FOREWORD

In this rich and interesting book Brian Lea looks back on a journey that begins in Birmingham and terminates, in retirement, in Eastbourne. In between, we are drawn into Brian and Gill's life as, like nomads, they move from country to country, culture to culture, and share the Christian message wherever they go. It is riveting narrative through which Brian displays a masterly gift for detail in which individuals, who had influenced them both, are brought onto the stage and take their bow.

Several features of the book are particularly noteworthy. First there is Brian and Gill's personal faith and love of Jesus Christ which is the compelling centre of their common life. In spite of ups and downs, disappointments and opposition, they keep the faith and see many rewards for their steady faithfulness and fierce commitment. Then there is the presence of Gill in the story. Like all outstanding clergy wives, Gill was not only entirely supportive of her husband but also exercised her own gifts and discipleship alongside Brian. The book reveals the nature of their united ministry and reminds us how much the church owes to women like Gill.

Lastly, Brian weaves into his story the lives of remarkable men like James Hannington, surely one of the Anglican Communion's great saints, and yet, today, scarcely known.

My final reflection after reading the manuscript is that this autobiography of a ministry that takes in Sudan, France, Spain and Holland is worthy of a wide readership. Not many people have been privileged to have had such a ministry: and among those who have, not all have pursued it with as much energy, humility and grace as have Brian and Gill Lea.

Lord George Carey.

AUTHOR'S PREFACE

"Did you have to preach in French?" I am sometimes asked when I have just given a talk describing the life of an English-speaking chaplaincy church in France. I realise that this particular listener hasn't even grasped the fact the vast majority of our Sunday services are in English. Part of the reason for writing this book is to paint a picture in words of the often varied and vibrant Christian life of many an expatriate congregation worshipping in English in different parts of the world. Many from Britain spend a part of their working life in an overseas environment. Others travel abroad in retirement seeking "a place in the sun". This book seeks to describe the kind of welcoming church life that they may well find, if not on their doorstep, then within reasonable travel distance from their new home.

Many family members and friends have encouraged me to write this book and have helped me prepare it for publication. David and Angela Marshall lent us their house in the south of France so that we could concentrate undisturbed on the task in hand. My wife, Gill, helped sort out letters and papers and often added wise words of advice. Our nephew,

Justin Hunt, the senior graphic designer for Weidenfeld and Nicolson, illustrated the cover of the book. Gill's brother, David Hunt, formerly head of the English department and Registrar at Haileybury College, proofread the manuscript as did our friend Valerie Thomas. We are particularly grateful to Lord Carey for his kind and generous Foreword. David Windsor offered to provide photocopies of the original manuscript for the proofreaders. Edward England, formerly of Hodder and Stoughton, read the original draft and offered much encouragement and useful advice. We are grateful also to Dorothy Lowe and to Andrew Wheeler for kindly allowing me to quote from their respective books: *Don't bother to unpack* and *But God is not defeated*.

Gill and I have both benefited in so many ways from the generous support we have received in times past from staff members of the Church Mission Society and later from members of the Intercontinental Church Society. Many Christians in the Sudan, the Diocese of Europe and the Diocese of Chichester have also inspired us on our faith journey. To all who have helped us on our way, we want to say, "Thank you".

CHAPTER ONE

THE TRAVEL BUG

An anxious, grim-faced group of adults was huddled around an old-fashioned wireless. The date was 3rd September 1939. Prime Minister Neville Chamberlain was addressing the nation: "I have to tell you . . . that consequently this country is at war with Germany." I was aged five at the time and of course I had no idea what it was all about, though even as a child I sensed that something serious was happening. And perhaps this was the beginning of a childhood awareness that there was a bigger world out there, way beyond the confines of suburban Birmingham.

After that broadcast events moved quickly for countless people and – certainly for our family – life would never be the same again. My mother took my brother Richard and me away from our home in Woodbourne Road, Birmingham, to live as paying guests on a farm in Herefordshire. There was no electricity and winter evenings were illuminated by oil lamps. My father was too old to be called-up so he continued to work in Birmingham and became an air-raid warden by night and coming down to the farm at weekends. Our stay in Llangarron lasted only three months and in January 1940 we moved to a rented house in Malvern owned by a Jersey family named de Carteret. This made it possible for me to attend a local day school.

Meanwhile, my grandfather left his home in Le Touquet, where he had been secretary of the golf club since 1931, and came to live near us in Malvern. I remember his telling me that the last person he said good-bye to when he left France was P.G. Wodehouse. The cinema in Great Malvern was popular during the war and newsreels were avidly devoured. One such film depicted in graphic detail the bombing of Rotterdam in May 1940. Little did I know that some sixty years later I would be preaching at a little Anglican church in that great city! From time to time I would ask my mother: "Are we winning the war?" Invariably I received the rather clipped reply: "Not yet, dear!"

The fall of France in the early summer of 1940 was followed swiftly by the German occupation of the Channel Islands. The de Carteret family, in whose house we were living, returned to live in Malvern so we were on the move again, this time to The White Cottage in the village of Pulbrook, on the edge of Malvern. My father continued to come home at weekends. He spent much of his time in the garden growing mountains of vegetables. Meanwhile I was packed off to a preparatory school which had been evacuated from Bromley to Malvern Wells. This was just as well, as the Bromley school building was eventually reduced to a heap of rubble by a flying bomb. The school was presided over by a bachelor headmaster who was extremely free with the cane. Wrong answers to questions in a geometry lesson would be rewarded with a beating inflicted with the help of a pair of wooden blackboard compasses.

The war tended to dominate the thinking of everyone during the 1940s and we youngsters at school were no exception. Newspapers carried maps which indicated the position of opposing armies and we would follow the ebb and flow of battles in the depths of the Soviet Union, the deserts of North Africa, and the jungles of Malaya. Graphic newsreels at the local cinema increased my awareness of a bigger world out there which was full of interest and excitement.

Most of my family were firmly rooted in England. My father worked in a long-established family firm of estate agents in Birmingham. The great exception to this rule was my Uncle Colin (Sir Colin Thornley as he later became). He served in the Colonial Service in West Africa in the 1930s and during the war he was private secretary to Oliver Stanley, the Secretary of State for the Colonies. Later he was to hold senior posts in the administration of Kenya and then Uganda before concluding his career overseas as Governor of British Honduras. In later life he entered a second career as the Director of the Save the Children Fund. I always admired Colin Thornley and his wife Betty and I followed their career in different parts of the world with great interest. Knowing them was certainly a factor in planting the travel bug within me.

Within our home, the Christian religion was very much taken for granted along with membership of the Conservative party. I believe my father had a very definite but also a very private faith. Every night he would kneel beside his bed and say his prayers and he was a regular 8 o'clock communion man all his life. During the war years my parents' marriage grew increasingly troubled as they grew further and further apart. My mother struck up a close friendship with a Mrs Polly Cartland who lived near us on the edge of Malvern. She was the mother of Barbara Cartland, the author, and a devout Roman Catholic. My mother started attending a High Anglican church in Malvern Link. I found the drama, the colours and the smell of incense in this crowded church attractive after a diet of dull old Matins and school religion. I was prepared for confirmation by the vicar, Canon Hartley. I remember little about the sessions I had with him, apart from being obliged to make my confession. The confirmation service was conducted, in June 1946, by the Bishop of Worcester, a former General Secretary of the Church Mission Society. My much-loved grandfather (ex-Le Touquet) rarely attended church but came and supported me at this service. He died from a heart attack a few days later.

In 1947 our family moved to the village of Barford, near Warwick, and I was sent as a boarder to Shrewsbury School. It was during the school summer holidays that my mother told me that she was soon to leave my father. The last time I saw them together was when they drove me to Shrewsbury for the start of that autumn term. I am sure that I gained much from life at Shrewsbury but I certainly would not describe my time spent there as the happiest days of my life! There were tensions between my parents as to how much holiday time was to be spent with each one of them and I found myself involved in sorting out the arrangements.

I was fortunate during those school years to have a sympathetic and understanding housemaster in Hugh Brooke. He was a glorious eccentric who managed to combine within his character both earthiness and godliness. Towards the end of his life as a schoolmaster, he was ordained to the priesthood and he ended his life as minister of a rural parish in Essex. I was a curate by the time I went to visit "Brookie" in hospital as he lay dying. Before I left him, he asked me to say a prayer for him and he handed me his prayer book. I chose one of the collects that was full of resurrection hope. After the prayer, he commented wryly that he was glad to see that I managed to combine faith, hope and clarity. He had heard every word of it and added his own "Amen". The late John Peel, the famous disc jockey and broadcaster, described Hugh Brooke as "the greatest man I ever knew." Such was the old boy network in those days that at the end of my time at Shrewsbury, where I acquired modest A-levels in French and German, I was offered a place at St John's College, Cambridge, where I studied for a degree in Estate Management in the expectation that I would eventually enter the family firm of estate agents based in Birmingham.

My years at Shrewsbury had done little to foster my interest in the wider world in spite of teaching me some French and German. In those days language study in schools was largely confined to reading and writing the language and the oral side of language study was for the most part neglected. There was no thought of exchange trips with French or German families, a custom which would be considered normal in today's world.

I arrived at Cambridge not at all sure about what I believed or what I wanted to do with my life. A new start at university seemed a good time to review my attitude to the Christian faith. If it were true, then I must take it seriously and live by it; but if were not true, then I must abandon it. My initial encounters with the Christian Union were not encouraging. I was pursued by one zealous member who was always trying to get me to attend meetings and services. I remember dodging into doorways to avoid him when I saw him approaching. I went to what was called a "freshers' squash" at which we were addressed by a retired army major on the merits of Christian belief, but this did little to stir my interest or my conscience. Later that term I was visited by a former school friend called Peter Whittome. He had discovered a living Christian faith during his period of National Service and I couldn't help noticing a remarkable change in his whole approach to life. At school he had been known as "scruffy Pete" and he gave the impression of being careless and idle in his very laid-back way. But the Peter who confronted me at Cambridge had discovered a fresh purpose in life and a new Person to follow. I was intrigued. It so happened that Peter's visit to Cambridge coincided with a mission to students led by the young Rector of All Souls', Langham Place, the Reverend John Stott. I was easily persuaded by Peter to start attending the nightly meetings in Great St Mary's Church, at which Stott was speaking. Here we were presented with a series of talks that explained the basics of Christian faith step by step. I remember being particularly struck by the sermon on the cross of Christ. The words: "The Son of God loved me and gave himself for me" were printed indelibly on my mind. It was being made aware of that sacrificial love that brought me to my knees and moved me to surrender my life to Jesus Christ. Thus I was set on a path of Christian discipleship in which I have sought to walk, however falteringly, ever since.

And it was during those three years at Cambridge that the travel bug, which had long lain dormant, was stirred into fresh life. For there was a strong interest in overseas missionary work amongst the Christian Union members. I found myself attending the occasional missionary breakfast in Cambridge restaurants which were addressed by well-known missionary speakers such as Joe Church and Cecil Bewes. We were challenged to ask ourselves whether God was calling us to serve him abroad. Biographies of former missionary heroes such as Hudson Taylor and C.T. Studd were eagerly devoured. Inspired by The Cambridge Seven (of which C.T. Studd was a part) a fellowship of students committed to overseas mission formed The Cambridge Seventy, which I joined. And yet there was a touch of unreality about our missionary enthusiasm. In the early 1950s the British colonial empire in Africa was still in place. The bishops who led the Anglican churches were still nearly all of Western extraction. Macmillan had not yet made his famous "wind of change" speech. Most people in our islands had not yet woken up to the fact that the demise of the British Empire was imminent and students at Cambridge were no exception. The Church Mission Society, however, under the visionary leadership of Canon Max Warren, did much to prepare missionary recruits to face with realism the changing world that they were about to face.

As a student at Cambridge I was brought into touch with C.M.S. by Dr. Donald Denman, the Head of the Estate Management department. Donald was a lay reader in one of the Cambridge churches and he became something of a mentor fo me. He could see that my interest in estate management was on the wane (I only managed to achieve a poor third class degree in the subject) and he suggested that I might meet a friend of his, Cecil Bewes, who was then the Africa Secretary for C.M.S. My estate management course included a wide range of agricultural subjects and it was thought that I might prove useful as an agricultural missionary. Stephen and Ann Carr in the Sudan had been showing how useful and effective such farming skills could prove in rural parts of Africa. Cecil Bewes paid quite frequent visits to Cambridge where one of his sons, Richard, later to become Rector of All Souls', Langham Place, was a student at Emmanuel College, so an interview with him was soon arranged. Little did I know at the time that a few years later I would meet my future wife, Gillian, in the Bewes home in Blackheath.

That Cambridge encounter with "Uncle Cecil", as he eventually became (since he was Gillian's uncle), was to lead on to an open offer of service with C.M.S. As a potential candidate I was obliged to report for interviews with three great C.M.S. stalwarts: Martin Parsons, vicar of a large church in Blackheath, Stanley Betts (later Bishop of Maidstone) and Cyril Bowles who was principal of Ridley Hall, Cambridge at the time and was soon to become Bishop of Derby. There followed a final interview with a large collection of venerable-looking dog-collared and besuited clerics around a huge oval mahogany table in a committee room at the C.M.S. headquarters which was then in Salisbury Square, just off Fleet Street in London. It was a somewhat awesome, and even terrifying experience, but their bark was worse than their bite. They dealt kindly with the rather raw student who appeared before them and I was duly accepted as a candidate in training.

Gill comes from what is best described as a large Christian clan, brimming over with clergy and missionaries, all interconnected by marriage. The clan includes such names as Bewes, de Berry, Hunt, Eddison, Guinness and Bridger. When it comes to a wedding or a funeral, the clergy are almost falling over each other in order to take a small part in the proceedings and it is not unknown for a small family choir to be formed minutes before such a service is about to begin.

Missionaries on leave were often invited to stay by Gill's parents, the ever hospitable Eric and Carol Hunt. Auntie Pearl de Berry, who served as a missionary with Scripture Union in South India, was a frequent visitor. She would arrive at a nearby railway station and perch herself on the platform surrounded by a motley collection of battered suitcases and parcels done up in brown paper and string. She would then summon her brother-in-law, Eric Hunt by telephone to come and fetch her, in much the same way as she gave orders to porters to carry her luggage in South India. She was a very forthright lady, famous for speaking her mind. On one occasion when she was addressed by a bus conductor as "ducks", she was heard to reply: "Do I look like a duck? Do I talk like a duck? Do I walk like a duck?" Another missionary relation of Gill's was Sir Albert Cook, the founder of Mengo Hospital in Kampala, Uganda. Later it seemed appropriate that Andrew, our son, should be born in that hospital.

Gill's uncle, Keith de Berry, was the youngest child in a large family with a host of older sisters. Sylvia and Carol came just above Keith in the pecking order. There came a time when these two sisters grew somewhat tired of their younger brother. So they conceived a cunning plan to dispose of their tiresome sibling without causing him any undue pain: they would initiate a missionary call to distant parts! So one night they hid under young Keith's bed and when lights went out the two little girls started to chant in unearthly tones: "You're wanted in Formosa. You're wanted in Formo–sa!" Poor young Keith ran screaming in terror from the room and the two girls were severely reprimanded. Keith grew up to be a distinguished clergyman who for many years was Rector of St Aldate's Church in Oxford. He was a gifted evangelist and many people of all ages were drawn into a lively Christian faith through his ministry. He and his wife Betty (née Eddison) enjoyed travelling abroad, especially during their retirement years. As as far as I know, however, they never visited Formosa!

In spite of missionary relatives and much interest in the work of Christian mission, both within her home and also at Clarendon, the boarding school in North Wales where she was educated, Gill felt no particular pull in an overseas direction. She enjoyed family holidays with her father in France and Spain as they toured around from one bed-and-breakfast to another in an ancient dormobile, but that was as far as her foreign interests went. Gill has always been fashion-conscious and she could never picture herself wearing the sort of clothes that most returning female missionaries were inclined to wear when they were invited to speak at school or at her local church. I suspect too that she suffered from a surfeit of interminable missionary slide-shows, which were meat and drink to the speaker but of limited interest to a teenage audience. Such shows always ended in a ritual "ah!" of relief when the inevitable sunset appeared on the screen to round off the performance.

Cecil Bewes, Keith de Berry and Gill on the day before our wedding – April 1963

Gill never turned away from the profound Christian faith of her parents, however. Their home could by no means be described as dull or dour. They both had a finely tuned sense of humour and an atmosphere of warmth, welcome and fun pervaded their home. And strangers always found a welcome there. It was a climate within which Christian faith was nurtured in all of their five children. But for Gill, holiday visits to Capernwray Hall (a Christian conference centre in Lancashire) and summer beach missions in Cornwall proved to be times when her faith was deepened. Gill's Auntie Ivy de Berry had been a police court missioner (a forerunner of the probation service). So it was no surprise to those who knew her well when Gill, with her great interest in people, decided to study for a diploma in social sciences at Leicester University, with a view to becoming a probation officer.

We first met in 1959 in the Blackheath home of Cecil and Sylvia Bewes when I was on my first home leave from the Sudan. I was staying with the Bewes family for a few weeks whilst doing a short Arabic course at the School of Oriental and African Studies in London. We met again several times during that leave and then I returned to the Sudan for a further two years, during which time we kept in touch through the occasional letter. I had not forgotten the attractive probation officer in training and I looked her up again as soon as I returned to the U.K. for a further leave. Time was short and we saw a good deal of each other during the course of two or three months, towards the end of which period we got engaged. Gill never felt that she had any particular missionary call, but she realised that in marrying me, she would be required to become a missionary with the C.M.S. in her own right. It seems that God uses a whole variety of ways in which to implant the travel bug in those whom he calls to serve in different parts of his world.

On our wedding day, 27th April 1963,
in Esher Parish Church

Almost immediately after we became engaged, I was back in the Sudan for a further nine months whilst Gill worked in South London in the Probation Service. We then had three months in which to get to know each other again and to rebuild our relationship before I returned to Omdurman and Gill embarked on a year's C.M.S. missionary training at Foxbury in Kent. The period of our engagement proved extremely difficult for both of us and it was due only to the grace of God and plenty of strong family support that we ever made it to the wedding service in the parish church of Esher on a brilliant late-April day in 1963. Uncle Keith de Berry took the service; Uncle Cecil Bewes preached the sermon (on our Lord sending people out two-by-two), and cousin Richard Bewes led the intercessions.

CHAPTER TWO

READY, STEADY, GO

I was a mere twenty-one years of age when C.M.S. accepted me as a candidate, and it was suggested that I should gain a year's work experience doing an ordinary job in the U.K. So I went to work on a farm near our home in Warwickshire where they bred Aberdeen Angus cattle for exhibiting at the annual Smithfield Agricultural Show. During that year, I helped with the village church Sunday School and ran a youth club which met in a freezing-cold barn close to the Rectory. In the summer we joined forces with the youth group from St Mark's Church in Leamington and ran a church-based holiday for young people under the leadership of John Ramell (a recently ordained curate) in a large rambling house overlooking the bay at Polzeath in Cornwall. For many of our young people in those post-war years it was the first seaside holiday that they had ever experienced. The discovery of the house in Cornwall, which had just been bought by the Revd David Bishop as a holiday home, came after weeks of searching for suitable holiday accommodation for this youth venture. It was a wonderful answer to my prayers just a few days before the holiday plans were due to be abandoned through failure to find anywhere to go.

My father had by now remarried a widow, Molly Payne. She and her three sons came to live with us in Barford joining forces with my father, my brother Richard, and me. The seven of us formed a happy and lively new family unit in a large rambling house with a grass tennis court, conveniently situated opposite the village church.

After a year on the farm I became a student again at Liskeard Lodge, the C.M.S. training college for single men and married couples with their children. The college was situated in Chislehurst, Kent, and there was a large intake of students that year preparing for missionary service in Africa, the Middle East, the Indian subcontinent and Japan. The Women's Training College was five minutes' walk down the road at Foxbury and most of our lectures were held there. There were courses in Biblical studies, mission and comparative religion. All the staff members at the two colleges had experience of living and working abroad under the C.M.S. umbrella. Our Principal, Douglas Sergeant, and his American wife Imogene had been missionaries in China before the Communist take-over. He was later to become a suffragan bishop in the York diocese. The training was valuable in preparing us to work as partners, usually in a subsidiary role, under national Christians. Max Warren was a frequent lecturer at the colleges. The regular routine of set times for daily worship and the occasional quiet days with a visiting speaker were useful in training us to be disciplined in our personal prayer and devotional life. Missionaries have often tended to be strong individualists and they don't always find it easy to live and work together in harmony. The community life of the colleges was a means of testing our ability to relate well to colleagues and to iron-out differences when they occurred.

After boarding school and university, I found community living relatively easy to handle. Such a shared existence had to include the parcelling out of chores. We took turns at washing-up and sometimes at cooking. I remember being part of a team that cooked apple pies for the college. We somehow misjudged the quantities and made enough apple pie to sink the *Titanic*. With my interest in agriculture and gardening, I was put in charge of the college garden and the huge vegetable patch that went with it. I exercised the art of delegation and assigned to my life-long friend, Richard Gill, the care of the compost heap. This experience planted within him a passion for compost that stayed with him until his dying day. A few years later I was to be best man at his wedding to Elizabeth Martin, a C.M.S. missionary in Uganda, and later still I became godfather to their daughter Susanna.

Towards the end of my training period, I learnt that I was to be posted to Equatoria Province in the Southern Sudan with a view to joining the staff of the Nugent School, Loka. This was an intermediate boys' boarding school which drew students from all over the Southern Sudan. By the time they arrived at Loka, the boys had completed four years of schooling at primary school, where the teaching was carried out using the vernacular languages. Although English was also taught at the primary level, it took time for the new intake to adjust to being taught by us in the English language. I was delighted to learn that Richard Gill was also being sent to the Southern Sudan to join the staff of Bishop Gwynne Theological College, where men were being trained (along with their wives) for Christian ministry. The students at the college came from both the Anglican and Presbyterian traditions.

We were booked by C.M.S. to travel by sea from London Docks to Mombasa on an ocean-going liner. My mother accompanied me to a firm in London which specialised in supplying and packing equipment for those embarking on life in the tropics. My C.M.S. equipment list included one rifle and one shotgun. I decided to forgo both these items and concentrated instead on domestic appliances which included a tin bath, a camp chair, sundry crockery, cooking-pots and utensils and an assortment of paraffin lamps.

Shortly before we were due to set sail, the shipping company called up C.M.S. and told them that all the cheaper passenger accommodation had been overbooked. Would Messrs Gill and Lea mind travelling to Mombasa in first-class berths at no extra cost? C.M.S. were quick to assure the company concerned that there would be no objections to this arrangement.

We sailed out of London Docks in September 1957 and headed for the Suez Canal. Port Said still bore the marks of the short-lived and foolhardy occupation of the port area by British troops during the six-day war. It was this exploit that led to the downfall of Sir Anthony Eden, the British Prime Minister. After a brief stop in port, we sailed on past Port Sudan and called in at Aden, where passengers were able to go ashore. I spent much of the voyage sitting on deck with a small portable typewriter wedged between my knees learning to type with the aid of a small volume entitled: *Teach Yourself to Type*. By the time I reached Loka, I had mastered the basics of touch-typing and acquired a skill that was to prove invaluable throughout my working life.

The next stop was Mombasa where friends of the Mission welcomed us and provided us with beds for the night and a brief tour of the city. Next day we caught the train for Nairobi where we were met by Jesse Hillman, the C.M.S. mission secretary, and given a brief tour of C.M.S. work in the city, which included the community centre in the down-town area of Pumwani where youngsters were being trained in carpentry and motor mechanics. And then it was time for the next lap of our journey on a train bound for Kampala, Uganda. Some of the scenery on the way was breathtaking as we passed through the highlands with vast stretches of agricultural land producing tea, coffee, sugar cane and pyrethrum. In Kampala we stayed for a few nights at the C.M.S. guest house and attended informal worship services with Ugandan Christians. Many of these had experienced a renewal of their Christian lives through the East African Revival movement which had swept through Rwanda, Burundi, Uganda and Kenya bringing much new life to the church. The meetings included the giving of testimony, which involved sharing with the group what faith in Christ meant to us at the present moment and the difference he was making in our lives. Bible reading and prayer were a regular feature along with the singing of hymns and songs. There was also space given for confession of sin and the restoration of relationships between members of the Christian family. All this freedom of expression was a bit daunting to uptight English Christians, who don't find it easy to bare their souls particularly in the company of people to whom they have not even been introduced! But the challenge to our sometimes rather staid expressions of Christian faith was good for us and it was heartening to be in touch with Christians who were so full of life and who welcomed us as brothers in Christ and part of the world-wide Christian family.

Ken Ogden who was on the staff of a vocational training centre in Lainya, a mere seven miles up the road from Loka, arrived in Kampala driving a lorry. He had come to collect Richard and me and all our belongings and to transport us through Northern Uganda and into the Southern Sudan. The journey took the best part of two days and it included an overnight stop at Gulu where we stayed with the Revd Maurice Lea and his wife. With its rich variety of plant life and colour the climate in that part of Uganda yielded a gardener's paradise. After crossing the border into the Sudan at Nimule, the first stop was Juba where we received a warm welcome from a number of C.M.S. missionaries who were gathered there for a business meeting. Our first night in the country that was to be my home for the next ten years was spent in the house of Brian and Eileen de Saram. Brian was the secretary of the Mission and was responsible for the business arrangements and pastoral care of missionaries. Shortly after my arrival at Loka a few days later, I received a pastoral letter of counsel from Brian. It contained some very practical advice: "As regards health, I would say – be strictly regular with your paludrine (an anti-malarial drug), take seriously the matter of a midday siesta, and make sure that your water is boiled." When discussing the siesta question with me, Brian commented that in his experience it was those missionaries with a streak of laziness in them that lasted the longest! I took his message to heart. In the Sudan it was my "raha"; in Spain it was my "siesta" and in France it became "mon petit dodo"! His letter closed with some words of Christian encouragement: "Above all, your primary task is to live a life of unbroken fellowship with Jesus Christ. Accept nothing less as your standard. It is your own experience of life in him that is your message. Allow nothing to come between you and God, but avail yourself quickly and constantly of the way back to God through the cross of Christ." I was indeed fortunate to begin my new life with such Christian colleagues close at hand. They certainly practised what they preached and they remained a fine example to me until the end of their lives.

It was exactly five years later, in the autumn of 1962, that Gill began her missionary training at Foxbury along with a good number of other single girls, about five of whom were engaged to be married to serving missionaries. Having lived away from home at boarding school and university, the community side of living came quite naturally to her. At the start of our training, it was true for both of us that our recent Christian backgrounds had been in Christian Union circles at university. Missionary training, however, brought us both into contact with wider elements of church life. Through chapel services at Foxbury, Gill was made aware of the changing liturgical colours through the Christian year. She learnt to appreciate quiet days and periods of silence as a means of deepening her relationship with God. The building at Foxbury was at one time the home of the Tiarks family who had made their fortune in the world of banking. There was a feeling of faded gentility about this centre for missionary training, with its grand staircase, its polished floors and its panelled walls. This setting seemed light years away from the somewhat basic accommodation for which most of the missionary recruits were destined. Some years later C.M.S. moved their missionary training to a far more functional set of buildings in Selly Oak, on the edge of Birmingham. Here the students were able to benefit from close contact with other theological training colleges and their teaching staffs. More recently still, the decision has been taken to close the C.M.S. college at Selly Oak and to train recruits in the areas where they will be expected to work. Certainly no training in England could prepare Gill for the dramatic change in lifestyle that would come about with her imminent move to the Sudan.

She found it hard to say farewell to the family, knowing that we would be away from the U.K. for the best part of two years. Her parents found it equally difficult, with all of their offspring living and working overseas at the time, in Rhodesia (as it then was), Malaysia, Kenya and Papua New Guinea. The travel bug had eaten badly into the Hunt family!

The journey to Omdurman is still vivid in Gill's memory. We sailed out of Liverpool in a cargo boat which also had room for a limited number of passengers. On board there were others who, like ourselves, were on their way to work in the Sudan. Some were going to work with the British Council; others were going to teach in government schools or work with international companies. I gave Arabic classes on deck every evening which would enable newcomers to exchange greetings in Arabic on their arrival in the Sudan. When the Captain discovered that we were missionaries, he invited us to take part in a worship service and to run a Sunday School for the children. The journey through the Mediterranean was like a second honeymoon for us. We called in at Port Said and paid a short visit ashore and then continued on south into the Red Sea until we reached Port Sudan where, with the help of a shipping agent, we were able to clear through Customs our boxes of wedding presents. After one night of sweltering heat in the Red Sea Hotel, we boarded a train for Khartoum. This was most certainly the hottest train journey of our lives, the like of which we hope never to experience again. The journey lasted some twenty-four hours and we were booked into a cabin with two bunk beds. For some reason the train came to a halt in Atbara in the middle of the day when the heat was at its most intense. The dining-car ran out of ice, so cold drinks were no longer available and there was only hot tea which poured straight through you in the form of sweat! The carriages had metal roofs which meant that we lay on our bunks and slowly cooked! When the train eventually pulled into the main station at Khartoum, we learnt that the temperature that day had reached 113 degrees Fahrenheit. The train journey had proved a real endurance test for a new young missionary wife and a rude awakening to a hot climate. Gerry and Rocky Nichol, colleagues at the American Mission School where I was teaching at the time, were at the station to meet us and they drove us to our new home in Omdurman.

The following morning I was required to attend school and invigilate some exams which meant that Gill was left in the house in the boiling heat, surrounded by boxes and unable to communicate with the various callers who dropped by to welcome her and greet her in Arabic. After the comforts of family life in leafy Esher, it was a case of culture shock for which she was ill prepared. It is small wonder that when Rachel Hassan, our mission secretary, called later that morning, she found her in tears.

CHAPTER THREE

LOKA AND LANGUAGE STUDY

It was about four-and-a-half years before our marriage that I had arrived at Loka and joined what was known as the Gordon Memorial Sudan Mission. This name must seem somewhat politically incorrect to modern ears. But General Gordon had at one period of his life been the Governor of the province of Equatoria in the deep South of the Sudan. Later he was to be Governor-General of the whole country when it was still a part of the crumbling Ottoman Empire. Gordon was a practising Christian and a fierce opponent of slavery, which was endemic throughout the Sudan during the nineteenth century. Slave raids amongst the southern tribes were carried out by northern traders. I remember passing through a place called Lui, where C.M.S. ran a hospital for many years, and being shown a large tree under which the captured slaves used to be secured and tied-up in readiness for the long journey to the slave markets of Omdurman. So it is hardly surprising that General Gordon, who had been killed in the Mahdi-led uprising against Ottoman rule in 1885, was something of an icon and inspiration for the first party of Anglican missionaries, all still in their twenties, who set off south to open up new mission work in 1906.

The group leader was Llewellyn Gwynne, who had arrived in the Sudan in 1901, not long after the battle of Omdurman and the conquest of the Sudan by the army of Lord Kitchener (which included amongst its number Captain Winston Spencer Churchill). Gwynne's aim in coming to the Sudan was to follow in the steps of Gordon and to proclaim the good news of the Christian message to the people of the Sudan. Most of his early years, however, were spent in Khartoum ministering to the needs of British troops and expatriate government officials. After serving as Deputy Chaplain General to British Forces during the first world war, he eventually became Bishop of Egypt and the Sudan, a huge diocese that extended for over 3,000 miles to the south. He was still just alive when I arrived at Loka in 1957. He died towards the end of that year at the ripe old age of 94. So the church which I was called to serve was a very young one. There was still a large missionary presence in the Southern Sudan, though numbers were beginning to dwindle, partly because of pressure from the new Sudanese government that had taken over the reins of power when the Sudan gained its independence in January 1956.

But in 1957 Loka still had three expatriate missionary staff plus their wives, all of whom were very active in the life of the school. That summer Christopher Cook, the headmaster, who had previously taught science at Rugby School in England, was transferred to Uganda. I was sent to fill the gap when Christopher and his wife Davie moved across the border. Stanley Toward took over as headmaster and was ably assisted by his wife Marjorie. Ronald and Olive Gray completed the expatriate contingent on the staff. They had previously worked in Egypt and were fluent in Arabic. They occupied a small house on the edge of the school site which consisted of two African-style round huts (or "tukls") joined together in the middle by two straight walls. One end of the house served as a kitchen. The middle section was their living room and the other circular room was their bedroom with a rudimentary bathroom area in one corner. Ronald had a unique storage system for letters and other papers: he threw them all into a long tin bath. Finding an appropriate document meant rummaging around in this sea of paper for an indeterminate period of time!

As the Towards, with their two small children Edwin and Hilda, were content with their existing house, I inherited the home of the Cooks. My new home was in some respects quite palatial. There was a large central room with a veranda on either side. I was told in passing that one of my predecessors had owned a dog but that a leopard had one night come in through one veranda, seized the dog, and escaped through the other veranda. Other rooms included a dining-room, two bedrooms and a bathroom area. The main kitchen area was a separate construction apart from the main house with space for an open wood fire. There was a cold water tap outside the back door which was a relative luxury. Other families and the school dormitories had to have water collected from a standpipe, and transported to their dwellings in large tin cans perched on wheelbarrows. A small generator provided electric light for the classrooms to allow the boys to do their homework in the evenings. Homes and boarding houses were lit by paraffin lamps.

The Towards and the Grays were extremely welcoming and hospitable. I was allowed to use a section of the Towards' paraffin-driven refrigerator for storing meat whenever a cow was killed locally. I had never taught before and I needed all the help and support that more experienced staff could give me. I was given responsibility for teaching both science and Scripture for the four year-groups. My knowledge of science was, to say the least, very basic. I relied heavily on a text-book for the teaching of science in the tropics written by a Mr Daniel. I was usually just one step ahead of my classes in the study of Daniel! Some of the teaching touched on com-munity health issues such as the best way to limit the spread of malaria. Formal Scripture classes were supplemented by voluntary informal Bible reading groups which explored the reading of Scripture in a devotional way with the aid of Scrip-ture Union notes.

Contact with the outside world was maintained through the arrival of the weekly mail lorry. Boxes of groceries could be ordered from a couple of Greek-owned stores in Juba and the lorry would deliver them for a small extra charge. In Loka village itself there was a tiny store which sold onions, salt and sugar. Local people would call at any time of the day and offer us their wares – a few eggs, perhaps, or a pawpaw or a chicken. One could buy a sack of groundnuts and have them shelled and then ground into paste at the cost of a few pias-tres. This paste, cooked with an onion and salt and diluted with water, made an excellent and very nourishing soup. Loka was about 3,000 feet above sea level so it was possible during the rainy seasons to grow a wide variety of crops. As a keen gardener, I enjoyed developing a vegetable plot which produced maize, groundnuts, sweet potatoes, tomatoes and beans. Grapefruit and pineapples also grew in my garden and mangoes were plentiful in season, so we didn't starve.

The day started at 6 a.m. with the beating of a drum fol-lowed by a roll call and brief prayers led by the headmaster. The boys then drank sweet tea and ate their breakfast. The morning was given over to classroom work and we stopped at midday for lunch.

Sudanese schoolboys share the world's passion for soccer so the school playing fields were put to good use during the afternoons. The boys played football bare-footed but, as a concession to western frailty, I was permitted to play in what we used to call gym shoes. I was told that an energetic former missionary wife once took to the football field but before the final whistle was blown she had had to be carried off with a broken leg.

The boys were easy to get on with and very eager to learn. Places at Rumbek Secondary School, which was the gateway for study leading up to the School Certificate exam, were limited. Everyone tended to study hard. Education was a precious privilege, especially at the higher levels.

Perhaps the main discipline problem arose when tension mounted between tribal groups and the occasional fight resulted. But the school provided an excellent opportunity for young people from varied tribal backgrounds to get to know each other and to learn to live and work together. The school chapel, which stood right at the centre of the school site, gave us a focal point for the life of the whole community.

Eyebrows are sometimes raised when it is mentioned that missionaries employed servants to work for them. I used to employ someone who spent most of his working day cutting and fetching wood from the forest to provide fuel for the fire upon which meals were cooked. In England our "servants" are gas and electric cookers and (these days) microwave ovens. We take such everyday amenities for granted but they are simply not available to most people in our world. Similarly water had to be heated over a wood fire and then carried to the tin bath. All clothes washing was done by hand. So I, and others like me, employed help to cope with the domestic chores and this enabled me to concentrate on the work of teaching and acting as housemaster to the boys who lived in one of the three dormitories. This was my reason for being there. The wages that I paid to Wani and Lojong, who helped me in the house, provided them with cash to augment the income they obtained from their subsistence farming.

Family Christmas presents pose something of a problem when you are living thousands of miles from your loved ones. Somehow I managed to obtain a gift catalogue and used this to order a few gifts for members of my family. I ordered for my father a plant-pot holder. How could I have guessed that it would turn out to be one of the most hideous objects he had ever seen, bilious yellow in colour with black legs? On opening this apparition on Christmas morning, I was later told that he looked glassy-eyed and speechless. I fared no better with a gift for my brother: it seems that I must have got the numbers mixed up when ordering him a book, the title of which turned out to be *Ballet Dancing for Beginners*. My father for his part played safe. He ordered me a luxury food parcel from Fortnum and Masons in London. The only problem was that it didn't arrive in Loka until Easter; by which time the rich fruit cake in the parcel had grown mouldy at the edges. But there were, however, other delectable items which provided me and various guests with some very welcome treats.

The approach of Christmas marked the beginning of the dry season and the end of the long school term which had started the previous April. A Christian conference for schoolboys was arranged at Bishop Gwynne College at Mundri, which was about a hundred miles from Loka. This was to be led by a team of Sudanese Christians along with some missionaries and I was invited to join the team. Our overall leader for this conference was David Brown, the Principal of B.G.C. who later became the Bishop of Guildford. He was a scholar of some repute who devoted himself to an in-depth study of Islam. Many years later he was to confirm our son Andrew into the Anglican church. Students came from a number of different schools and tribal backgrounds. The daily programme began at 6 a.m. and the mornings were taken up with worship, Bible studies and discussion groups. Football again featured in the afternoon, with four competing teams: the Lions, the Leopards, the Elephants and the Hippos. One evening there was a student-organised concert. On Christmas Day we celebrated the birth of our Lord with hundreds of local Christians in Mundri parish church and the service was followed by a shared feast. One of the Sudanese leaders at the youth conference was John Malou, who later became a prominent and inspirational leader in the Presbyterian Church. Sadly he was killed in an air crash, while still quite young. His untimely death was a great loss to the church in the Sudan.

Once the conference was over, I was sent to Omdurman in the North to commence a three-month course of Arabic study during the school holiday period. January and February are relatively cool months in Omdurman and thus ideal for study. I was billeted with two single lady missionaries who lived in a large house opposite the C.M.S. hospital. My chief language teacher was a remarkable lady called Sitt Faith. She was of Ethiopian extraction and a Christian convert from Islam. Her conversion to Christ and baptism aroused the wrath of members of her family and an attempt was made on her life. But Faith persevered in the way of Christ in the face of persecution and loneliness and when I met her she was a radiant Christian and an inspiration to all who met her. She taught many generations of missionaries to speak colloquial Sudanese Arabic. I don't consider myself to be a particularly gifted linguist, but I love languages and I enjoy studying them. I have discovered that the essential thing is to "have a go" when it comes to speaking and not be worried if you make mistakes. So during those three months I made some progress with learning the spoken language and made a start with the study of written classical Arabic. For relaxation, I paid an occasional visit to the Sudan Club in Khartoum which boasted a fine array of grass tennis courts which were irrigated once a week from the Nile. The Omdurman Church was led by the Revd Philip Abbas, the Sudanese pastor, and the Sunday evening services were crowded with worshippers, many of whom came from the Nuba Mountains region which covers an area roughly between North and South in the Sudan. I sometimes treated myself to a service in English in Khartoum Anglican Cathedral, an imposing building in the centre of Khartoum and close by the presidential palace. Early morning communion services were followed by breakfast in the adjacent clergy house. These meals were presided over by the ever hospitable and generous George and Lena Martin. George was Provost of the Cathedral and Archdeacon of the Northern Sudan.

In April it was back to Loka for the beginning of the long school year, which was to last until the following December. I was able to get away to Uganda for a few weeks' local leave during the summer months. Independence had not yet reached Uganda and the Colonial Administration was still in place. The journey south by road and rail and in a steamer across two lakes, during the course of which I picked up a stomach bug which laid me low for about a week.

Bishop Oliver visits the Nugent School, Loka

I eventually reached Entebbe where I met up with my mother and her husband, General Dimoline, who was at the time the Colonel Commandant of the King's African Rifles. I witnessed him taking the salute at a huge parade of East African troops at Jinja. The K.A.R. were slow to provide officer training for potential Ugandan officers. At this stage Idi Amin, later to become a ruthless and paranoid dictator, was still a sergeant and famous chiefly for his prowess as a boxing champion. The army's lack of preparation for the independence that was soon to come did not bode well for the future of Uganda.

As I neared the end of my first tour of service in the Sudan, discussions took place concerning what I should do next after a period of home leave. Loka school was due to be taken over by the government at the end of 1959, so the missionary staff there would all need to be relocated. One possibility suggested for me was to join forces with Stephen and Anne Carr at their training farm project at Undukori, not far from Yei; this option was eventually dropped in favour of a proposal that I should become a diocesan youth worker for the church, visiting schools, encouraging Scripture teachers and the formation of Christian fellowship groups in the schools, as well as running Christian youth camps and conferences during the school holiday periods. I was to be based in Mundri at B.G.C. so that the college staff there would be available to offer advice and support. It was with this plan in view that I returned to the U.K. in the spring of 1959 for home leave.

CHAPTER FOUR

TEACHING IN OMDURMAN

After about eighteen months in the Sudan, I was back in the U.K. for a period of home leave. This included time for holidays with my the family alongside visits to parishes supporting C.M.S., several of which were in the York diocese. I also enrolled for a nine-week study course in classical Arabic at the School of Oriental and African Studies in London, during part of which time I received generous hospitality from Cecil and Sylvia Bewes in their Blackheath home so I could commute to London. Cecil was still Africa Secretary for C.M.S. but was soon to become the vicar of Tonbridge Parish Church.

In Blackheath they ran a club for youngsters from a nearby housing estate in their home once a week. The whole house was taken over by table-tennis, billiards, and other games and the evening always ended with refreshments and a simple talk on some aspect of the Christian faith.

One evening Eric Hunt called in with his daughter, Gill. She was a niece of Cecil and Sylvia so it turned into something of a family get-together. We all settled down to bowls of cornflakes, a Bewes late-night custom at the time. Gill was in the middle of her practical training as a probation officer and recounted a number of quite lurid stories of her experiences dealing with wayward girls. I was fascinated – in more ways than one! Later that summer I attended the Keswick convention, having been invited to speak at the missionary meeting. I stayed in a men's student camp and was pleasantly surprised to find that Gill was a member of the team of cooks. I found myself unusually eager to help with the washing-up and can even recall a moment of frisson when Gill tied an apron around my waist! Back in London I plucked up courage and invited Gill out to lunch. The occasion went well and lasted far into the afternoon. The day before I flew back to the Sudan, I went down to Esher and spent the afternoon seeing Gill and meeting up with some of the family. And that was it for something like eighteen months. Apart from the occasional rather dull letter from me, there was no further contact for the time being.

Then it was back to Omdurman for further Arabic study. For part of this time I shared a mud-brick house in a suburb called Abu Qadog with Dr. Roland Stevenson, a fellow missionary who was a brilliant linguist and anthropologist. I lost count of the number of languages that Roland could speak The house we moved into had been unoccupied for some time and it took a while to clean it up and make it reasonably habitable. The house had once been the home of Sophie Zenkovsky, a former missionary nurse who used to run a mothers' and children's clinic in Abu Qadog, and in the course of tidying up we found a discarded set of her false teeth in one of the drawers. Roland owned a large library and most of his books and belongings were stored in boxes in one of the rooms. Roland simply shifted some of the boxes to make space to move a bed into a corner of the room near the door, thus providing himself with enough room for sleep.

The aim of my Arabic course was to bring me up to a level of fluency so that I could work in the language when visiting schools in the south, where Arabic was fast becoming the universal medium of instruction. This study period lasted about six months.

My bachelor bedroom in Omdurman 1961

When Roland's wife, Rowena, arrived back from England, where she had been keeping an eye on their daughter Janet, she soon took the situation in-hand and our home in Abu Qadog became more civilised. Eventually the Stevensons moved to another house nearer the hospital and some time later I welcomed John and Dorothy Lowe and their young twins, Michael and Catherine, into my Omdurman home. The parents had both come north from Bishop Gwynne College to study Arabic. I enjoyed having a family around and the children adapted wonderfully well to Omdurman city life and our shared home,which was enclosed by high mud-brick walls with a strong metal gate. Dorothy began to share the cooking with Zebediah who, up to that point, had been looking after the domestic needs of my bachelor existence. On occasions I, too, ventured into the kitchen to prepare a dish. I was rather proud of my lemon pudding. One day I served up this culinary masterpiece to the Lowe family. Michael, who was aged about five at the time, took one mouthful of this delectable offering, screwed up his face and uttered the one word: "ghastly!" It was an unforgettable moment !

I was busy with Arabic study until the Spring of 1960 – and then the blow fell. Permission to return to the south to take up the role of Diocesan Youth Worker was turned down and I was given orders to leave the country within four weeks. Chris Cook, who had returned to Juba as Mission Secretary, suggested that I relocate to another country where a youth worker's post might have been a possibility. But having laboured at Arabic for many months and attained a reasonable degree of fluency, I was eager to explore the possibility of other employment in the north which would meet with government approval. The American Presbyterian Mission, which worked in partnership with the Egyptian Evangelical Church, was still running both an intermediate and a secondary school in Omdurman not far from where I was living. They were willing to take me on as a teacher of English and in due course the necessary government approval was obtained for this change of plan.

Another reason for staying in Omdurman was that about five miles from my home was the University of Khartoum. Whilst studying Arabic, I had begun to get to know some of the southern students who were from a Christian background.

Tennis proved a useful means of socialising with some of them and before long I found myself sharing in small Bible study groups. The Christian students were a small minority in a predominantly Muslim environment and they needed all the encouragement they could get. One of the students with whom I shared Bible study was Oliver Duku who is now the Principal of the Bishop Allison Memorial Theological College for the training of Sudanese clergy. Friday was the Muslim rest-day in Khartoum and the day when students were free from lectures. So the Provost of the Cathedral at Khartoum organised Holy Communion services on Fridays, which attracted a number of students and helped build up their faith. Michael Green (then on the staff of the London College of Divinity and later to become my college principal) stayed with us one summer and was the guest speaker at one such service.

The American Mission owned a conference centre at Geraif, which was to the south of Khartoum close to the river Nile. It was a refreshing place to visit, away from the bustle and noise of the city and surrounded by fruit trees and cultivated farm land. A few of us would take parties of schoolboys or students from the University away for a weekend retreat at Geraif so that together we could explore the Christian faith in greater depth. Sometimes we would invite outside speakers to come and help if they happened to be available. John Holmes, a travelling secretary with the Evangelical Fellowship of African Students, was one such speaker; while Ian Watts, who was teacher training in Nigeria, came to us on another occasion. Ian had previously worked as a District Commissioner in the Sudan before the country became independent (He was many years later to become the chaplain to the Anglican Church in Cannes). Another very welcome speaker was Professor Hugh Morgan, Professor of Medicine at Khartoum

University. At one such conference the topics studied included: "The Christian and his Work"; "The Christian and his Home"; and "The Christian and other Religions". As some may observe we were living in a very male-dominated society. But at least such weekends helped strengthen the faith of schoolboys and university students, living as they did in an environment that was not always friendly to Christians.

After an initial period at the Intermediate School, I joined the staff of the Secondary School alongside Gerry Nichol, who taught commercial subjects such as typing and book-keeping. Gerry and his wife Rocky and their young daughters lived in a house adjacent to the school buildings. Within their compound was a further block consisting of two bachelor bed-sitting rooms between which there was a shared bathroom. A short distance away from this block was the "little house" which contained a pit latrine. I was fortunate in being able to move into one of the bed-sitting rooms and to take my meals with the Nichol family. A friendship developed then which has lasted until the present day.

Our headmaster was Fahmi Suleiman, a distinguished Christian layman and an inspiring leader. With the commercial training that the school was able to provide, our school-leavers had no difficulty in finding employment in banks and businesses in Khartoum and Omdurman. Some of our students went on to take the Sudan School Certificate which was the entry examination for Khartoum University. I was given responsibility for teaching English language and literature in preparation for these examinations. I particularly enjoyed teaching English literature. There were some amusing moments. For most of this period the Sudan was ruled by a military dictatorship that was growing increasingly unpopular. When we were studying George Bernard Shaw's

Arms and the Man, we came across the line: "And remember, nine out of ten soldiers are born fools" – a little unfair perhaps to vast numbers of intelligent people in the armed forces, but at the time it raised a morale-boosting laugh. Any form of protest under dictatorship rule can prove dangerous and such a moment helps to reduce tension.

With my commitment to teaching English and our friendship with a number of British Council staff, I found myself drawn-in to taking part in amateur dramatic productions put on by the Council, principally for the benefit of those studying English in schools. I acted in one very ambitious production of Shakespeare's *Richard the Second*, playing the part of the Duke of York. Our producer worked with Sudan Airways, but his great passion in life was the theatre and he and his wife owned a small theatre in Nairobi. He was a brilliant director, gifted in his ability to inspire a collection of very amateur actors to produce a high-level performance. The play was performed once in Omdurman and a second time in a large university auditorium in Khartoum.

For relaxation I turned to tennis. There was one court in the school complex in Omdurman. The playing area was covered with a mixture of mud-clay and manure beaten flat and smooth and left until it was bone dry. It produced a surprisingly good, if rather slow, surface for tennis, which was on the whole reliable. My partners on this court included our headmaster, Fahmi Suleiman, who was a good all-round sportsman and Arkasha Giffen, who ran the dispensary at the C.M.S. mission hospital. Many years previously Arkasha had been found as an abandoned baby on a rubbish heap in Khartoum North. He was brought up and adopted by a couple of American missionaries. I remember attending a very joyful Christian wedding ceremony when Arkasha married Mary.

*Tennis in Omdurman with Arkasha Giffen, Willard Galloway
(American Mission) and Fahmi Suleiman*

Most of my tennis, however, was played either at the Sudan
Club in Khartoum, with its very expatriate ambience, or at
the Sudan Lawn Tennis Association Club in Khartoum South.
There were two open tournaments each year: one at each
club, and both of these events were keenly contested. I was
fortunate for a while in being paired with a very good doubles partner, a British army officer, Robin Crawford, who was
training Sudanese army officers at the local equivalent of
Sandhurst. He and I usually made it to the semi-finals and
on one memorable occasion we beat the top Sudanese doubles pair in the Sudan Club final. For a few years the tennis
scene was greatly enhanced by the arrival in Khartoum of
Baron Gottfried Von Cramm, who was by then a prosperous
business man in his mid-fifties. In the summer of 1939 he had

lost in the finals of the men's singles at Wimbledon and in Khartoum he helped coach some of the younger Sudanese players as well as playing regular doubles games with the rest of us. He certainly lifted the general standard of play. When Gill arrived on the scene, she also shared in the tennis expeditions and we managed to win a mixed handicap doubles competition before the onset of pregnancy meant that she had to give it up for a while. At the hotter times of the year, play usually started around 4 p.m. and ended when it got dark at 6 p.m. When tennis was over, we would gulp down huge quantities of iced drinks, usually diluted fresh lemon drink or Coca-Cola.

My teaching career in three different schools lasted for six years and although I wasn't a trained teacher, I felt I had a bit of a gift in this direction and was usually able to keep a class interested even if I was not particularly hot on the discipline side. As my sixth year in teaching was drawing to a close, a vacancy occurred in the C.M.S. hospital as the manager and his wife returned home to Switzerland. Having read estate management at Cambridge I began to wonder if I could turn my hand to managing a hospital. I discussed the whole question with Dr. May Bertram, the hospital superintendent. They needed to fill the post as quickly as possible and my reasonable competence in Arabic helped my cause. May was in favour of taking me on and approaches were made to the Ministry of Health. The fact that I had the word "management" in my degree subject was enough to convince the government authorities that I could do the job. So permission was granted for my transfer from the school to the hospital, on condition that we trained a Sudanese to take over my post in a few years' time.

CHAPTER FIVE

OUR RIVER HOUSE HOME

I had moved into the River House, which was owned by C.M.S., some time before I went on home leave to get married. With Gill due to arrive shortly, I thought that I had better try and spruce the place up a bit. Some of my schoolboys offered to come and give me a hand. Together we painted the interior of the lean-to, mud-walled kitchen bright blue and the one large kitchen cupboard, in which mice had a habit of nesting, a lurid shade of orange. Hitherto cooking had been carried out by Zebediah using primus stoves. I thought that it was time we modernised, so I bought a set of three gas rings that were fuelled from a portable cylinder on the floor. I also found in the market a metal box oven that could be lifted from the floor and placed on a stand which had to be positioned over the gas rings. "What more could a new bride want?" I thought to myself.

In my naïvety, I was ill-prepared for the culture shock that Gill would soon experience. I had grown used to the Sudan and its blazing hot climate. After five years of living there, it had become my home. I could speak the language and I enjoyed communicating with friends and neighbours. Our

Our River House by the Nile

River House was surrounded by Arabic-speaking neighbours most of whom spoke not a word of English. Gill is a very gregarious person and her inability to relate and converse with those living around us was very frustrating for her. Furthermore we arrived from the U.K. in June at the hottest time of the year, and there would be no appreciable let-up in the temperatures until the following November. Gill tells of how the heat knocked her for six. For some reason she was not over-impressed by the makeover of certain parts of our home that my team of schoolboys and I had achieved before her arrival. It was still pretty basic, to say the least, after home in Esher and life at Foxbury. The bucket latrine under a wooden box in a small room built up against the outside wall of the garden held few attractions for her. There was an outside flap to this latrine which could be lifted at night by members of what had become known as "the camel corps", who were responsible for changing the buckets each evening; but in fact they did their rounds far less frequently than this and the smell could be pretty intense. There was no main drainage at the time (I believe that a mains drainage system has now come into effect in the area of Omdurman where we used to live) and the waste water from taps ran out into open drainage channels and was used to water the shrubs.

Gill soon found that the best time to do any cooking was before nine o'clock in the morning when the temperatures were still reasonable. Her chief priority in those early months was Arabic language study. She used to make her way to her language classes in a taxi, and her teacher was Sitt Josephine, a substantially-built, Egyptian, Christian lady. The taxis would take four passengers along a specified route. The driver would pick people up and drop them off at any place they chose along that route. This means of shared transport meant that the fares were cheap and not much more than the cost of a bus ride. Gill was often squeezed into the back seat beside two much larger Sudanese. But everyone was very friendly and the taxi was always a good place to practise the few Arabic greetings and phrases that she had learnt in class.

Our home, built in an "L-shape", consisted of four rooms. There were three rooms in a row with the central room forming the dining/living room. The remaining rooms were bedrooms. Each area of the house "benefited from", as estate agents would say, high ceilings with ceiling fans while at the front of the house there was a long veranda. Around the time our son Andrew was born, we invested in an air-cooling system. This was a cheap, easy-to-install, apparatus and much more economic to purchase and to run than the more sophisticated air-conditioning. At the very hot and dry times of the year, it could bring the temperature inside the house down by twenty degrees Fahrenheit. Rain never came except during the months of July to September so evening meals were frequently taken out of doors. Our house enjoyed a view of the Nile and it was possible to use tap water to irrigate the garden. We developed a patch of lawn and grew a variety of shrubs which included bougainvillaea, poinsettia and oleander. Familiar bedding plants grew well during winter months from November until the middle of March. At one stage we kept chickens in the garden, a useful source of eggs. We had the usual basic mission furniture, but were able to use our wedding gifts to add a personal touch to our home.

The main Omdurman thoroughfare

Most of our shopping was done in one of the markets in Khartoum or in Omdurman and Gill soon picked up enough Arabic to buy vegetables, fruit and meat from the different stall-holders and she learnt to bargain over the price which was an acceptable part of doing business. Goat's milk was delivered to our front gate every morning by a milk-seller who arrived with two large churns on either side of a donkey.

For a short while Gill taught English at Unity High School, a Christian high school for girls in Khartoum. The church had pioneered girls education and both the Unity High School and the C.M.S. girls' school in Omdurman were held in very high regard. It was the arrival of our son Andrew on the scene that eventually put a stop to these teaching expeditions across the river to Khartoum.

Gill's gift for hospitality soon came into play. From time to time we invited home to tea one of my classes of secondary schoolboys. We learnt to make rather heavy sponge cakes, using oil as the main fat ingredient since butter and margarine were not available. We plastered these cakes with brightly coloured icing thickened with cornflower and the results were eagerly devoured. Neighbours would sometimes drop in to pay their respects and would be offered a cold drink. Our house was some distance from the hospital where most of our missionary colleagues lived, so with our spare room we were able to offer some of the single missionary staff a restful day away from their place of work. Missionaries passing through Omdurman on their way to and from home-leave often stayed with us for a night or two. Rather less welcome were the young people who dropped in on us, sometimes with little or no warning, and stayed with us for several days. They delighted in telling us how they were doing Africa on a shoestring and enjoying the hospitality of missionaries along the way! Our own salaries, as was the case with most missionaries, were at an adequate but pretty basic level, so such visits from tourists travelling around on the cheap were a bit irksome.

We always looked forward to visits from members of our family. Gill's parents both came to see us as did my mother and stepfather at different times. Gill's mother got rather a shock once when she paid a visit to the "little house" at the corner of the garden: she had just perched herself on the seat when she heard strange bleating sounds coming from below. A passing goat had stuck its head through the flap in the outside wall, and when she looked down to see what was happening, a bearded face peered up at her. It was a far cry from Esher.

We also made friends with British Council staff and their families: David and Alison Latter, who ran the Omdurman Council Centre for a time, became our particular friends; while the Barclays Bank staff were also very supportive. On the day of Andrew's baptism, we had invited all our neighbours and a crowd of Sudanese Christian colleagues and their families back for refreshments in our garden after the service, when the power supply broke down. It was imperative that we supply our guests with ice-cold soft drinks. Monty and Molly West, who were connected with Barclays and ran the Omdurman branch, came to our rescue and brought in huge blocks of ice so that we could serve cool refreshments.

Becoming pregnant inspired Gill to acquire new sewing skills and to master a sewing machine so that she could make maternity dresses. Rocky Nichol, Alison Latter and Sitt Josephine all gave valuable help with this new learning process. The powers-that-be decided that our first baby should be born at Mengo hospital in Kampala, Uganda, rather than in Khartoum or Omdurman where the blood banks were less well stocked. So when she was seven months pregnant, Gill boarded a Cessna plane for the flight to Entebbe. She felt very vulnerable, leaving home and husband and travelling to yet another country at such a crucial time in her life. Looking back she realises that God's loving protective hand was over her in all the arrangements that were made. She was booked into the C.M.S. guest house in Kampala for two months, the prospect of which seemed rather bleak and uninteresting. What on earth was she going to do during those two long months as she awaited the arrival of our first child? But on her first day in Kampala, she bumped into Dr Raef Leach and his wife Bertha. They both worked on the staff of Mengo hospital where Gill would eventually be having her baby. They immediately recognised the loneliness of her situation and invited her to come and live with them in their mission bungalow. They welcomed her into their home and made her a part of their extended family. Gill was asked to help entertain the many visitors who poured in and out of the Leach home. Raef and Bertha were sometimes away on medical safaris, visiting outlying clinics, and it was helpful for them to leave someone in charge of the house. Gill was only too happy to take on this new role, so she readily accepted their invitation.

In that busy household time passed quickly and our son Andrew was born in Mengo hospital on 11th May 1964. I was still in Khartoum making daily visits to the government immigration offices and spending hours trying to obtain exit and re-entry visas, without which we could not return to the Sudan at the end of our leave. So Gill had no family around her. But other missionary colleagues, whom she had got to know during the training period at Foxbury, such as Bryan and Vera Rogers, and Robin and Joan Church were a great support and treated her like one of the family. They visited her regularly in hospital where she shared a ward with a lovely Ugandan lady who had just given birth to her fifth child. The presence of Gemma Blech in the hospital as a patient with a troublesome back was also a great help to Gill. They had been at Foxbury together and Gemma was a qualified midwife and was able to be present at Andrew's birth. It was in such ways that Gill experienced what it means be a part of God's worldwide Christian family. Having eventually managed to obtain my visas, I arrived in Uganda two weeks later. It was a joyful reunion after a testing time in our lives.

We were then able to enjoy a period of leave together, first at a tea plantation not far from Kampala, and later in Karen, not far from Nairobi, with my stepsister Jane Sleap and her husband Peter. Our train journey to Nairobi was a novel experience as we shared a compartment with a delightful newly-married Indian couple. From time to time they cooked spicy meals for themselves which filled the carriage with a distinctively Eastern aroma. They very kindly babysat for us whilst we ventured forth at meal times to find the restaurant car.

The birth of Carolyn eighteen months later in October 1965 took place at Kingston Hospital in Surrey. Husbands were kept well away from the labour ward at that time, so I was not present when she arrived on the scene either. We enjoyed plenty of support from Gill's family at Esher throughout this leave period and when Carolyn was only six weeks old, we travelled back to the Sudan by plane having just enjoyed a family Christmas with grandparents. We were also able to celebrate Carolyn's baptism with family members in the church to which they belonged in Surbiton.

The children had few toys at the River House but, provided they kept out of the direct rays of the sun, they could play outside for much of the day. My old tin bath from Loka days came into its own again. It was filled with sand and placed outside the kitchen in a covered area thus providing hours of amusement for our two young children. Each day, however, before the children entered the sand pit, we had to sift through the surface of the sand to ensure that no scor-

pions were present. The shock of a scorpion sting was sometimes enough to kill a child so we couldn't afford to be
careless. Gill once discovered a scorpion scurrying around the
seat of our latrine in the corner of the garden.

Our son Andrew and his great friend Jeremiah

As Andrew grew a little older, he began to make friends with
the local Sudanese children living close by. His greatest friend
was a little boy of his own age called Jeremiah. They would
spend hours together in the garden and Andrew began to pick
up a few short Arabic sentences. He soon learnt to say, "I want
some water", as well as, "I want a banana". Having acquired
his banana, he would toddle off and share it with Jeremiah.

Picnics were popular in Omdurman, particularly when
there was a public holiday. Sometimes a party from the school
would drive out of town in a bus to a farmland area near the
river where the meal would be eaten under the shade of the

trees. If it was a very special occasion, a sheep would be killed and roasted over a fire. Sometimes we would go with a group of friends for a night-time picnic in the desert. An *al fresco* meal in the cool of the evening was a refreshing experience at the end of a very hot day. At the end of one such picnic, we were stopped on the way home by some police. "Don't you realise that there is a curfew in force?" they asked. We had had no idea that trouble was brewing and we were allowed to go home in peace. It turned out to be the first rumblings that led on to a coup d'etat which overthrew the existing military regime and opened up the way for an elected democratic government.

We were often invited to attend the weddings of Sudanese colleagues, neighbours and former students. These were joyful occasions and, like those in New Testament times, they could last for up to a week. At each evening celebration, the bride and groom would be the centre of attention, dressed in their finery and seated on chairs like a royal couple on their thrones. Marriages were normally arranged by the families of the couple as in Muslim society young men and women live very separate lives. The women wore long, flowing garments which enveloped them and partially covered their faces. But beautiful eyes would peer out from this mass of flowing material. The young men would survey the scene at a wedding reception and if they saw a pair of eyes that they fancied, they would have a discreet word with their parents and marital negotiations would probably follow. There would be much to arrange, including the dowry that the groom's family would have to pay to the bride.

One of the days towards the end of the wedding celebrations was known as *yom ad duxla* – the day of entry. That night the groom would lead his bride into a specially prepared bedroom for their first act of intercourse. Female circumcision, which was common in Omdurman, rendered this a painful experience for the bride and she was expected to scream so that everyone in the next room would know that she had entered the marriage bed as a virgin.

Funerals were very public affairs which had to take place within twenty-four hours of the death. If you had had any contact with the bereaved family you would be expected to attend what was know as a *biqa* (literally a weeping). As you entered the house of the bereaved, you would approach the chief mourners and exchange a greeting. There was a prescribed form of words for this: "The blessing of God be with you!" You would then go and sit on a cushion or a chair at the edge of the room in silence for five or ten minutes. Sometimes a small cup of sweetened coffee was served. I came to respect this simple way of expressing sympathy and solidarity with a family during a time of grief. In Britain we are often not sure how to behave in times of bereavement and there are few clear customs to guide us. Sometimes people simply can't face the situation and they avoid those who have lost a loved one for fear of not knowing what to say. The Sudanese pattern seems infinitely superior to the rather confused British response to death.

Our local church was in Omdurman and the building was shared by the Anglican Episcopal Church and the Evangelical Presbyterian Church. Each congregation had its own pastor and all the services were in Arabic, punctuated in our case by hymns and songs sung in Nuba vernacular languages by different tribal groups. Our services were held on Sunday evenings after dark. They tended to be rather drawn out and the sermons were long and it has to be admitted that Gill in particular, with her limited Arabic, found these services a bit of an endurance test. Sometimes it was only the promise of supper with the Nichols', who lived next door to the church, which provided light at the end of the tunnel.

As the children grew old enough for church, Gill would take them on Sunday mornings to a Cathedral family service in English in Khartoum. On Palm Sunday the children would be given real palms from genuine palm trees to take home with them. Soon after we were married, Patrick Blair took over the post of Provost of the Cathedral and we came to know him and his wife Gillian well. The Blairs had two small children of their own and were keen to develop the Cathedral's ministry to young families. They also started a midweek pram service for mothers and toddlers. Gill was drawn-in to help with the work amongst the children. An important part of Cathedral life was the supper club that took place on Sundays after the evening service. It was a simple meal, the basis of which was a huge pot of groundnut soup. This was a social occasion that drew together people of all nationalities, and different speakers were invited by the provost to give a talk after supper was over.

It could well be that this supper club taught us the value to the church of shared meals, a practice which became a key ingredient of our ministry in later years.

There was a considerable number of expatriates living and and working in Khartoum. Some were in business attached to local firms or banks; others were involved in education. The different embassies were well represented and the numbers were swelled by foreign aid workers. With the arrival of John Twidell to teach physics in the University and some new Christian teachers at Unity High School for girls (including a certain Mary, who was later to become Mrs.Twidell!), we found that there was scope for starting up some informal

Bible study groups in homes. These became known as The Three Towns Bible Study Fellowship. They drew together people from all sorts of races and religious backgrounds. Those who attended included foreign aid workers, teachers, missionaries, business people and students. There were Sudanese, Egyptians, Greeks, British and Americans and at least one Indian! One Sudanese Muslim convert to Christianity came regularly and another Muslim seeker, who worked at the airport, came from time to time. Sometimes a group of Muslim students would attend and listen and observe. Some of our number moved from a nominal attachment to Christianity to a living faith in Christ and these included a Greek business man, an Indian student and another student from an Egyptian Coptic Christian background. We moved around each week from home to home. Numbers tended to be around thirty, so we would divide into two groups for the study period. Afterwards we would share a simple sandwich supper together followed by cakes and coffee. This form of fellowship provided us with something of a spiritual lifeline and was a huge source of encouragement to us. The fellowship was enhanced by the arrival of Keir and Shelagh Downing, a young and newly married English couple. Keir had come out under the auspices of C.M.S. and was teaching at the American Mission School. From time to time they used to babysit for us.

During all of our years in the Sudan, our spiritual leader in the Anglican Church was Bishop Oliver Allison. He was a larger than life character with huge *joie de vivre*. He was one of four brothers, all of whom became clergymen and two of them became bishops. Oliver sailed for the Sudan in 1938. He began his missionary career in Juba where he learnt the local Bari language. He was involved in the educational side of C.M.S. work in the south and also worked as a pastor to the English-speaking congregation in Juba. In 1954 he succeeded Bishop Maurice Gellsthorpe as Bishop of the Diocese of the Sudan.

Oliver was a confirmed bachelor. He certainly enjoyed the company of women without ever forming a close attachment to anyone in particular; although it was at one time rumoured that he was getting interested in a certain lady missionary. If this were so, the course of true love was not exactly enhanced when at the end of a missionaries' conference, he ran over her cat. His ministry involved constant travel over bumpy and rutted unmade-up roads in a Peugeot van with all his camping gear in the back. He travelled thousands of miles visiting isolated churches, taking confirmation services, and offering encouragement to Sudanese pastors and lay leaders. His journeys were often fraught with danger. There was civil war between the Northern Sudanese government and various rebel insurgent groups which were active in the Southern provinces for most of the second half of the twentieth century. This added greatly to the burdens that Oliver had to bear as leader of a church in a time of conflict. Throughout his time as Bishop he remained an outspoken champion of his Christian flock, who often suffered persecution at the hands of Government forces.

Oliver was sometimes dismayed but never downhearted for long. He would always bounce back and he offered warm friendship and encouragement to thousands. If he had been a married man, he could never have undertaken the arduous and costly ministry to which he was sure God had called him. He died in 1989. In a tribute to Oliver in the book *God is not defeated* Gordon Tikiba writes of him, "His smiles, voice, jokes, and the way he used to walk is still vivid in the minds of his friends, sons and daughters. The Sudanese people consider him as one of the cornerstones of their church."

There was nothing grand or pompous about Oliver and he loved children. My favourite photograph of him is reproduced in Dorothy Lowe's book: *Don't bother to unpack*. It shows Oliver with head bowed, on his knees in front of Patrick Lowe, aged five. Patrick had just said, "You must be tired, Uncle Oliver, of always blessing people. Now I am going to bless you." Oliver immediately responded by kneeling down in front of the child who stretched out a hand over Oliver's head and uttered these words: "Uncle Oliver, I bless you in the name of God." At one level it looks like just a game but there was a serious side to this play. Jesus once said, "I tell you the truth, unless you change and become like little children, you will never enter the kingdom of heaven." Oliver Allison lived out this kingdom faith to the full and we give thanks for this true friend and father in God.

CHAPTER SIX

A HOSPITAL IN OMDURMAN

The C.M.S. Hospital could trace its roots back to 1899 when Dr. Harpur opened a small clinic in a simple mud hut in Omdurman. This work was taken over by Dr. Alexander Hall who, with his wife Eva, opened a clinic on a different site on the outskirts of Omdurman. The nickname given it by local people was The Poisoner's House which was a sign of their deep suspicion of Western medicine in those early days. The men would bring female slaves to the clinic before risking the doctor's treatment on their own bodies. Dr. Hall died in 1903 but the work reopened in 1908 with the arrival of Dr. Lloyd, who worked as a doctor in Omdurman for twenty-five years. The hospital itself was built and opened in 1914 and two further clinics linked with the hospital centre were later developed in other parts of the city.

When I joined the staff as hospital manager in 1964, there were four other British staff and an Egyptian Christian doctor, Ramzy Muawad. Dr. May Bertram was the medical superintendent and Ruth Pakenham the matron. Hazel Caren was a hospital sister, Beatrice Coggan was sister tutor in charge of the nurses' home.

May had formerly worked in the Upper Nile region of the Southern Sudan at Ler hospital amongst the Nuer people. Her husband, the Revd Charles Bertram, worked at planting and building up a new church, whilst May ran the medical side of their work. In 1944 Charles died of black water fever and a few years later the work at Ler was handed over to the American Presbyterian Mission. This allowed May to move up to Omdurman, where she became leader of the medical work until her retirement in 1966. She was immensely hard working and gave herself unstintingly to the care of her patients. On one occasion, for example, a blood transfusion was needed for a very sick patient and no relatives with the right blood group were to be found – so May, whose blood was a perfect match, supplied the necessary pint herself.

Beatrice Coggan, the sister tutor, was another remarkable character. She kept a watchful eye on the nurses' home, since many of the girls were very attractive and there were plenty of possible male suitors for them in Omdurman. But it was a Muslim country and discipline had to be strict. An unwanted pregnancy would be an utter disgrace for the girl and her family, and a subsequent marriage would be difficult to arrange.

Beatrice remained remarkably thin. She seemed to subsist mainly on a diet of goat's cheese, a local green salad plant and bread. Part of her responsibilities lay in the care of a number of destitute, very elderly people who lived in what was known as the "poor hosh" (a home for the very poor). The hospital provided them with food, a bed and a roof over their heads. They were very infirm and many of them were incontinent. The local authority in Omdurman provided us with a grant from which we were able to take care of these folk. It was the nearest thing to an old people's home in

Omdurman at the time. Beatrice would personally take care of these older people when they were ill and needed attention. She would make a daily round of this compound and talk briefly with all the residents. It was with great care and devotion that she took care of this aspect of the work.

We kept in touch with Beatrice after we left the Sudan and she came to stay with us both in Barcelona and in Hove. She was a very skilful needlewoman and upon arrival at our home, she would gather up anything that needed mending and set to work. After she died, I wrote a letter of sympathy to her brother the former Archbishop of Canterbury, Donald Coggan. We told him of all that our friendship with Beatrice had meant to us. In his reply, he mentioned her ministry of mending and said he reckoned she would probably have a front seat in heaven, but that she would be greatly embarrassed by such an honour.

There were different sides to the work of the hospital. There were two main wards: the children's ward and the women's ward. Relatives of the patients would sleep on adjacent verandas and would look after their loved ones' food requirements. There was also a hospital theatre which was used for minor cases of surgery. The more serious surgical cases had to be transferred to one of the larger government hospitals.

The leprosy compound played an important part in the life of the hospital since we were the only hospital in the country at the time that specialised in the treatment of this disease. Out-patient clinics were held each week and most of the patients were able to continue with their treatment as out-patients. Sulphonamide drugs greatly improved the ability of the medical staff to treat the disease successfully. But when patients were suffering from severe ulceration of feet or hands, they would often be admitted to the leprosy compound in a separate part of the hospital, so that their ulcers could be treated on a frequent and regular basis. There was, and probably still is, a great fear of this disease throughout the world, but it is transmitted from person to person only through close physical contact.

One of the difficulties the staff faced was that the officials at the Ministry of Health refused to acknowledge the presence of leprosy in the Sudan. They were inclined to maintain that it simply didn't exist. My Swiss predecessor, in a moment of extreme exasperation, had taken an ambulance full of our leprosy patients and paraded them in front of government officials in the offices of the Ministry of Health. This somewhat unorthodox approach at least led to the renewal of the government grant for their treatment for another year.

Alison Chater was an expatriate wife living in Khartoum who had trained as a physiotherapist. For a while she proved very helpful to us in supplementing the treatment that we were able to offer to the more disabled patients. Tutu Tia was one such patient. He was a Christian evangelist who came from the Nuba Mountains. Parts of his feet had been destroyed as a result of his illness but it proved possible to have a special pair of shoes made for him. In the course of time his ulcers were successfully treated and he was able to return to the Nuba Mountains with his new pair of shoes and to continue with his work as an evangelist, walking over the hills and telling people the good news of Jesus.

My task in the hospital was to handle as many of the administrative non-medical tasks as possible, thus relieving the medical staff of unnecessary burdens and freeing them to get on with tending the patients. I had to oversee all the repair work that needed attention such as blocked drains and leaking roofs. When rain storms came in July, although few and far between, they could be very severe. I was fortunate in having an excellent colleague in the hospital office who took care of the bookkeeping and the accounts as well as coping with the weekly paying of wages to the hospital staff. Sheikh Aziz was a pleasure to work with. He and his family were members of the Presbyterian Church in Omdurman. I also had to keep records of patients and their treatments, copies of which had to be submitted each month to the Ministry of Health. Drugs and other supplies had to be ordered and collected from Khartoum. There came a time when the government drastically reduced their grant to the hospital. This meant laying-off a number of workers, including the man who drove the ambulance. So I combined my role as manager with that of ambulance driver. My tasks included collecting little plastic packets of blood from the blood bank. I have always been a bit squeamish where blood is concerned, so this was a task that I did not relish. I would leave the blood bank holding the offending but life-giving packets out of my direct gaze and would hurriedly deposit them in the back of the ambulance and head back to the hospital.

A regular visitor to the hospital was Muhammed the builder. My Arabic didn't often let me down but on one occasion I must have ordered two pairs of gates for the hospital instead of one. Muhammed swore that this was so and in the end I was obliged to believe him! Within the hospital grounds we eventually found a home for both pairs of gates. Whenever a major building project was in-hand, such as an extension to the nurses' home, Muhammed would bring us an estimate for the job that was about to be undertaken. Once we had agreed a figure for the building work, he would ask me for a down-payment of around ten per cent for the work that he was about to commence. The word for this in Arabic was *arabone*. He required this sum so that he could go and buy the materials that he would be using for the new building. A few years later when I was studying New Testament Greek, I was fascinated to discover that the same word crops up in Greek in Paul's letters. He describes the gift of the Holy Spirit as God's *arabone*, or guarantee, or down-payment. The Holy Spirit given to us is the foretaste of the fuller resurrection life that God promises his people when the dead are finally raised.

The reason for the existence of a mission hospital such as the one that existed for so many years in Omdurman was to demonstrate in a very practical way God's love for all people, regardless of race or religious background. Most people had little time or concern for the destitute people in the poor compound, or the ones who suffered from leprosy. It was important – and it still is – that Christian people show just how much God loves and cares for all. It was not easy for expatriate staff to speak of the Christian message to Muslims who came to the hospital but two Sudanese members of the church, one man and one woman, would visit the hospital and tell of Jesus Christ and all that he had come to do for us, sometimes in one of the wards and sometimes in an out-patients' clinic. Pastor Butrus, our Sudanese pastor, also came and took prayers for us from time to time.

The coup d'etat which overthrew the military government affected us all, including those of us who were at work at the hospital. It began with some university students demonstrating and protesting against the government. They were soon joined by a wide range of professional people parading down the streets and joining in the protests. Street demonstrations spread throughout the towns with people parading, shouting abuse and waving banners that bore anti-government slogans. We used to drive around Omdurman and Khartoum in a little Citroen 2CV car (there were only two of them in the country). When we saw a demonstration approaching, we simply put the car into reverse and retreated in the opposite direction. Most of the demonstrations were peaceful and there was little loss of life. On one or two occasions, tear gas wafted through the hospital compound with unpleasant effects. In the end President General Abboud and his government stepped down and handed power to a provisional government which paved the way for countrywide elections. Sayyed Sadiq al Mahdi became the next head of state. He was a direct descendent of the Mahdi who threw off Ottoman rule in 1885 with the capture of Khartoum and the killing of General Gordon.

But whilst changes were taking place in Khartoum, there was trouble in the south. In 1964 the government had ordered the expulsion of all foreign missionaries from the three southern provinces. It was believed by those in power that the best way to unite the country was to Islamise these provinces and to bring everyone together into one religious family. So new mosques were built throughout the south and every effort was made to convert southerners and to bring them into the fold of Islam. The schools were a major target as a part of this policy.

By now, however, the church in the south was well established with two relatively new assistant bishops and a growing number of pastors coming out of training at Bishop Gwynne College. Bishop Allison remained in Khartoum until his retirement in 1974 but his movements were severely limited. Civil war broke out in 1959 with southern rebel fighters in the south seeking greater autonomy and freedom from northern rule. The attempts to Islamise the south only added fuel to this conflict. There were some times of fierce persecution for the Christian church. In 1965 government troops surrounded Bishop Gwynne College when seeking to arrest Bishop Elinana, who was staying overnight in the college while en route for a Synod meeting further north. Here is a quotation from Andrew Wheeler's history of the church in Sudan, *But God is not defeated*: "During the night at about 3.00 a.m. the army surrounded the college and attempted to arrest the Bishop as well as the staff and students. Forewarned, the staff and students were able to escape into the surrounding bush. Only one person was killed; the college bursar. Bishop Elinana himself had to spend the night hiding in a ditch next to a hedge, listening to the soldiers passing nearby looking for him. In the morning he was able to escape from the compound and to join the rest of the college community. The whole college community then began a three-month journey through Congo into exile in Uganda." Most of the students were able to continue with their studies at other colleges in East Africa. John Lowe had already left and was teaching at Bishop Tucker College in Uganda, a college which some of the B.G.C. students were able to attend.

Many Sudanese refugees found a home in Uganda. These included Jeremiah, the other Assistant Bishop. There was a a brief peaceful interlude in the Sudan civil war following the Addis Ababa peace agreement which was signed by the various parties concerned in 1974; but by 1984, with the introduction of sharia law into the whole of the Sudan, fresh conflict erupted in the south and it has continued until the present day.

But God is not defeated is the title given to the book describing the first one hundred years of the Anglican Church in the Sudan from 1899 until 1999. It is a very appropriate title because clearly God has not been defeated by all that has happened during that century. Missionaries were expelled but the gospel seed had already been planted and no amount of persecution could wipe it out. Perhaps the departure of missionaries was a blessing in disguise, since it left the initiative for evangelism and growth in the hands of Sudanese leaders and they in their turn were cast back onto God and had to learn to trust in him alone. Over the last forty years there has been massive growth in this still young church. The small Dinka church which was the fruit of the labours of Archdeacon Shaw, the de Sarams and the Sharlands has, partly through a period of revival, grown from a tiny plant into a large tree. As I write this chapter, reports have recently come through in the press of a new peace accord signed in Nairobi. There is a fresh spirit of hope in the air. Indeed, God is not defeated!

The Sudan we left behind in 1968 was still in conflict, however. When I was appointed manager of the hospital, it was agreed with the Ministry of Health that we would train-up a Sudanese who would in a few years be able to take over my post. So, as I began work in the hospital, Ayyoub Bishara, a former student of mine at the American Commercial High School, became my understudy. When we left for the U.K. in the spring of 1968, Ayyoub stepped into my shoes. The hospital itself was finally taken over by the government in 1971 and since then it has been run as a psychiatric hospital. Our departure from the Sudan in 1968 was, for us, the end of an era. Ordination now beckoned.

*A royal state visit to the Sudan. Her Majesty Queen
Elizabeth arrives in Khartoum – February 1965*

CHAPTER SEVEN

COLLEGE AND CURACY

Our journey home from the Sudan took us in different air-craft via Egypt, Libya and then Malta, where we stopped off for a few days for a very welcome holiday. All the farewells and the packing-up in the heat of April had left us somewhat exhausted. In St Julian's Bay we rented part of an apartment from the mother of a staff member in the British Embassy in Khartoum. The rent was very modest and Mrs. Speers was a kind and gracious hostess, who had no problems sharing her kitchen with us.

The next stop was Northwood, on the outskirts of London. On a previous home leave in 1965, we had purchased a small two-up and two-down semi-detached house, knowing that I might possibly soon become a student at the London College of Divinity. But first there was a clergy selection conference that I was obliged to attend. This took place at a retreat house in Hampshire and it was very competently run by Colin Semper, who was later to become a canon at Westminster Abbey. I cannot remember a great deal about that weekend. But the layman who was part of the examining team was a somewhat unusual character. He was a farmer in the west country who kept a herd of Red Poll cattle. During my interview with him, I managed to steer the conversation in the direction of cows and the merits of the different breeds. I told him of my year spent with a herd of Aberdeen Angus before the commencement of missionary training. I like to think that my knowledge of cattle helped to persuade him that I would make a suitable parson, at least in a country parish! Later he gave a talk to the assembled candidates and spoke quite vehemently of his dislike of dirty vicars. This was a sentiment with which I felt we could all agree, regardless of our churchmanship. Since he went on to mention his distaste for grimy finger nails, I am now inclined to think that he he was referring to the bodily cleanliness, rather than the morals, of the clergy. I made a mental note to make sure that, if I were ordained, mine would be carefully scrubbed after a spell in the garden on a Saturday; so that my hands gave no offence at worship on a Sunday.

The selection conference report was positive so, at the advanced age of thirty-four, I returned to student life. One option was to follow the older men's essay course which lasted for two years. The alternative was to have an attempt at the London Bachelor of Divinity course. I decided in favour of the latter. With my interest in languages, I was eager to study Greek and Hebrew. The one disadvantage of choosing the B.D. course was that it lasted for three years rather than two, but I felt the extra year spent in study would be worth it.

I was able to obtain grants for my own personal support and also for the expenses of college but there was nothing forthcoming for the support of Gill and the children. We sold-off a number of wedding presents before leaving the Sudan and some very generous gifts from friends and family also made a great difference. An allotment helped to keep us in vegetables. Then, just as we were starting college life, a legacy came through from the estate of an uncle of Gill's, so by one means or another we never lacked anything essential. In such varied ways we felt that God was providing for all our material needs.

The college was staffed by a very gifted team of lecturers. Hugh Jordan, who was shortly due to retire, was the college principal and a specialist in Old Testament studies.

Others on the staff included Michael Green, already well known as the author of many books and a passionate evangelist as well as a very stimulating New Testament lecturer. Julian Charley taught doctrine whilst it was Colin Buchanan (later to become Bishop of Woolwich) who gave lively lectures in liturgy. Charles Napier had formerly been a Jesuit priest and he added a whole new and very welcome dimension to the life of the college. He was a keen gardener and his vegetable patch was within view of the room where he lectured, which meant that he was liable to get a bit distracted if he espied a pigeon starting to devour his cabbages. It was a formidable line-up and those of us who were students at that period were indeed fortunate.

But a huge upheaval was soon to confront the whole college. Northwood was a long way from the centre of London and London University. So it was thought that the college would benefit from closer links with one of the provincial universities. The college council of governors eventually took the bold decision to sell the Northwood site to the London Bible College and to move up to Bramcote in Nottingham, where we would be within easy reach of the Nottingham University campus. The theological faculty at Nottingham were also happy to have closer links with a theological college close by, so the die was cast and the move was made in the autumn of 1970. Massive building work had to be completed on the new site, including lecture-rooms, a dining-hall, kitchens, living quarters for married and single students and a row of new staff houses. It was a mammoth undertaking. Not all the buildings were complete when the new autumn term started and there seemed to be mud everywhere. By this time Michael Green had taken over as principal of the college and new staff had joined us, including Steven Travis to teach New Testament, George Carey (the future Archbishop of Canterbury) to teach doctrine and John Goldingay to teach Old Testament. It was a truly dynamic team.

We managed to let our Northwood home to some students and we moved the family into a rented house not far from the new college. By now our family had increased again with the arrival of our youngest daughter, Susanna, late in 1969. I was allowed to be present at her birth in a London hospital and stayed in the delivery room rubbing Gill's back until the very last moment and then got out of the way and moved into the next room. My defence of such cowardly behaviour was the argument that if I was to keel over at the sight of blood and lie prostrate on the floor, I would be a thorough nuisance to everybody.

The B.D. group of students was small so we came to know each other well. Our numbers included Pat Travis, married to Steven who was on the staff. Pat was a gifted education-alist who had a career in teacher training. She and Steve visited us in later years in all our overseas chaplaincies. Steve often preached for us and Pat would run a weekend train-ing course for all involved in teaching the faith to children. Pat is a good friend and a great enthusiast, with the ability to encourage people to develop their gifts. I was not altogether pleased with her, however, when in one of our churches she got me to do the actions to the rather dreadful chorus: "If I were a butterfly". I was wearing clerical robes at the time and with a white surplice on I felt rather like an outsize cabbage white!

Another member of our B.D. group was Michael Sanders, who years later was to take over from me as the Anglican Chaplain in the Hague. In our final year he became the Senior Student and was heavily involved in entertaining Prince Charles when he came to declare the new college officially open.

While I was studying, Gill's time was fully occupied in running the home and taking care of our three small children. Jane Napier and Di Buchanan became close friends and she enjoyed the Wives' Fellowship group meetings which were led by Eileen Carey during that final year at Nottingham. In order to allow me some peace and quiet at home in the afternoons, Gill would take the children off, with Susanna in a large pram, to the nearest local park.

The B.D. course was very demanding and it kept me studying at full stretch but it was also very rewarding. I revelled in the chance to do some in-depth theological study. The years passed all too quickly and suddenly the finals were upon us. Our morale as we set off for the exams in a car was not helped by a fellow student called Roopsingh Carr, who approached this big test in a mood of the darkest pessimism. As we drove to the university to sit the first of our many papers, the conversation in the car went something like this:

Roopy: "I'm going to fail; I know I am."
Pat Travis: "Don't be so silly Roopy; of course you're not going to fail."

Roopy: "Yes I am; I am going to fail. This is only a trial run."

Pat: "Come on Roopy; you'll be all right. Just think positive".

Roopy: "No, I shall fail; this is only a trial run and I shall
    take it again next year."

We were delighted that Roopy's gloomy predictions proved
ill-founded: he passed with honours and went on to teach in
a Bible College in South India.

Shortly before the college move to Nottingham, David
Bubbers, the Vicar of Emmanuel Church in Northwood, had
invited me to join his staff at the end of the next academic
year as his second curate. His senior curate was John Went,
who is now the Bishop of Tewkesbury. Emmanuel was a
thriving suburban church to the north west of London with
large and active youth groups and a good number of families in the congregation. It stood firmly within the evangelical
tradition but David enjoyed good relations with neighbouring churches and clergy. In some ways Emmanuel seemed to
me to be a soft option. Should I not perhaps be looking for
a struggling parish that would be more demanding? The college staff gave helpful advice to students seeking a curacy:
"Go for a vicar who will train you well." They were all agreed
that David Bubbers was an excellent trainer of curates. I
believe that events were to prove them right.

David was not one to sit his curates down and give them
instructions as to how things should be done. His method was
simply to take a wedding or a funeral and leave us to learn
by observing him. David accompanied me to my first few
funerals before allowing me to "fly solo" (as he put it). I still
remember my first funeral. I was terrified. "How did I do?"
I asked David when the service as over. "Fine," he replied,
"but I think next time it would be a good idea to allow the

congregation to sit down at some points during the service."
It dawned on me then that I had been so keen to get my own
part right that I had hardly noticed what was happening to
the congregation.

Emmanuel had an excellent choir in those days led by
David Iliff, a brilliant choirmaster and organist, who set very
high standards. Our son Andrew was fortunate in being able
to join this choir as a treble during some of his most formative years. Gill took over the running of a wives' group,
which flourished during that period and proved a major part
of the outreach strategy of the church to younger families.
At one time there were as many as sixty on the books. When
we left the group continued under an older and different
guise calling itself, After Eight. It still meets a real, if different, need within the church family.

At times husbands were invited to special events such as
the annual supper with entertainment to follow. There was
the usual problem of not being sure what was going to be
served up in the guise of "entertainment". At one such event
a lady who was related to a member of a famous pop group
seized her opportunity. She sang in a husky, sultry and rather
gravely voice a song which had the well-known line in it: "a
little bit of what you fancy does you good." We had never
realised before the potential for interpretation that could be
read into such a song. Gill was overcome with embarrassment
but we were relieved to see that David and Evelyn, who were
sitting right behind us, were both roaring with laughter at
Gill's discomfiture.

David and Evelyn were a pleasure to work with. They were
hardworking and inspiring leaders of a parish team but also
great fun. From time to time Evelyn would take Gill and
Rosemary Went for a day-trip to London where they would

wander round the shops and have a meal together. Evelyn herself ran a highly successful women's fellowship which met one afternoon a week in the church hall. It provided a spiritual home for many elderly women in the parish, most of whom were widowed or single and living alone. They all valued the warmth of the fellowship and the love that Evelyn lavished on them.

I was asked to run the older of two teenage youth fellowships which went by the rather quaint name of Guild. The group was greatly enriched when three young members of the Buckley family, David, Lois and Liz joined its ranks. They were all extremely talented musicians, able to play a variety of musical instruments and it was through their initiative that a youth choir was formed with a membership of about thirty. They sang contemporary Christian songs, and performed not only for our own church but also in concerts in other churches in the surrounding area.

Emmanuel invited a variety of gifted speakers to address its members. There was an embarrassing moment for me when John Stott, of All Souls', Langham Place, was due to speak and respond to questions at a meeting after the evening service. First, however, we were obliged to listen to a selection of songs sung by a Guild singing group that called itself The Grape Vine (this was shortly before the Buckleys came onto the scene). I am afraid it was a rather painful performance. John Stott, I am glad to say, was his usual patient and gracious self.

Our strong youth base was able to attract a wide range of musical and dramatic talent. Graham Kendrick, now well-known as a writer of hymns, performed at a concert for us one evening. He began with what he called "a warm-up song." It contained a line in it (I think there probably was only one line) that went "Big Vera, boom, boom, boom." It was perhaps a slightly unfortunate choice of song as, unknown to Graham, the leader of our Mothers' Union group was called Vera. This was not the kind of event to attract members of the Mothers' Union and mercifully Vera was not present.

At Emmanuel there was a strong emphasis on mission. Support for overseas mission partners was strong. The church had invested in a house which provided a home within the parish for missionary families when they came back to England on leave. But mission at home was not forgotten. The God First mission, as it was called, was held towards the end of David's time as our vicar and it made a considerable impact on both the church and the parish, putting evangelism on the map and challenging us all to be unashamed in our confession of faith in Christ. This period in church life proved quite a turning-point for our son Andrew in his personal faith journey. Paul Carter, who later was to marry Lois Buckley and who went on to be a Chaplain to the Forces, also looks back to a moment during that mission when he committed his life to Christ.

It was during our final year at Northwood that David Bubbers moved on from Emmanuel and became the General Secretary of the Church Pastoral Aid Society. There was then a short period of interregnum before Richard Bewes arrived. He and his wife Liz and their three children came to us from Harold Wood in Essex. It was an unusual situation for us, since Richard and Gill were first cousins. I had in fact met Gill in Richard's family home in Blackheath and we had known each other as students at Cambridge. But as things turned out there were no problems and we were glad to be in Northwood as the parish welcomed its new vicar. Richard's personality and style were very different to David's and, although we overlapped only for a few months, it was good to have the experience of working under two different but extremely gifted vicars. We learned much from them both as we started out on a new stage of ministry in Barcelona.

It was when David was still with us that we had begun to think about the next possible move. With growing school-age children, we had assumed that we would go on to parish ministry in England. But we had reckoned without Symon Beesly, who was the General Secretary of what has since become the Intercontinental Church Society. He was responsible for finding chaplains for certain English-speaking chaplaincies in mainland Europe. One day as we were travelling on a train to London together, he asked me whether I would consider working overseas again. I explained that for reasons relating to the children's education, we were hoping to move on to an English parish. Symon went on to point out that there were a number of good English-speaking schools in most of the larger European cities. Would we be open to suggestions if the education side of things was sorted out? Gill and I talked and prayed together and we felt that we should consider such a possibility, if a suitable offer were made. Symon's first suggestion was a chaplaincy post on the outskirts of Paris that covered two churches which were some distance apart. Having explored this possible opening, it was felt both by Symon and by us that this would not be right. Then came a further suggestion: "What about Barcelona?" Quite soon we were on another plane heading for Spain. We took a taxi from the airport and arrived at a late hour well after dark at the church premises, which also contained the chaplain's flat. The place was all locked up and there was no sign of a bell, so Gill gave me a leg-up over a high perimeter wall and I dropped down on the other side. I was eventually able to rouse the locum chaplain and his wife, who let us in. At the interview with the church council the following day, I think it was our determination to gain an entry to the church premises that helped convince them that we were the right people for the job.

CHAPTER EIGHT

AT HOME IN BONA NOVA

In late August 1974 we set out from Gill's parents' home in Pyrford, Surrey in our rather elderly dormobile. We were travelling with our daughters Carolyn and Susanna and Polly our cairn terrier. The latter had all the correct papers to allow for her entry into Spain. The vehicle was piled high with our personal effects. We were moving into a furnished apartment but we took with us photographs, table lamps and ornaments to make it feel like home. Kind friends had undertaken to store most of our furniture for us while we were abroad. Some heavier items went overland and by sea, including a small piano. We had recently installed Andrew as a boarder at Monkton Combe Junior School near Bath, in large part thanks to a very generous grant provided by Hillingdon Council. Monkton was to provide far more opportunities for sport than would have been possible in Barcelona.

The journey across France took us several days. It was my first visit to France and I was unaware that green card insurance cover was obligatory in mainland Europe. So we travelled across France with no insurance cover at all. Divine protection must have been looking after us as we reached our destination unscathed. I was ignorant, too, of the geography of France and so drove the dormobile on a road through the middle of the country which traversed mountainous regions in the Massif Central. Somehow the dormobile kept going. Our first evening after the channel crossing was spent at Abbeville and later in the journey we stopped for the night in a hotel in Clermont Ferrand. One afternoon as we sat by the roadside outside a bar sipping cold drinks, Susanna, who was approaching five at the time remarked: "The one thing I don't like about France is the language." We often remembered this remark in later years, when Susanna became fluent in French and went on to acquire French nationality.

As we approached Barcelona, it occurred to me that I had failed to obtain directions for finding St George's Church. We turned off the main thoroughfare into Barcelona and began to climb into a hilly area. I remembered from our previous visit that the church complex was sited on the slopes of a hill. It was a Sunday evening and we noticed a small group of Spaniards leaving a church and clutching their Bibles. We stopped and asked one of them in halting Spanish if they knew the way to St George's English Church. One of the group stepped forward and offered to lead us there in his car as we followed behind. So as darkness fell, we arrived at our destination thankful to God for His gracious provision of a Christian guide to lead us to our new home situated just above the Plaza Bona Nova.

Freddy Witty, a churchwarden at St George's, was there to meet us with his wife Peggy. They had already stocked up the refrigerator ready for our arrival. Freddy and Peggy were like parent figures, not only to the church family at St George's but also to the wider expatriate community. Freddy's family had founded a shipping firm in Barcelona during the previous century and Freddy himself was born in Barcelona. His war time service had taken him to the intelligence centre at Bletchley Park in England. He had married Peggy and brought up a family in a large apartment not far from where the new church complex had been erected and completed about a year before our arrival. The new buildings consisted of a church with a hall area to the rear of the worshipping area, which could serve either as a worship area or as a church hall. This was on the ground floor of the building and there were doors leading off from the hall into a kitchen, a church lounge and toilet areas. On the first floor there was space for crèche, Sunday School teaching, table tennis and the chaplain's office. The next two floors consisted of apartments. The first of these was the chaplain's flat whilst the top floor flat housed Doug Macnamee, the church organist, with his wife and daughter.

Our own flat contained four bedrooms, two bathrooms, a dining/living room, and a kitchen. There was a large balcony leading out of the hallway onto the church roof, which was ideal for barbecues. Another smaller balcony was situated on the other side of the apartment adjacent to the living room. We were delighted with our new home.

The following day, however, was Monday and life began in earnest for our two girls. We drove them to St Peter's school for the start of their new academic year and left them standing together in the school playground. We felt terrible! St Peter's is a Spanish private school which generously gave free places to our two girls. The teaching in class for the most part was in English and the presence of a few native English girls helped the Spanish girls to pick up the language. But in the playground, it was Spanish that was spoken so our girls picked up the language very quickly and were fluent in no

Brian, Gillian, Andrew, Carolyn and Susanna on the balcony over
St George's, Barcelona

time at all. John and Eleanor Copestake had children of
roughly the same age and their Barcelona flat was quite close
to the church so Gill and Eleanor shared the school run
between them.

Our induction to this new post took place a few weeks
after I had started work and the service was taken by Bishop
Edward Capper, who in his retirement helped out in the diocese. He came to us quite often for confirmation services and

was a good friend to St George's. A number of guests representing other churches in the locality were invited to attend my induction. It suddenly occurred to us that there ought to be some kind of reception for invited guests after the service so we asked Freddy if he would like us to lay something on. He was pleased at this suggestion so Gill arranged a meal for all who had received a special invitation.

We received a warm welcome from many in our new church community but it was a very small congregation after Emmanuel Northwood and it took us time to adapt to our new environment. On arrival we spoke only a few words of Spanish so one of our first priorities was to get to grips with the language. At that time Franco was still alive – just. He died about two months after our arrival. During the long years of his rule, the speaking of Catalan, which was the mother tongue of most of those who lived in and around Barcelona, was strongly discouraged. So when we arrived Spanish was still widely spoken. We went to language classes and made some headway, at least enough to greet people and to find our way around and do our shopping in the markets.

The tap water in Barcelona was very heavily chlorinated and virtually undrinkable. If someone made a cup of tea using tap water, you could smell it across a room. Our problem was solved when we discovered a spring further up the slopes of Tibidabo (the hill just above where we lived). Gill would drive our car up to the place where water poured out from a pipe that was linked to this spring. She would fill a number of demijohns with the water which then supplied our family needs as well as the requirements of the congregation whenever they met for social functions.

It wasn't long before Doug Macnamee and his family moved out of the flat above us and found other accommodation. Their place was taken by an English couple, David and Helen Melliar-Smith who had recently retired from the Madrid Embassy. David took a retirement post working with the British Consulate in Barcelona. They were both a tower of strength to us in different ways during the four years or so that they were our neighbours. David acted as an assistant warden to the community centre and was quite brilliant at mending anything that went wrong. Helen for her part was a great hostess and she was an enormous help to Gill with all the church catering that took place. David and Helen were also very ready to accommodate guests who required a peaceful stay in a child-free zone. Their spare bedroom was ideal for the use of visiting bishops.

We arrived at the end of a year's interregnum. Our predecessor, Harry Wilson, with the aid of some skilled lay helpers, had done a terrific job overseeing the construction of the new church plant in a suburb of the city. This had replaced a small gothic church building in the centre of town. The old church had no space for community activities apart from the worship area so the potential for growth in such surroundings was severely limited. The bold decision was therefore taken to sell up and move. But a year's gap between vicars is a long time for a church when there are no retired clergy on hand to help out. Visiting locum clergy and some lay assistants had worked hard to keep things going but midweek at St George's was relatively quiet when we arrived and there was just the one Sunday morning service.

Not long after we had unpacked, there was a newcomers' welcome picnic at Tordera, some sixty kilometres to the north-east of Barcelona. It was to the country home of John and Eleanor Copestake that we all headed. Everyone took their own food but Eleanor and John provided wine and *pan con tomate* (delicious local bread spread with olive oil and crushed tomato) It was an excellent opportunity for us to get to know the community which we had come to serve. The annual Tordera picnics are a St George's tradition which have lasted until the present day.

Quite early on we attempted to start an evening mid-week Bible study. This was not a success. One evening a Japanese lady and a young man from West Africa joined us in our flat. I cannot remember what we were studying but when we tried to engage in group discussion, the Japanese lady simply smiled sweetly and bowed her head; not a word passed from her lips! Meanwhile the West African did have something to contribute: "What I want to talk about is divorce." he said. Divorce, unfortunately, had nothing whatsoever to do with the subject in hand. We soon decided to abandon mid-week Bible studies for the time being and to try again during the forthcoming Lent.

Our first attempt to start an evening service was also a total failure. No one came. The two of us sat in the church for a while in gloomy silence. Gill wept and thought back to Emmanuel. After a brief prayer together, we made our way up the stairs to our flat.

Some time later we tried again with an evening service once a month. We followed the service with a supper club not unlike the one we had encountered at Khartoum Cathedral. After a service of worship, we laid on a two-course supper with wine and this was followed by a speaker on some subject of interest. The Melliar-Smiths were much travelled in the course of their embassy career and David was a brilliant photographer so we were treated to slide shows of some of the countries where they had worked, with erudite commentary from Helen who was passionately interested in art and architecture. Sometimes a group of us would get together and put on a play-reading such as *The Importance of Being Earnest*. We encouraged people who were away for the weekend to come back a little before the rush hour to worship with us and also have a meal before going home. The new plan certainly worked quite well and the monthly services were well supported.

During our first year we were greatly encouraged by the arrival of several new committed church families. Several of these came from the United States but none of them were Anglicans. Our church was an Anglican church and part of the Diocese in Europe. Our church stayed within the limits of Anglican liturgy which even then was becoming increasingly flexible. But we were glad to cater for an interdenominational congregation and our hymns certainly drew on other traditions. Some of our Baptist members put together a hymn book containing some of their preferred hymns and this was welcome alongside our existing Anglican hymn book. We all had to learn to give and take and to make room for people from a Christian background that was different from our own. At one stage we had three church wardens; one was an Anglican, one was a Methodist and the third was a Baptist.

There came a time when we felt that it was right to arrange for a church weekend away. The first of these was held in and around a small hotel at a place called Begas just outside Barcelona. We took over the complete hotel and many of us camped at night in the grounds. Doug Greenfield, who had worked with David Watson as a lay member of staff at St Michael's, York, was our guest speaker. He gave Bible talks at morning and evening sessions and there were opportunities for group discussion and plenty of time for relaxation in the afternoons. This weekend and many others in subsequent years did much to weld together our very mixed and often transient congregation. Since we were a multinational group and most of us were in Barcelona on short term contracts, it was important to build up a sense of community and fellowship.

These weekends soon became a highlight of our Christian year. For subsequent weekends we moved much further north to a retreat centre called Casademunt deep in the countryside, which was run by a group of Roman Catholic nuns. They were quite delightful and always gave us a very warm welcome, assuring us that they would be praying for us during their regular times of worship. Our speakers at these weekends included Branse Burbridge (a friend from Northwood days), Julian Charley (who was on the staff of St John's Nottingham and later a vicar in Everton, Liverpool) and John Collins (vicar of Holy Trinity Brompton in London). I shall never forget how, at one of our final communion services, a small group of nuns came forward and took communion from us. For a few moments communion barriers that had stood for centuries came down. My eyes filled with tears. It was a foretaste of heaven.

One of the snags of the ministry in Barcelona lay in the fact that many of our longer-term and more permanent members lived in their Barcelona flats during the week and went out to a second home in the country at weekends. There was a high level of air pollution in Barcelona and we had every sympathy with those who sought to escape from the city at the end of a hard week's work in search of peace and fresher air. Skiing was a further attraction that drew people away at weekends. And those who could not afford a second home in the country often had tents and would go away on weekend camping trips during the summer months. We adopted

*The setting for a Communion service on a campsite
at Cambrils, Spain*

the principle "If you can't beat them, join them" and organised at least once a summer a church camping weekend further south on the coast. We packed up cars and trailers and headed off as a church group to somewhere such as Cambrils where we pitched our tents together in a corner of the camp site. The evening meals would normally take the form of potluck suppers with everyone sharing food. There were times of informal worship and discussion sitting in the shade of some trees. One Sunday morning communion service was held in the open air in the site bar and patio. The site manager provided us with bread and wine and a couple of families camping near us came and joined us in the service. The children, who had had their own programme, mimed the story of Jesus washing the disciples' feet, which was the gospel reading for the day. A number of other campers observed the service as they sipped their drinks beside the bar. It was good to have people looking on as the Lord's death was proclaimed through word and sacrament.

On Wednesday mornings there was a short communion service followed by coffee, which led into a Bible study discussion group. This drew in a small number, mostly women married to Spanish husbands. They often found it difficult to get to church at weekends with family commitments. So for some of these, the Wednesday worship and Bible study became their church.

When we arrived at St George's, we discovered that all the financial efforts of the church were devoted to paying half of the chaplain's stipend, plus all his expenses as well as keeping the buildings going. The new church complex had made huge demands upon the small church community, proving very costly. The Intercontinental Church Society had helped them out with a loan and were still paying half of the chaplain's stipend. We felt strongly that the church had to learn not only to pay its way but also to start to look outwards and to support mission projects at home and abroad. There was some resistance at first to this latter suggestion but eventually it was agreed to hold a weekend of prayer and gifts. Friday evening was given over to prayer and people came and went over a three-hour period. Gifts came in over the weekend and as a result we were able to make substantial donations in the first year towards the work of a hospital in Chile (run by missionaries working with the South American Missionary Society, with whom we developed links). A contribution was made towards the purchase of a Land Rover for the church in the Sudan; money was sent to the Diocese for the Bishop's Ordination Fund and another donation went to the local branch of the Cheshire Homes. This weekend of prayer and gifts became a regular feature of our church life.

The appointment of Ed Stone, an American Baptist, as our church treasurer who not only believed in tithing but practised it was a great boost to the financial impetus of the church. His testimony at a church service made a considerable impact. Before long the church was able to repay the debt on the building that was still owed to I.C.S. and they were also able to take over full responsibility for paying the chaplain's stipend. With an increase in church attendance and a growth in church income, it became possible to consider employing an extra lay member of church staff to work with children and young people.

Church-giving was supplemented in various practical ways. Spain is the home of Seville oranges and a team of ladies would turn these into marmalade, the results being sold in aid of the church. As is well known the British cannot survive Christmas without their annual input of Christmas pudding. Eleanor Copestake cashed-in on this national weakness and each year organised a large team to stir and steam vast quantities of this heady mixture, which was generously laced with local brandy. Christmas puddings were unheard of and unobtainable in Spanish supermarkets at the time so Eleanor and her team cornered the market. Most of the ingredients were donated by friends of the church returning from Britain. Considerable profits resulted from this enterprise which made a healthy contribution towards the church bank account. And then there was an annual sale as Christmas was approaching. This drew support from all sorts of people, many of whom had only very loose connections with the church. It was a real community effort. A barbecue on our balcony provided lunch for all the visitors and it became a very festive occasion which everyone seemed to enjoy. The proceeds were most welcome and helped to pay the bills.

Some clergy are a bit sniffy about such fund raising efforts and regard them as unspiritual but I have never found them a problem. On the contrary, especially in overseas church situations, they are most helpful in building a bridge between the church and the community at large, many of whom seldom come near the church. It has never prevented me from teaching the need for direct giving in accord with biblical principles. At the same time I recognise there are some with few cash resources who have time on their hands and who can devote some of their time and skills to the service of the church by making something that can sell. In such ways people's hobbies and creative gifts can be offered to God as a part of the stewardship of their resources.

We were fortunate in having Andrew Williamson to direct our church choir for most of our years at St George's. He built up a very able choir with some outstanding solo singers. Under his leadership the carol services were always special and concerts were arranged from time to time. The choir were happy to lead us in a variety of music styles and their repertoire ranged from Handel's Messiah to a modern musical version of the passion of Christ entitled *Jerusalem Joy* by Roger Jones.

As the church grew, we were able to establish home groups for at least part of the year, meeting in different people's homes. We were keen to encourage Spanish partners of mixed marriages and so one such group was held in Spanish. We found that inviting mixed-marriage couples to meals helped make it clear to Spanish partners to a marriage that they were very welcome in our church. At the same time we tried to make Spanish the vehicle for conversation at the supper table, thus improving our facility with the language.

Spain is a country which many love to visit and it was

never difficult to persuade speakers from the U.K. to come, often with their families. The Mardens and the Lowes (both ex-Sudan friends and colleagues) came and provided cover for us whilst we were away for summer holidays.

One day we received a telephone call from Rosemary Green in Oxford. Michael Green had recently left Nottingham and become the new Rector of St Aldate's Church at the centre of Oxford, having taken over from Gill's uncle, Keith de Berry. But during a recent visit to South Africa, he had become seriously ill with pneumonia and was still well below par. Could we have Michael to stay for a couple of weeks so that he could recuperate in the Spanish sunshine? We happily agreed to this suggestion. Michael is a man of many gifts but sitting quietly in the sun doesn't go well with his very energetic nature. "Would you like me to preach for you next Sunday?" was a question he put to me not long after his arrival. How could I turn down such a tempting offer from the one who had been my college principal? He duly preached at a service during one of our weekends for prayer and gifts. While Michael was staying with us, we also a had a young man and his girlfriend staying in the flat for a few days. He was not a practising Christian but came along to church one Sunday morning and was struck by something that was said during the sermon. Afterwards Michael sat down with the pair of them in our kitchen and over a cup of coffee explained in simple terms how the young man could enter into a new relationship with Christ by turning from sin and turning to Christ, as the baptism service so clearly puts it. The lad prayed a simple prayer accepting Jesus Christ as his Saviour and Lord. The girlfriend, who was already a convinced Christian, looked on in wide-eyed amazement. "You should have been a missionary!" she exclaimed to Michael.

"Well, in a kind of way I am," was his reply.

There were times when visits took on a somewhat comic turn. One visitor to our home some years later described our residence as being a bit like Fawlty Towers. He even began his thank you letter to us after his stay with, "Dear Sybil". This description was never more apt than when a visit from Beatrice Coggan coincided with that of a newly married couple. Beatrice took it upon herself to take them an early morning tray of tea and unfortunately she forgot to knock on the door before entering the bedroom. The couple hastily disentangled themselves from an amorous embrace. Fortunately Beatrice was fixing her gaze so intently on the tea tray that she noticed nothing out of the ordinary!

For some clergy chaplaincies can be quite lonely undertakings. Our Archdeacon was hundreds of miles away in Madrid. Our Bishop's home was in London. There were no other Anglican clergy in any direction north or south, for several hundred miles. Archdeaconary synods were held only every other year. When there was a crisis, you were very much on your own.

One day the British Consulate phoned us to say that a man had suddenly died that morning in a Barcelona hotel. His wife and young daughter were stranded in the city. Could we possibly help? We agreed to have them both to stay with us whilst things got sorted out. Ursula Ure came to us for about a fortnight, while arrangements were made to fly her husband's body home. Our two girls were much the same age as Ursula's daughter and the three of them played together. We learnt from our girls that their new friend had somehow picked up the fact that her daddy had died, even though her mother had not yet spoken to her on the subject. Ursula was a sad but charming guest and it was a privilege to have her to stay at a time of such great need. When she left us, she presented us with a lladro porcelain dog with a very mournful expression on its face. In the circumstances it seemed a most fitting gift and it is one that we still treasure in our retirement home. Twenty-five years later we met up with Ursula at a service in Andorra at which I was the guest preacher.

Another call from the Consulate alerted us to the fact that an English single mother had just lost her only daughter in a road accident. Could we please visit her? Her home was just down the hill from where we lived. I walked that short distance to her apartment with a heavy heart, praying for wisdom as I went. I found Pat in a state of shock surrounded by friends and neighbours. There was nothing that I could say that would alleviate her grief. I assured her of our church's prayers and concern and promised to keep in touch. Gradually Pat started coming to church and became a real friend to our family. There was a moving moment when she came up to St George's with all her daughter's toys and presented them to the church crèche. Later she was happy to see our children playing with them. Bit by bit Pat was able to enter into a living faith of her own. Eventually she married and had another child. She was helped through that period of intense grief and loss through the loving support of our church family.

As a family we, too, passed through a sad time when Gill's father, Eric Hunt, was diagnosed with terminal lung cancer. His illness dragged out over a period of about nine months as he slowly grew weaker. It was especially hard for Gill living so far away from her parents' home at such a time. We were so grateful to Ed Stone, our treasurer, who at his own expense gave Gill an open return air ticket to allow her to travel to and fro between Barcelona and Heathrow. She was able to make use of this ticket to pay a crucial visit to the family, who were now living in Pyrford, Surrey. We were all home for the summer holidays and so were able to see something of Eric and Carol during the last weeks of his life. He died in September 1977 and the funeral was in his parish church, where he had served as a lay reader. His example of courage, good humour and Christian faith was an example to us all.

CHAPTER NINE

CHILDREN IN THE WAY

I have borrowed the title of this chapter from an excellent
Church of England report on children in the church that
came out a few years ago. It was master-minded by Bishop
Gavin Reid, who was Bishop of Maidstone for a number of
years. Sadly it failed to secure the full attention that it
deserved. I love the double entendre of this title. There are
still far too many churches in England where children are
seen as being a bit of a nuisance. They get in the way; they
disturb the ordered and peaceful rhythms of our liturgical
worship, and so no provision is made for them within the
structures. There is no crèche, no special instruction, no toilet, no concessions for them in the liturgy, and no mid-week
activity – nothing! And yet we claim to worship the Lord who
said to his earliest followers, "Suffer the little children to
come to me. Don't hinder them!"

At St George's in the 1970s we began to realise that we
had to do more for the children of families who came to us
on a regular basis. We had a crèche and a Sunday School
which were functioning well, but with the families often away
at weekends, the instruction in the Christian faith that the

children were receiving was limited and there was little for them on week days at the community centre. There was a limit to what Gill and I could do on our own and on weekdays most of our lay people were busy earning their living.

So we decided to look for a lay worker to come and help us, particularly with work amongst the children. Aid came in the form of Jill Edkins, a girl from South Africa who had been teacher-trained. She had a great love for people and was a delight to work with. She wore long loose-fitting flowing dresses and boasted a mop of naturally curly hair. On one occasion when she arrived at the centre wearing a short dress, my Gill was heard to exclaim, "Oh, so you have got legs!" Jill loved life and was a great enthusiast who enjoyed a challenge. She had considerable gifts in the area of children's work and the children loved her. With Jill's help, we were able to start a Discoverers' group for younger children and a youth group for the teenagers. The groups each met once a week at the church centre for games, creative activities and a time at the end of each session when they received some basic Christian teaching. Jill Edkins wrote in our church newsletter, describing some summer activities in June 1976, "They ate and romped their way to a rousing party finish. There were thirty children of various shapes and sizes ranging in age from seven to eleven. Some of the activities of recent weeks have included bare-chested boys being covered in chocolate, the chocolate apple race, girls cooking their own drop-scones and much football (the boys) as well as a table tennis tournament.

During the quiet times held in the lounge, we read and discussed different parts of the Bible. One night a mum noticed her son busily poring over his Bible and a piece of paper.

"What are you doing?" she asked.

"I'm discovering Christ", he replied.

The week-day activities were supplemented by weekend camp-outs for the different age groups. One of the great assets of Spain is the weather, which greatly contributes to the enjoyment of outside activities such as camping. Freddy and Peggy Witty kindly lent us their country home, called Can Blanc, situated in a small village in the foothills of the Pyrenees. This was the base for our first-ever youth weekend away. We were greatly assisted in this pioneer venture by the loan of three youth leaders from our former church at Emmanuel Northwood. These were Tom Parker, Paul Carter (both of whom would eventually be ordained) as well as Ann Harwood. The local scout group and many of the parents lent us tents, which were pitched in a field behind the house for sleeping purposes. We had a short "thought for the day" each morning at the end of breakfast and every evening there was a session held around the log fire in the sitting-room during which Tom led us in singing and played his guitar. This was followed by a talk on some aspect of Christian faith and living. Masses of food was cooked and eaten. Cathy who cooked for us used up surplus rice from the night before by turning it into rice pudding and serving it up for breakfast. They were so hungry that they lapped it up! Activities included hikes through the beautiful rugged countryside, hill-climbing, volley-ball, table tennis and wide games.

Freddy Witty was a former golf champion for Catalonia. At Can Blanc he invented his own unique form of golf for playing in the scrub land around the farmhouse. Where greens were an impossibility, if you could hit the ball to within a golf club's length of the hole, you could count it as duly holed! It provided hours of amusement for the many visitors to their home who enjoyed their hospitality, including our young people.

At the end of that first youth camp, one of our youngsters commented afterwards when writing about it: "It started you thinking about Christianity and we were in a wonderful setting to think about the big issues in life. It was through this great trip that I (among others) became a Christian."

Jill Edkins also describes a teach-in weekend at the church centre for youth group members. "There was a speaker called Soapy Dollar who was of American Apache Indian descent. Subjects looked at ranged from, Who is Jesus? to Christian Apologetics. The kids listened and talked in turns, sprawled on the carpet or on chairs."

After a couple of good years at Can Blanc, the youth camps moved to an ancient and rather dilapidated rectory at a place called Baget high up in the Pyrenees. The house was situated in a tiny but picturesque village at the end of a very long track. It was several miles from the nearest town. It provided us with a good base for several more youth camps. One year, however, a young man was taken seriously ill with an acute attack of asthma and had to be transported by car to a doctor who was on emergency duty in the nearest town. Such are the hazards sometimes confronted in running any young people's venture.

Jill Edkins' term of service came to an end and she moved to St John's Nottingham to take up a course of study. Whilst she was there, she met Dennis Bailey, also a student at the college, whom she eventually married. They came out to visit us as man and wife and were the speakers at one of the Baget weekends.

Meanwhile, regular Sunday School work continued at church under the devoted and effective leadership of Judith Baum and others whilst a team of helpers took it in turn to run the crèche.

After Jill Edkins left us, Alma Harward was our next lay helper. She was an American girl from Northampton, Massachusetts, in the United States. She came to us after spending a period of time studying at Oxford and worshipping at St Aldate's Church where Michael Green was her vicar. With so many of our congregation coming from the United States, it was good to have an American on the staff of the church. Alma approached her work with the children with great zest and enthusiasm. But sometimes her enthusiasm outran her experience. There was one afternoon when Alma had planned for a candle-making session. The children were due to arrive in a about a quarter of an hour when Alma approached me with a troubled look on her face. "Do you know how to insert wicks inside candles?" she asked. Anyone who knows me well will appreciate that when it comes to making candles, I am a bit lacking on the creative side. In fact, I am not particularly strong when it comes to making or mending anything. Alma had come to the wrong person. I never did find out what happened to the candles.

On another Discoverers' afternoon Alma had arranged for a papier mâché exercise. Everything was carefully prepared. There was a basin full of a thick, glutinous substance which was an essential ingredient for the project and beside it there was a jug of water. A somewhat naughty boy called Caspar was one of the first to arrive. Quick as a flash, he rushed into the room, seized hold of the jug, and poured its contents into the glutinous mixture, which quickly dissolved into a thin soup. Poor Alma's carefully laid plans were ruined in ten seconds flat.

A local theatre group put on a production of *Godspell*. Alma offered to take part and the show was a great success. But for me there was one anxious moment. Alma was a well-built young lady and at a certain point in the drama she had to hurl herself into the air with a view to landing in the arms of the young man playing opposite her. I was somewhat afraid that he would either drop her or be flattened by her. In the event my fears proved to be unfounded. He may have buckled slightly under the strain, but he passed the test with flying colours and the show went on.

Alma Harward carried forward the good work that Jill had begun and the young people's work continued to prosper. In due course it was Alma's turn to move back home to the United States and she was replaced by Mary Dow who came to us from Cheltenham. Mary was a quieter character than either Jill or Alma, though deeply spiritual. I think that she would agree that children's work and youth work were not her strong suit, but she tackled the task with enthusiasm and dedication and also with the help of other lay members of the church community. Elsa Day in particular was a great help with the children's ministry and she and Mary worked very well together. Elsa's husband, Les, was a church warden at the time and together they often hosted home Bible study groups. Mary also had other gifts and she contributed to the church's ministry to the older generation. She would lend a hand whenever help was needed and she continued to serve the church well under the leadership of Struan Dunn who came to Barcelona as my successor.

It was good to be part of a church which, in spite of not being large numerically, valued the younger members of our community and was prepared to invest time, money and effort in ministering to them. Our years in Barcelona proved to be an invaluable preparation in equipping us for our future ministry both in Hove and later still in Paris.

CHAPTER TEN

OPEN DOORS

How can a church live and grow if its doors are closed to those who don't belong? Whilst we were always eager to build up the core centre of our church with Christians who were keen to grow and move on in their faith, we were also keen to ensure that the church remained open at the edges. We encouraged any who were unsure and yet were prepared to explore the possibilities of Christian faith and living. St George's was a community centre as well as a church, so we would welcome groups to the centre which were not necessarily specifically Christian, provided they were not against what the church stood for. So, for example, the local Alcoholics Anonymous group met in our church lounge and quite a number of their members came to our services. From time to time Guides and Brownies would meet on our premises. Helen Melliar-Smith welcomed a small sewing group to her flat for tea once a week. This drew in women of different faith backgrounds and doubt-less some of no faith persuasion at all. There was one Jewish lady who came whose husband's parents had perished at Auschwitz. Our openness to different groups sent out a signal that all were welcome at St George's. Towards the end of our time in Spain, government funding for the Barcelona Queen's annual birthday party was withdrawn. So we offered our premises to host the annual get-together which brought all sections of the British community into our church grounds for a glass of wine and some snacks. After such an occasion, at the very least, everyone knew where the church was situated and the message was given that all were welcome there.

At the same time we were very aware that the church is far more than a social club. We have good news to share concerning the kingship of Christ Jesus, our one true Lord, and his longing to rescue people from self-absorbed living and to bring them into a fuller life centred on God and inspired by His Spirit. So from time to time we invited old Christian friends with a gift for making the Christian message clear to those who were still uncertain or unconvinced. Gill's uncle Keith de Berry was one such visitor. He spent the last twenty years of his life, after retirement from parish ministry, taking missions. He was a remarkably gifted evangelist. One of us once overheard him on the telephone remonstrating with a vicar who was proposing to limit his preaching time to ten minutes. "That's not long enough", said Keith, "I cannot convert anyone in less than half an hour!" He sometimes found patience a difficult virtue to sustain. Years later in Paris, he was invited to speak at a midweek meeting on the subject of mission. The preliminaries at the start of the meeting seemed interminable and at one point when the lady leading the meeting announced yet another song, Keith was heard to utter in a very audible stage whisper: "Oh, not another ditty!" He had a number of endearing and amusing foibles, but he was a man God mightily used to bring many to faith in our Lord and so we were more than happy to welcome him to preach for us in Barcelona.

Other gifted evangelists included Bishop Cuthbert Bardsley, who had just retired as Bishop of Coventry, where he had made the whole diocese very conscious of the church's responsibility to look outwards in mission. During his episcopate he had organised a diocesan wide call to mission. The Bardsleys came to us for just over a week and the Bishop spoke at a variety of meetings at the church centre as well as in homes. Perhaps he was at his most effective when he gave an address to a men's luncheon which was held at the Liceo, a place that had about it something of the flavour of the Athenaeum in London. He brushed aside the microphone that had been put in place for his use and delivered a stirring Christian message in almost Churchillian tones. He was clearly audible at the far end of the room. His coming was a great boost for our church and many were stirred and encouraged by his preaching.

Nevertheless, even Cuthbert Bardsley found it difficult at his age to adapt to a different culture. In one home where he was due to speak, he became quite impatient when the evening meal was not served until a time that he regarded as being far too late! In Spain evening meals usually are served around 9.00 p.m. Our host had phoned to say that his plane was delayed in Madrid and that he wouldn't be able to get to us until around 9.00 p.m. Our poor hostess was in something of a state. Finally as a result of the Bishop's pressure, the meal was served, even though many of the guests had still not arrived. When the Bishop eventually started to speak, his talk was interrupted by a group of late comers who all wanted their dinner. Needless to say, the whole evening was something of a disaster. It was a painful reminder of our need to be adaptable when encountering another culture.

I believe Bishop Cuthbert was at his best before a large

crowd in a massive cathedral inspiring his flock and challenging the unbeliever as well as the doubter. But although he was a very imposing and at times an imperious figure, there was also a very humble side to his character. Before we entered one of our meetings in Barcelona, we would spend a few moments in prayer together. The Bishop would usually commence his prayer with the words: "Lord we can't, you can." This spoke volumes of the deep trust in his Lord which under-girded his whole ministry.

Another weekend of mission centred around the visit of Garth Hewitt, the singer and song writer, and Richard Bewes. Garth sang at a number of different venues. either in the centre or in the homes of church members. There was always an evening meal followed by an impromptu concert. The songs were designed to make people think about the Christian message and its personal challenge. They also spoke to us of the Christian's responsibility to care about issues of justice in a world of suffering. It was easy to invite guests to such evening meals at which Garth was singing. They provided a relaxed and unthreatening convivial setting within which people could reflect upon the implications of the Christian message. As a result of this visit, Garth was invited to return to Spain for a further concert by an American working in the oil industry, Don Walton hired a restaurant near Tarragona where he and his family were living and he invited all his friends to come along and hear Garth sing. All expenses of the visit were covered by the very generous Don. On the Sunday of our Barcelona weekend, Richard Bewes preached at both the morning and the evening services. We enjoyed meeting up with the Bewes family again and after the weekend was over, Richard and Liz and their children joined us for a few days holiday up at

Can Blanc in the Witty's country home which they kindly lent to us.

Because there was no other Anglican church anywhere near us, appeals for help would come to us from far and wide. I was asked to take funerals at distances of up to a hundred miles from Barcelona. On one occasion a call came through from Lloret de Mar further north on the coast. I was asked to conduct the funeral of an English visitor from England who had died during the course of a Saga holiday. I duly took the service and later found myself in conversation with the Saga representative who was handling the arrangements. I suggested that it might well help Saga in the future if they were to make room in their holiday parties for a clergyman, who would be given a free holiday and also be attached to the Saga staff. He would be required to offer care and support to any of the the elderly Saga holidaymakers who fell ill and he would also arrange for services on Sundays in a hotel for any who wanted to attend. The idea was taken up at a higher level and the Revd Pennel came out as visiting chaplain to Lloret for a trial period in the spring of 1975 and he came again for a longer period in the winter of 1975/76. In January 1976 Mr. Pennel wrote a contribution for our St George's church newsletter.

I have been licensed for this winter season to continue the work we set on foot in the spring amongst English holidaymakers. It all began through the Revd Brian Lea and I.C.S. responding to the offer of a secular travel company (Saga) to sponsor a chaplaincy for their Lloret hotels.

What we (my wife and I) do is to move about during the week amongst the English, sometimes in the hotels, more often just by walking around meeting people. "Will the chaplain go through this business document with me?" "Would his wife take a blind lady for a walk?" All sorts of human needs and problems arise; and of course illnesses and accidents, breakdowns and deaths.

On Sunday we have services where we can – a bathroom, a T.V. lounge – always a 9.30 a.m. Holy communion and an informal "people's service" at 11 a.m. Think of us at these times. You would be impressed by the pool of quiet in the midst of the holiday racket. All kinds of people come; old and young, Church of England and many other church loyalties or none. An electric piano, a microphone, a table borrowed from the bar, but the promise holds that where two or three meet in the name of Christ, his presence is there.

Mr. Pennel was followed by other chaplains at Lloret de Mar, the first of whom was the Revd S.J. Archer. All of these did valuable work during the winter holiday seasons. They were recruited and briefed in preparation for their ministry by I.C.S. Thomson Young at Heart Holidays also joined in with this programme of providing short-term holiday chaplains for their resorts. Saga dropped out of the picture in the early 1990s, but Thomson continues with this pattern in partnership with I.C.S. right up to the present day.

During our time in Spain, an increasing number of expatriate families were settling in Casteldelfels, a seaside town south of Barcelona. We explored the possibilities for services in this town and eventually these were established on a fortnightly basis in the evenings at 6.00 p.m. Once again we accepted the hospitality of the local Roman Catholic Church. Our numbers hovered around fifty. At one service the singing was accompanied by someone playing a rather tired church organ; while a lady played a piano accordion and Andrew, our choirmaster, played his violin. On another occasion

Louise Wolf was playing a little portable organ on a freezing cold evening. She was wearing a woolly hat and mittens. During one of the hymns one particular note got stuck but, undaunted, she ploughed on to the end of the verse. It was at this point that I suggested that we sing the rest of the hymn unaccompanied. After the service, many gathered in a local pizzeria for an evening meal. Our children's favourite treat on such occasions was chicken and chips. At a later period, the pattern of services during the summer altered to one morning service a month followed by a picnic lunch in the garden of a church member. Attendance at the annual carol service in Casteldelfels before Christmas 1976 was around eighty. Some of the St George's choir came along and contributed a few carol items and their presence boosted the quality of the singing. Refreshments were served afterwards in the local American School.

Our first service in the Principality of Andorra, high up in the Pyrenees and tucked in between France and Spain, was held just before Christmas 1976. In those days the roads in the north of Spain were not as good as they are today and the journey took around five hours to complete. We stayed with Dan Parsons and his wife, whom we had known slightly in Khartoum. They had retired to Andorra and we were installed for a few days in their guest room. We led a carol service in the local Roman Catholic church in La Massana which was attended by about one hundred people and some sixty stayed on for a shortened service of Holy communion afterwards. This was the first of a number of visits that we paid to Andorra at special times of the year and services have continued there in English until the present day. Those who organised this first service also arranged a lunch in a local restaurant afterwards for any who wanted to take part.

Christmas could be a very lonely time, especially for single people living far away from home and family. We always tried to invite any who were on their own, whether church people or not, to a Christmas dinner. Gill worked hard in our kitchen preparing a turkey and all that went with it, together with a plum pudding (one of Eleanor's). Tables were laid out and decorated throughout the church hall and lounge. We put a name beside a place for each invited guest and everyone received a small gift. There were usually a few anxious moments at the last minute as people were arriving and we tried to ensure that everyone had somewhere to sit and an appropriate gift. One year we had a few sailors from an American ship which was in port to share Christmas dinner with us. To our horror we found that we were one place short for one of the group of sailors; an extra place was laid quickly and I rushed upstairs to find yet one more gift. I seized hold of a shaving set and brought it down all wrapped up. It was only then that I noticed that this final sailor was sporting a beard! A further hasty switch of parcels proved necessary.

The port of Barcelona was often visited by naval vessels. These were mostly ships of the American Sixth Fleet which was stationed in the Mediterranean. We often had visits from sailors coming ashore from these ships and we did our best to make them feel welcome.

One year just after Christmas we arranged a party at the centre to which we invited a group of American sailors. Between sixty and seventy of us gathered for this party which took the form of a buffet supper. After the meal there were games and entertainment. The latter included Elsa Day (who, it has to be admitted, was rather a large lady) singing a Noel Coward song in which she sang: "I wish I wasn't such a big girl." It brought the house down. The evening ended on a quieter note with the singing of a few carols.

On one such visit of a major warship to the port, there was a terrible accident in the harbour. A liberty boat laden with sailors who had gone ashore for the evening was on its way back to the warship when it collided with another larger boat going in the opposite direction. The liberty boat capsized and many of the sailors drowned in the oily waters of the harbour just offshore. There was a profound sense of distress and shock amongst the surviving members of the ship's company. Many of them had lost friends and close colleagues with whom they had been working only the day before. I visited the ship and attended a memorial ceremony on board. We invited any who wanted to come and visit us to share in our worship and take a meal with us. A number responded to this invitation and we did our best to offer them comfort in their loss. This incident is just one example of the kind that occur in chaplaincies across Europe from time to time. Chaplains are called up suddenly to come and help in a time of crisis. This happened to colleagues of ours in the Diocese of Europe at the time of the Zeebrugge ferry disaster. In such situations the chaplains and the local church communities act as ambassadors for Christ as they reach out and offer a helping hand to people in time of great need.

It has to be admitted that quarrels and divisions among Christians do nothing to help our attempts to communicate a message of love and reconciliation through Christ to an often divided and hurting world. So we were always glad of those occasions when we were drawn together with members of other traditions especially during the week of prayer for Christian unity in January. As has already been made clear, the Roman Catholic Church offers generous hospitality to Anglican congregations right across Europe and in

Spain we were certainly no exception.

A shared service with other congregations and churches took place one year at the German Lutheran Church in Barcelona. This was where Dietrich Bonhoeffer had been the chaplain at one time, before the outbreak of the second world war. He was eventually executed by the Nazis early in 1945, not long before that war came to an end.

On another occasion I was asked to give a lecture in Spanish on some of the recently produced Anglican Roman Catholic International Commission reports. This was to be delivered as part of the celebration of the week of prayer for Christian unity at a Roman Catholic ecumenical centre. My Spanish was nowhere near good enough to write out the address myself in Spanish. So I duly prepared the text of the lecture in English and got a Spanish friend, Carmen Black (whose English husband was a member of St George's) to translate my address for me into Spanish. I was then able to deliver the lecture in Spanish and was told later that I had spoken with a Catalan accent – which I took to be a compliment. At any rate the talk seemed to go down well and perhaps helped to foster good and friendly relations between our two church communions.

In January 1979, just a few months before we left to return to parish work in England, there was a united service with the Roman Catholics in the parish church of Bona Nova, just down the hill from where we were living. Members of St George's came as guests and received a warm welcome. We came together as fellow members of the body of Christ and met around the Lord's table. We sat in a circle round a central table on chairs rather than in pews. Wicker baskets contained the wafers, and pottery chalices were used. It was all very simple and reverent. There was some lively singing of hymns both in Catalan and in Spanish. I was asked to preach and to assist at the administration of the communion. After the service, which all greatly appreciated, we agreed to invite members of the parish church to come to a service held at St George's church later in the year for a return visit.

This "return of service" (to borrow a phrase from tennis), took place on the following Ash Wednesday. This time the sermon and readings were in Spanish and we followed the Series Three order of service which was in use just before the Alternative Service Book came out in 1980. The Imposition of Ashes was offered for all who wished to receive it but there was no obligation or pressure. This was not a tradition that I was used to but I knew that it was important for our friends from the parish church, so I was happy for their priest to take this part of the service. When it came to the Eucharistic prayer, we concelebrated. In inviting our church members to take part in this service, I wrote: "Please come and share in this joint act of worship which will emphasise the essential oneness in Christ of all Christians who truly love our Lord and seek to serve him."

As we prepared to leave Spain and return to Britain, I wrote in our church newsletter: "God has taught us so much through a host of different people and for all this we praise him and thank him that we have been allowed to spend part of our lives and ministry here in Spain." These words came truly from the heart.

CHAPTER ELEVEN

IN THE STEPS OF GORDON GUINNESS

In 1979 I was appointed vicar of Bishop Hannington Memorial Church in Hove. The church had been in existence only for about forty years. It was during the nineteen-thirties that Bishop George Bell of Chichester set in motion plans to build five new churches within his diocese. One of these was built to serve what was then a major new housing area to the west of Hove. It was named in memory of Bishop James Hannington, a Sussex man who, soon after he had been appointed Bishop to serve in East Africa, was martyred near the Uganda border in 1885.

Gordon Guinness was the first vicar of the new church, the building of which was completed in 1940. Gill was distantly related to Gordon and Grace Guinness by marriage and remembers as a child being taken to tea with Uncle Gordon and Auntie Grace in the vicarage that was about to become our home. Gordon was every inch a church-planter and the new congregation had grown under his leadership. When we arrived in Hove, there were still many who looked back fondly to those early years and they included some who discovered a living Christian faith through Gordon's ministry.

Bishop Hannington Memorial Church, showing the new Church Centre in the foreground

Three successive vicars had served in the parish after Gordon's departure and had built up the work that was begun when the parish was created in the 1930s before the new church building was completed. So we were coming to a well established church with a lively congregation.

We were given a marvellous send-off by the church in Barcelona with gifts that included a television set and a washing-machine, a great help as we were setting up a new home in the Holmes Avenue vicarage. Friends had driven a Budget van out to Barcelona and we drove it back loaded with all our possessions. Church Warden Donald Grover plus a team helped off-load the contents of the van and deposit them in the vicarage.

As far as our family were concerned, the transition to England meant less of a change for Andrew than for our two daughters, Carolyn and Susanna. Andrew continued with school at Monkton thanks to the ongoing grant from Hillingdon Council, but the girls both had new schools to contend with. Carolyn found it quite difficult to adjust to life in a huge newly formed English comprehensive school after her small and much more intimate international school in Barcelona from which she had just come. Eventually both girls settled very happily in Hove and made many new friends.

In September 1979 Gill's mother, Carol Hunt, moved into a house in the road next to where we were living. It was good to have her close by and she was a very positive influence in the parish and Carolyn could drop in to see her on her way home from school.

B.H. (the church was normally spoken of in this short-hand form) was fortunate in having a good number of young families attending. Many of these were professional people who were ready and willing to give active service within the life of the church. I saw it as part of my job to harness this talent and to encourage, train and utilise more and more lay ministry and leadership.

When I arrived there was a pattern of fortnightly Bible readings, usually delivered by the vicar and held in the church hall, alternating with home groups. Attendance was in the main usually confined to the elderly, whose heads it seemed to me were already crammed full of Bible knowledge. They all came to church on Sundays, some of them twice. Quite soon we moved over to a pattern of weekly home Bible study groups that were led by lay people apart from one central meeting for prayer once a month. We sought to encourage the growth of these home groups, a policy which has been pursued by successive vicars at B.H.

With so many families attending, there were well established children's groups ranging from a crèche through pathfinders and on to King's Own, the name given to the older teenage group. The Pathfinder group for youngsters aged eleven to fourteen was particularly strong at this stage. The church arranged a summer camp for this group in the New Forest.

B.H. was a busy church with a host of different groups meeting midweek and at weekends. We sought to strengthen the men's side of the work by holding quarterly men's breakfasts. Our men seemed quite happy to escape from the demands of home early on a Saturday morning provided they were served with a full English breakfast! Speakers at these events included Malcolm Muggeridge, Bishop Peter of Lewes and Brian Hogbin, a local consultant surgeon whose subject was "living on a knife edge"!

Gill started a Tuesday Group in our home for mothers and small children. A crèche was provided in one room and the mums gathered in the sitting room. A team of leaders included Anthea Collard and Meriel Vincent. Our Jack Russell dog would wander through a gaggle of tiny tots at refreshment times. The trouble was that when the small people clutched a biscuit with a view to popping it into their mouths, Sheba assumed that the biscuit was meant for her and would gently gobble it up leaving behind a tearful two-year- old. Gluttony was Sheba's besetting sin! The programme for this group ranged through a variety of family and faith subjects. Sometimes there was a speaker and at other times a taped talk followed by plenty of lively discussion. It was a good group to which one could invite a new young mother who was just trying out the church.

In an area that contained many young families, there were frequent requests for baptism. Some of these families had little or no connection with the church but were under pressure to "get the baby done". On the one hand I had no wish to send out a message that such families were not wanted in the church by excluding them through a very strict baptism policy. On the other hand, I didn't want them to make promises in a public service the meaning of which they were unlikely to understand. So we devised a three-part Introduction to the Christian Faith and invited couples to work through this course so that the baptism service, when it happened, would mean something to them. The promises and affirmations of faith that they were making having been explained. Nearly all the couples agreed to take part and the first two sessions of the course were taken by lay couples from the church. They would normally take the course to the parents' home so that babysitting would not be a problem. I would then visit the home for the third and final session. For quite a lot of young parents, this course was an important step along the road towards Christian commitment and active church membership.

We continued the practice of holding church weekend house parties with a visiting speaker that had been established long before we arrived. These were usually very helpful in building up the fellowship and helping people to get to know each other and to explore their faith at greater depth. There was, however, one particular houseparty that was held at Ashburnham Place, a Christian conference centre in East Sussex and in the depths of the countryside, which had about it more than a touch of Fawlty Towers. Things got off to a shaky start thanks to some faulty directions to Ashburnham sent out from our church office. These resulted in some of our number wandering around the Sussex countryside, hopelessly lost. One couple arrived very late indeed and the husband was red in the face with rage. Our treasurer tried to smooth things over and offered to show the steaming couple to their room. Unfortunately he got his numbers mixed up and when he threw open the bedroom door, one of our elderly parishioners was to be seen standing only half dressed in the middle of the room, preparing for bed. Our friend Gareth beat a hasty retreat and led the couple down the stairs again and eventually found them the right room. The following night we held the Saturday evening entertainment. All went well until two of our men performed a Peter Cook and Dudley Moore sketch. To many it seemed fairly innocuous if perhaps a bit borderline. But to some others, it seemed deeply shocking. If we had had some smelling-salts handy, I am sure we could have put them to good use with a few of our conference members. Meanwhile our guest speaker, George Duncan, was completely unfazed by these goings-on and and did much to pour oil on troubled waters. The remainder of the weekend passed off happily.

Whilst we were still in Spain, with the help of my father we had been able to develop an old and derelict water mill into a home base. It was situated in a small village not far from Ross-on-Wye where there was some trout-fishing close by. This provided us with a place to which we could escape for family holidays. It also gave us an ideal setting for retreat weekends for our confirmation candidates. Sheba, when still a puppy, had to come along for the ride and tended to wreak havoc with human underwear if given half a chance. It all added to the excitement as teenagers pursued her with a view to rescuing an endangered garment. In spite of her mischievous traits, she had a placid temperament; she was a great favourite with the children and an asset to vicarage life.

On arriving in Hove, we soon discovered that there would be work to do on some of the church buildings. The congregation had developed a very commendable passion for the support of overseas missionary work. Just over half of the church's annual income was being given away to missionary projects. But this enthusiasm seemed to be leading to the neglect of some of our own church buildings. The Pathfinder group for young teenagers was meeting in what had at one time been a scout hut. When we arrived, it was rather grandly called the Tudor Room but it was in a poor state of repair. If a health and safety team had paid it a visit, I think they would probably have closed it down. The church hall itself was also in a bad state of repair. The kitchen was very small and totally inadequate when it came to catering for a large church family function The lavatories were a disgrace, with green mould growing on the walls of the men's urinals.

It was in the church hall that all the children's work took

place on a Sunday. It was situated towards the end of a street and a good distance from the church. This was highly inconvenient for parents who had to drop their children off early at the hall, then make their way up the road to the church and finally collect them from the hall after the main church service. The church itself had only one lavatory and that was situated at the end of a short passage and could only be approached via the vicar's vestry. There were no proper coffee-making facilities at the church.

This was the urgent situation that the church council had to address. Eventually it was agreed that we should approach an experienced church architect, Ken White, with a view to his drawing up plans for a new church lounge that would be joined on to the church. The extension would also include a kitchen, some toilets (including one with disabled access), a crèche room and a further meeting room that would eventually be used as a church office. A new entrance way into the extension and the church was also envisaged. It was an ambitious set of plans that was finally produced and the total estimate for this new work was £220,000. This was to include a complete renovation of the car park area and a new heating system for the church and the adjacent centre. The Diocesan Arts Council was brought fully into the picture and gave its approval to the plans. Planning permission was also sought and obtained from the local council.

When the plans were presented to a special congregational meeting, there was something of a shocked intake of breath when the full costs of the proposed project were revealed. Could we raise such a large sum? Would it be a right stewardship of money to spend it in this way even if it could be raised? Should a large sum be donated towards the support of missions abroad as had been the pattern in the past? Would the raising of money for new church buildings undermine and drastically reduce our existing support for missionary work? These were some of the questions which were being raised and which had to be addressed.

I arranged an open meeting at the vicarage for all who had such questions and we had a full and frank exchange of views. I stressed the fact that if we were to sustain our overseas mission support in the future, we could not afford to neglect our home mission responsibilities towards those who were living immediately around us. And if we were to have a credible ministry to local people towards the end of the twentieth century, we needed to have good facilities as a community base from which we could operate. I also believed that once people learned to give more generously than they had ever done before, the giving to missions would not suffer but rather it would increase. In the event this prediction proved to be correct. The scheme was approved, first by the P.C.C., and then by the whole congregation at an extraordinary general meeting of the whole parish.

Once the work got under way, a small group of people kept a careful watch on the work as it progressed. John Puttock, who was professionally involved in one aspect of the building trade, put in many hours of work on our behalf. John Head took care of any legal matters as they arose. And Gareth Stacey was the treasurer for the building fund. We were fortunate in having James Clark, a retired bank manager and a very devout and gracious Christian, as the man who handled all the covenants. He had the impressive gift of being able to explain the details of a covenant form and to allay any fears that a potential donor might have. He answered every query and reassured the most reluctant. With his gentle encouragement, the covenant forms poured in and the giving to the fund mounted more quickly that anyone had expected. An auction of people's treasures raised the total by a further £5,000.

Bishop Festo Kivengere talking to Grace Guinness (widow of Gordon Guinness) at the opening of the new Bishop Hannington Memorial Church Centre in 1983

The building work started early in 1982 and was completed by the following October. With our historic links with the church in Uganda, we invited the Rt Revd Festo Kivengere, a well known Ugandan bishop, to preach at the opening dedication service for the new building. Bishop Festo had a world-wide ministry of preaching and teaching. It was he who was famously once asked in an interview: "If you were in a room with Idi Amin and he handed you a revolver, what would you do?" He replied: "I would hand the gun back to Amin and say: 'Mr. President, this is your weapon, not mine.

Mine is the weapon of love.'" Festo was the obvious choice to do the honours and preach at the opening dedication service. The new lounge was to be called: "the Luwum lounge" in memory of Archbishop Janani Luwum who had been shot and killed during the Idi Amin regime in Uganda. The opening service of thanksgiving and dedication was a time of much praise to God and great rejoicing.

The opening of the new centre enormously increased the scope of our ministry. Children and parents could now be catered for on a Sunday under one roof as they all worshipped on a single site. There were excellent new crèche and Sunday School facilities. This led to an almost instant growth in the work amongst the families. The Tuesday Group moved from the cramped conditions in our home into the much more spacious church lounge. In time we took the step of offering a second morning service at 9.30 a.m. on a Sunday. This was designed for young families with small children, and many lay people were involved in leading the worship and the length of service was kept to under the hour. Numbers at this extra service were not large, perhaps hovering around sixty, but it was meeting an important need.

A new group which was developed in the lounge was called Cameo (short for "come and meet each other"). It was the brainchild of Margaret Weir, who led the group for a number of years. It was designed for elderly members of the community of whom there are a considerable number in Hove and it was entirely lay led. It met once a week for coffee, chat, and usually a talk on some subject. A whole range of topics of interest were addressed with a view to enhancing the lives of those who came along. From time to time a talk would follow a specifically Christian theme, particularly around the festivals. Many older people were gently nudged into the family of the church through this gentle approach. And many others who were often quite sad and lonely experienced a sense of belonging and received much loving support through the work of Cameo.

As the work developed, we were able to take on more staff. Helen Snider came to us for a few years as a deaconess after studying at Cranmer Hall. She did valuable work amongst all sections of the community and her work was much appreciated. When it was time for her to move on, Ann Ballard took her place. She came from Wycliffe Hall Oxford and had a beautiful singing voice. She was often quite visible around the parish in somewhat striking pink dungarees! When we moved to Paris, she took possession of our cat who was aptly named Sherlock as we were living in Holmes Avenue. Just before we left the parish, Mark Plater joined the team as a youth worker. He and Ann were both in place when Alex Ross replaced me as vicar.

At one point during our time at B.H., our Rural Dean, Hugh Glaisyer, suggested that it would be a good idea for us to invite Bishop Eric to conduct a service for us other than a confirmation service. I thought back to curacy days when the Bishop of Willesden had carried out a parish visitation at Emmanuel that lasted a day. So I invited Bishop Eric to come and spend a whole day with us. The date was duly fixed a year in advance.

Bishop Eric and B.H. were at opposite ends of the ecclesiastical pole. Needless to say, the Bishop was at the higher end! I felt that it would be most helpful if we arranged a day's programme that would give him as typical a view as possible of our church life. So the day began with a simple 1662 service of Holy Communion which was the norm for a Wednesday morning. The Bishop, of course, presided. During the course of the day he visited an old people's home in the parish and called in at our church school. He had lunch with Peter Davies and his wife Linda; Peter was priest-in-charge of our daughter church of Holy Cross. After lunch the Bishop came back to the vicarage and I made allowance in his schedule for an hour spent horizontally in our spare bedroom (I was still a great advocate of the siesta!). I felt that by this stage in the day, he would need a break from meeting and talking to people. Alas! This plan was sabotaged at the last minute by a clergyman in trouble who came to see him. I left them closeted for an hour or more in our sitting-room.

The two of us managed to sit down quietly together for a glass of sherry before it was time to make our way across to the church lounge for a parish supper. It has often been said that while evangelicals know how to eat well, it is the Anglo-catholics who know how to drink well. On this occasion I made sure that some decent wine was served with the meal!

The visit happened at a time when Bishop Eric was celebrating a decade of his episcopate. So we presented him with some gifts to mark the occasion. The Bishop's son had revealed in a local newspaper article that our honoured guest had a weakness for bath salts. So I paid a visit to the Body Shop and we began by presenting him with a packet of purple bath salts done up with purple ribbon. I had sounded-out his chaplain as to his taste in wine and so we were able to give him two bottles of St Emilion, a liquid designed to reach those parts which the bath salts could not reach. Finally I had heard that John Stott and the Bishop were in touch with each other with a view to establishing a greater mutual understanding concerning issues that divided evangelicals from Anglo-Catholics. So we gave him a copy of John Stott's book, *Issues Facing Christians Today*, to reach those parts which neither bath salts nor wine could reach! Bishop Eric took this presentation ceremony in very good part and seemed appreciative of the various offerings that came his way.

We then moved into what was for us a fairly typical type of prayer meeting. We sang a few hymns and songs and then Bishop Eric, after a reading from Scripture, spoke to us as a true pastor of his flock about Jesus the Good Shepherd who knows his sheep and is known by them. We then broke into small groups for a time of open prayer and the Bishop joined one of these groups. And then it was time for us all to go home after what had been a very rewarding day. I gathered later that the Bishop had enjoyed his day with us. We got to know our Bishop better and he got to know us.

Gill's mother, Carol Hunt, took an active part in the life of the church and was always very supportive. She had been a very able public speaker in her day but by 1984, she was finding it difficult to get about. Her driving was getting increasingly hazardous. When she offered people lifts in her car, they would quickly make alternative arrangements. Her doctor finally persuaded her to cease driving. She found this hard but we were able to provide transport for her whenever it was needed. Carol was always on the lookout for people to befriend and frequently invited lonely people home to tea. There was no doubting her great love for people.

She was weakened by a stroke early in 1984 and died in May of that year. Her funeral in our church had something of a family service atmosphere about it which is just what she would have wished. Children who knew her were encouraged to attend. A family group sang a hymn that Gill's brother David had written many years previously. It began with the lines: "In his beauty shall mine eyes see the King upon his throne." Keith de Berry gave a tribute to his sister and

Richard Bewes, one of her nephews, preached a sermon on the text, "Here we have no continuing city, but we seek one that is to come." The service ended with the singing of the hymn "Thine be the Glory." It was accompanied by two schoolgirls who had known Carol well, playing trumpets with tears streaming down their faces. It was a truly remarkable send-off for a great Christian lady. The open scripture reading beside her bed the night she died contained these words: "Forgetting what is behind and straining towards what is ahead, I press on towards the goal to win the prize for which God has called me heavenwards in Christ Jesus." Philippians 3, verses 13 and 14. Carol never ceased to press towards that goal while breath remained in her body.

CHAPTER TWELVE

THE PRICELESS LEGACY OF JAMES HANNINGTON

As far as I know, there are not many churches which are named after James Hannington. The only other one that I have come across is situated in a tiny African village on the borders of Kenya and Uganda. At first sight, it seems an odd choice of name but a glance at the Church of England lectionary reveals that on October 29 James Hannington, Bishop of Eastern Equatorial Africa, was martyred in Uganda, in the year 1885. James Hannington came from a well known Sussex family who owned a large department store in Brighton so he is better known in that part of the world than elsewhere.

James was born in 1847 at Hurstpierpoint, about eight miles inland from Brighton. His parents were very comfortably off and he grew up in a large country house set within extensive grounds on the edge of the village. His mother was a gentle soul and James remained devoted to her. For many years, however, he was somewhat afraid of his father, who was very strict. Even as a young boy, James was very adventurous. On one occasion he managed to blow-off his thumb while manufacturing an explosive device with a view to destroying a wasps' nest!

He was educated first by a tutor at home and later at a school in Brighton. He left school at the age of fifteen in order to start work in the family business. In his journals he has not a good word to say about his education. He spent six years in the family firm but was never at ease in the business world. He loved the outdoor life and was fascinated by plants, birds, beetles and other insects.

As a young man James visited Paris with a tutor as his guide. On one Sunday morning he attended a morning service in the "Ambassador's" chapel which was a forerunner of St Michael's church, the very church which was to become our next spiritual home. With considerable family wealth behind him, James was able to travel across Europe visiting places such as Moscow and St Petersburg. His father had given him a shotgun when he was seventeen and he later became a very good shot, winning prizes for marksmanship. In 1864 he was commissioned as a second lieutenant in the first Sussex Artillery Volunteers. He had an enormous zest for living. Much of his time was spent as a gentleman at leisure on the family yacht. And yet even at this stage, he was not wholly satisfied with a life apart from God.

His father had built a chapel in the grounds of the Hannington home, which for a number of years was a Free Church chapel. But in 1868 the family switched from nonconformity to membership of the Church of England and the church building became an Anglican Church within the parish of Hurstpierpoint. Soon after this James began to think seriously about ordination. He was much moved by the Christian example of a cousin who died in the peace of Christ. With the help of a family friend, he began to study the Greek New Testament. Eventually his parents agreed to his seeking ordination and he was sent up to Oxford to study at St Mary's Hall. As a student he failed to apply himself to his studies and instead enjoyed a fairly boisterous social life. When he was not at Oxford, he went to Devon where, under the guidance of the Revd Scriven, he helped out in the parish of Martinhoe and slowly worked towards obtaining a degree. He was awarded a B.A. degree some five years after starting his studies at Oxford. Had his studies been in the natural sciences, it is probable that he would have achieved a much better degree in a far shorter time.

Soon after coming down from Oxford, a college friend began to pray for him. He also wrote him a letter describing his own journey into a lively Christian faith and he urged James to follow the same path of Christian discipleship. He received no reply to his letter for thirteen months and he assumed that the letter must have been thrown away. In fact, however, it had been set to one side but not forgotten. Meanwhile James was struggling to prepare himself for further examination test papers, success in which would lead on to ordination. At his first attempt he he scored a very low mark in a paper on the prayer book and he failed. He was sent packing by the Bishop of Exeter. A year later he surmounted this hurdle, was duly ordained deacon in 1874 and began working as a curate in the Martinhoe parish. He was a popular young man who related easily to all sorts of people, but at this stage he had little understanding of the good news of Christ and he felt totally unfit to be a minister within the church. He became increasingly depressed, until he remembered the letter that his friend had written to him. He made contact with him again and his friend sent him a book to read which explained in straightforward terms the way to find peace with God.

It was during a visit to his old home in Hurstpierpoint that he read this book and it was as if the scales fell from his eyes and he could suddenly see the glory of the good news of new life in Christ. He describes what happened in these words: "I sprang out of bed and leaped about the room praising God that Jesus died for me. From that day to this, I have lived under the shadow of His wings in the assurance of faith that He is mine and I am His." He still had his struggles to face but he was a changed man. His preaching, hitherto dry and moralistic, now came alive.

After leaving Martinhoe, he became curate-in-charge of St George's, Hurstpierpoint and remained there seven years. But before taking up this new post, he gained further temporary experience sharing in parish missions in a church in Derby. He was always eager to share his faith with others but managed to do this in his home parish without causing everyone to run for cover whenever they saw him coming. He was quite happy to converse with people about things that interested them, particularly if it related to sport or country life. He spent much time visiting people in their homes and was able to build up a strong men's Bible study in the village.

In 1877, after a short engagement, he married Elizabeth Hankin-Turvin and they went on to have four children. She was a great support to him in his parish life but she was not a keen walker and did not enjoy travel. So when James was away taking missions in other parishes and later serving with C.M.S. in Africa, she stayed at home with the children.

In terms of churchmanship, James was most at home within the evangelical tradition, but he was not strictly-speaking a party man and was happy to mix with Christians of all traditions. He preferred to describe himself as first and foremost simply a Christian. During his travels in Africa he was grateful for the tender care he received from Jesuit missionaries at a time when he was desperately ill and close to death.

The latter half of the nineteenth century was a time of vigorous missionary expansion by many different societies, including the Church Missionary Society. The much publicised travels of men like Livingstone, Stanley and Speke had brought Africa very much to the forefront of people's minds and C.M.S., along with other church organisations, was eager to send missionaries to territories that were fast opening up. So it is hardly surprising that James Hannington, with his strong passion for the mission of the church, was challenged and stirred when he heard that missionaries were wanted to take the gospel of Christ to East Africa. In 1882 James responded to an appeal for recruits from C.M.S. He offered to serve with this society on what he described as a short-term basis, by which he meant for a period of between three and five years. He was aged thirty-four at the time and he was asked to lead a team of six recruits to travel out to Uganda to support the work of the two missionaries who were already there. The team set out from London docks in May 1882 and sailed to Zanzibar. James busied himself during the voyage with the study of Swahili. They arrived at their destination in June of that year and after a period of time sorting out luggage and porters, they set off into the interior towards Lake Victoria Nyanza. At some of their stops en route, the party was able to stay with missionaries of various societies but for most of the journey, it was a case of camping for the night. James soon contracted malarial fever and was ill for most of the journey. He also suffered from rheumatic fever and dysentery and by the time the party eventually reached the Lake, his health had completely broken down. During that arduous journey he was often at death's door. Sometimes he had to be carried in a hammock by a team of porters. His very poor state of health persuaded the rest of the team that James must return to the coast and go back to England. Bitterly disappointed at not being able to stay and pursue his calling, he nevertheless accepted this decision. In May 1883 he set sail for home and a month later he was back amongst his family at Hurstpierpoint.

Back in Sussex his health rapidly improved, until just over a year later he was passed as fit to return to missionary service in East Africa. At C.M.S. it was decided that there was the need for a bishop to oversee the growing work of church and mission that was spreading inland from Mombasa. In June 1884 James Hannington was duly consecrated by the Archbishop of Canterbury as Bishop of Eastern Equatorial Africa.

In late 1884 his wife gave birth to a fourth child and it was planned that she and the new baby should eventually travel out to East Africa to be based in Mombasa, a plan which was destined never to come to fruition.

The new bishop set sail in November 1884 and headed first for the Middle East where he travelled through Lebanon and the Holy Land taking confirmation services on behalf of the Archbishop of Canterbury in both Beirut and Jerusalem.

He eventually docked in Mombasa in January 1885. The working staff under him in East Africa at that time consisted of twelve clergy, eleven lay people and four missionary wives. He set about visiting local schools and initiated the construction of a new church in Mombasa. The mission owned a steamer in which he travelled up and down the coast visiting Zanzibar to the south.

In March and April of that year he undertook an arduous journey two hundred miles into the interior to visit a lonely missionary who was carrying on bravely in a famine-stricken area. There were various stops along the route and at least one was at an established mission station. They would frequently start as early as four o'clock in the morning to make the most of cooler weather conditions. Mr. Wray, to whom the Bishop's party brought relief supplies, had to withdraw to the coast as his position had become untenable. But during this visit the Bishop made good contacts with surrounding Masai tribesmen and caught his first glimpse of Mount Kilimanjaro.

Soon after his return from this expedition, Hannington began to plan a journey to Lake Victoria Nyanza, taking a shorter northern route rather than the one he had taken from Zanzibar on his previous tour. The southern route from Zanzibar was perilous health-wise with the constant threat of rheumatic fever, malaria and dysentery. His plan was to establish a chain of mission stations along this new route from the coast right into Uganda. He took advice from many whose knowledge of the interior was greater than his and they all encouraged him to explore further this northern route. The Bishop was completely unaware of the fact that the Ugandans were extremely fearful and suspicious of any aliens who approached their territory via this route, which they regarded as their own back door.

The Bishop visited outposts to the north of Mombasa. He was a man of boundless energy, frequently walking as much as thirty miles a day in the course of his visiting. His May diary for that year records that he had walked six hundred miles since March. On Trinity Sunday he ordained two African deacons, and on a Sunday in June he conducted his first African confirmation service, confirming thirteen candidates. A further visit into the interior gave him the opportunity to choose sites for further future mission stations. A hunger for education was already evident and he was beginning to receive requests from chiefs for missionary teachers.

In July 1885 the Bishop and his party were ready to depart on what was to be his final journey to the Lake. In Uganda hostility was already mounting towards foreigners and Christians, with the ascent to the throne of the young King Mwanga, who had already had a number of Christian pages at court tortured and burnt to death. They died singing hymns to Christ their Lord.

Provisions for the journey included bales of cloth, coils of wire and beads, to be used as gifts and as payment for provisions along the route. The diet was supplemented by guinea fowl and, on one occasion, an elephant! In spite of all such preparations and precautions there were times on the journey when they came very close to starvation. The party numbered two hundred, most of whom were porters, along with a newly ordained deacon, the Revd Jones. Bargaining for food when passing through Kikuyu country proved particularly difficult, since Masai warriors were at times very demanding and threatening.

On October 12th, the Bishop left Jones and most of his party behind and pressed on alone with fifty porters. Jones would never see his bishop alive again. There were three missionaries installed in Uganda at the time who realised the danger that Hannington was in and they tried hard to intercede on his behalf with the young king but it was all in vain. King Mwanga sent a group of his warriors to intercept the Bishop and to execute him along with his entourage. The Bishop was taken prisoner on the twenty-first of the month and was held captive for just over a week before finally being executed. Details of those final days are recorded in his journal. His final words were remembered and passed down to future generations: "Tell the king that I am about to die for Baganda and that I have purchased the road to Baganda with my life." Of fifty who accompanied the Bishop on his final journey only four survived to tell the tale.

His biographer, E.G. Dawson, comments: "To us he bequeaths the priceless legacy of a devoted life." That tribute provided the title for this chapter. His life and the manner of his death as a Christian martyr deserve to be remembered and to become the inspiration for devotion to Christ for succeeding generations. Bishop Hannington Memorial Church has a great name to live up to.

With the legacy of such a life to motivate them, it is hardly surprising that we came into a church where there was so strong an emphasis on the need to support overseas mission work. Links had been forged with a number of missionaries serving abroad. Francis Iliff was working in Afghanistan and her mother was an elderly member of our congregation. Richard and Christine Viney were working at a mission school in India. Links were forged with the South American Missionary Society and we gave support to Nicholas and Catherine Drayson working with the church in Argentina. During our time at B.H. Alan Butler left us for Nepal to work as a water engineer with a missionary society and Peter and Sandy Renew, whose faith had come alive through the life of B.H., offered for missionary service in Afghanistan. A number in the church were keen supporters of the Rwanda mission and one of our young people spent a year abroad in Rwanda during our time in Hove. Our daughter, Carolyn, spent her gap year after leaving school with S.A.M.S. at a school in Asunçion, Paraguay. Other societies also received considerable financial support and on the home mission front we gave support to David and Alice Fanstone who were working with an evangelistic team called Open Air Campaigners.

The fact that our massive support for mission was helping

to peg our quota payments to the Diocesan Common Fund brought us sadly into a time of conflict with the Diocesan Board of Finance. The Diocesan Treasurer managed to get agreement for a new policy for estimating quota contributions. Henceforth this was to include all income that passed through the church accounts, including that which was being passed on to missions. At a stroke, this would probably have doubled the amount that we would then have been required to pay into the common fund and it could well have done serious damage to the support we were committed to giving to missionaries and their supporting societies. I have to confess that I sent off an angry letter to the treasurer with copies for all the members of the Diocesan Board of Finance. They would not budge, however, and the new method of estimating quota went ahead. At this point it was agreed by members of B.H. that a group of us would set up a new trust fund which would be called the Bishop Hannington Memorial Fund. Its accounts would be kept entirely separate from the church accounts and the congregation members would be offered separate coloured weekly mission gift envelopes via which they could contribute to the new trust fund. The trustees of the fund were all members of the church and they were given responsibility for administering any income that came their way in accordance with the expressed wishes of the donors. Looking back, I regret the intemperate nature of my correspondence with the Diocesan officials. It would have been so much better and more satisfactory all round if those on both sides of the dispute could have sat down and worked out some compromise agreement. But both the Treasurer and I were obstinate people and no halfway measures were even considered. Later when I was Archdeacon in northern France, I was responsible for seeing that all our churches paid their share into the European diocesan fund and it was rather a case of poacher turned gamekeeper! In that later instance our Synod came to the conclusion that it was reasonable for a church to be allowed to give away ten per cent of its income to mission without incurring quota liability; but beyond that, all income would be subject to quota. Some such arrangement could perhaps have been worked out and agreed with B.H. but it was not to be. Some time later the Diocese of Chichester reformed its system of assessing common fund payments and introduced a much fairer system. If any system is to work, it has in the end to be seen to be fair. Otherwise people will be encouraged to find loopholes to avoid payments.

As for B.H., the new trust fund flourished and, even with the new building programme that came in early in the 1980s, its income continued to rise as recruits were sent overseas. But overseas mission was not the Church's only concern. We were encouraged to engage more actively in mission to our local community by different visiting preachers who came to us from time to time for guest weekends. These included Keith de Berry, Roger Simpson, Ian Knox and Gavin Reid. They usually stayed for two or three days and the programme often included supper parties in different homes to which our members invited neighbours to come and meet whoever was the weekend guest speaker. After supper, a talk was given and then there was opportunity for questions and debate. An evangelistic address was then given at both the main Sunday services. Over each of these weekends there was nearly always a handful of people who expressed interest in exploring faith issues further or who prayed to invite Christ to become central in their lives.

On two occasions we attempted to take the Christian gospel to other parishes in our area. I led a team of lay people first to Henfield and later to Ardingly and in both places the pattern was much the same, with supper parties on Friday and Saturday evenings followed by questions and debate. The preaching on Sunday contained an evangelistic thrust. How effective these visits were I am not sure but they certainly gave our team a taste for parish-based mission.

In 1985 B.H., along with the churches in Hurstpierpoint, were celebrating the centenary of Bishop Hannington's martyrdom on the borders of Uganda. I was able to take six weeks off from parish duties to visit East Africa. After a brief stop with friends in Nairobi, I travelled on to Entebbe and was the guest there of Bishop Misaeri Kauma and his family. My first few days were spent at the Namirembi diocesan guest house. I had stayed there years before when arriving in Uganda with Richard Gill. Time was spent visiting old haunts in Kampala such as Mengo Hospital where our son Andrew had been born. I was taken by Bishop Misaeri to visit Namugongo Diocesan College, which had suffered much in the Idi Amin regime but was now running certificate courses for ordinands. I was also able to visit memorials to the young Christian martyrs who had perished one hundred years before during the reign of King Mwanga. These included a newly built memorial church which Robert Runcie, Archbishop of Canterbury, had opened the previous year. Whilst in Kampala I ran into Canon Shalita, the Diocesan treasurer, who had visited B.H. during the time of my predecessor, William Filby. I went on a parish visit with Misaere one afternoon and there was a tremendous welcome awaiting the bishop and a great feast prepared in his honour. On my first Sunday in Kampala I preached in Namirembe Cathedral on the theme of "Christ our Peace". Outside that cathedral stands a memorial to Bishop Hannington. I received wonderful hospitality from Misaere and his family but the political situation all around was insecure and the regime of President Obote was tottering. At night you could hear bursts of gunfire coming from different parts of the city.

One afternoon Misaere came home all of a sudden and said that he was off again to Gayaza High School for girls. Would I like to jump in and come a long with him and by the way, would I preach when I was there? I had no idea who the congregation would be but it turned out to be a Communion service for the staff. I hastily had a look at the readings for the day, jotted down a few headings and that was it. It was one of those occasions when one simply had to rely on the Holy Spirit for instant inspiration.

A few days later I was off to Busoga in the east of Uganda from where I was taken to Kyando and was able to see the actual spot where Bishop Hannington was martyred. I was also able to visit the small thatched roof village church, also called the Bishop Hannington Memorial Church. I was taken to a local village school which catered for three hundred children. Bishop Cyprian of Busoga and his family gave me a very warm welcome when I stayed with them. One could not but be impressed by the warm hospitality of all the people of Uganda. It was soon time to leave Kampala and to move on to the second leg of my trip. I spent my fifty-first birthday in Nairobi en route for Khartoum. I visited Nairobi cathedral and worshipped there on the Sunday and listened to Michael Bourdeaux preaching a sermon on the suffering church in different parts of the world. That was before the collapse of communism. On January 21st I flew to Khartoum where I stayed at the Sudan Interior Mission headquarters and met up with friends we had known back in the sixties who were now running their guest house. The following day in Khartoum I caught up with a few of my old students from the American Commercial School and saw them frequently during the following few days. In Omdurman I was able to see many old friends including the now very aged Aziz who had been my colleague in the hospital office and Fahmi Suleiman, the former headmaster of the school where I had taught. During this visit I preached three times in all, two of these sermons being in Arabic, thanks to a friend who helped correct the script of my sermon. My Arabic was very rusty but was beginning to come back.

January 28th was Gill's birthday. I tried all morning to get through to her on the telephone. In the end she managed to put a call through to me to tell me that my mother had died that morning. It was a great shock and totally unexpected. A few years earlier she had got married again, this time to a man she had known in her youth, Tom Grieve, a Scotsman who had two daughters by his previous marriage. I didn't feel that I would be much use supporting him and in the end I decided to stay on in Khartoum and fulfil commitments I had already undertaken there. Our three children went to my mother's funeral on February 1st in the parish church of Remenham near Henley-on-Thames, which was where she and her husband, Tom, used to worship.

Gill was due to join me on the 31st and duly arrived that evening. She was just getting over a very bad bout of 'flu and was badly in need of a change. The weather in January in Khartoum is sunny and pleasantly warm, which was just what she needed after a period of illness. In between other engagements, I managed a few games of tennis at the Sudan Lawn Tennis Association courts, not far from the guest house where I was staying. I met up with a former Minister of Education with whom Brian de Saram used to play tennis, now an old man. The following Sunday I went with a Sudanese pastor to take a service on the outskirts of Omdurman at which I preached and baptised a number of candidates. Gill grew weary shaking hands with hundreds of people! On visits to Omdurman we found signs of tension and division within the church family, probably with tribal conflict at its roots. We were able to visit Sitt Josephine and her family: she had been Gill's Arabic teacher twenty years earlier! The return journey took us home via Sofia in a Balkans airline plane.

It had been a very emotional few weeks with my mother's death in the middle of a time of revisiting a country where I had made my home for ten years. In spite of many problems, we found a church that was full of life and growing.

When she reached Khartoum, Gill told me that the post of St Michael's Paris was being advertised. On arrival home, I got in touch with Don Irving, the General Secretary of I.C.S., who was handling the appointment, and put in an application. We attended interviews a few weeks later and as a result I was appointed as the new chaplain in succession to Peter Sertin, who had recently suffered a heart attack and was returning to England for health reasons. The Rt Revd John Satterthwaite, the Bishop of Gibraltar in Europe, telephoned a short while after that and invited me to become the next Archdeacon of Northern France, an area that in ecclesiastical terms covered all of France except for the Riviera.

I had made it plain that we would not be able to leave B.H. until the end of the year because in the autumn there were to be special celebrations marking the centenary of Bishop Hannington's martyrdom. These duly took place the following October, when we were able to welcome as our special guests Bishop Misaere and his wife Geraldine, from the Diocese of Namirembe in Kampala. The highlight of this

Bishop Misaere Kauma from Namirembe, Kampala, with Brian and Gill at the centenary celebrations in 1985 marking the martyrdom of Bishop James Hannington

visit was a wonderful celebration of James Hannington's life in a service at which Bishop Misaere preached. The church was packed with many invited guests and there was much joyful singing as well as a dramatic presentation of the life and death of Bishop Hannington. After all the kindness that I had received in Uganda, we were so glad to be able to return hospitality to Misaere and Geraldine, who stayed with us for about a week. It was a very special and memorable time, which emphasised the links between B.H. and the Church in Uganda. After a series of warm and rather emotional farewells, our next journey took us across the Channel to Paris where fresh challenges awaited us at St Michael's Church in the centre of the city.

CHAPTER THIRTEEN

A MOVING TRAIN

For a short while after leaving school, I used to travel on a commuter train between Warwick and Birmingham. There was a certain octogenarian who travelled regularly along this route too. One day a seventy-year-old man ran to catch the train as it was moving out of the station. He just made it; swinging himself into the carriage, provoking the octogenarian to mutter, "Silly young fool," to no one in particular.

I am reminded of this incident as I think back to the start of our life in Paris which we shared with St Michael's Church. Starting work there was rather like jumping onto a train that was already moving at some speed. We arrived in Paris in the depths of winter in January 1986. Gill in particular had found leaving our home and many friends in Hove especially difficult. We had spent the previous seven years amongst many contemporaries of our own age and all our children had grown up together. I was fifty-two soon after we arrived in Paris (perhaps not yet just a silly old fool!) and we knew that we were moving to a much younger congregation. Would we find new friends within this new community?

And then there was the apartment into which we were

moving. We had just left behind a vicarage with a garden. We had visited Paris some months previously and seen the flat but we were not all that impressed. It was on two floors adjacent to the church. The bedrooms, which were on the lower floor, resembled cabins on board a ship. Our own bedroom was one floor up from a busy street and right over a car lift, which descended to two floors of underground car parks. The doors to the lift opened and shut making loud clanking noises. Gill was quite frightened that one day she would be stuck in our car inside this lift when it broke down. Such a breakdown was a real possibility. So we approached this new home and new job with some misgivings.

Steve Wookey, the assistant chaplain, had held the fort at St Michael's during a nine month interregnum. For a short while he had been helped by Brian and Eileen de Saram, our former friends and colleagues from the Sudan. Steve was a very fine cricketer who had distinguished himself by playing for both Oxford and Cambridge. His moment of greatest sporting triumph came when he bowled out Geoffrey Boycott for a duck. Steve was a great colleague to work with. He was very gracious in showing me the ropes and in helping me to adapt to a very different job to the one I had held in Hove. He had a lively sense of humour which is always a help when one is working under pressure, as we often were. We were once both faced with a sheet of paper inviting us to send in prayer requests for the I.C.S. quarterly prayer diary. For some reason we decided to send in a spoof request along with all the more serious ones. So we composed a request from Sheba the dog which read as follows: "Sheba is praising for Toc-H. teas and was heard to bark, 'the half was not told me'." To our amazement Charles Bonsall, who was responsible for this prayer diary, printed it!

Steve's main area of work was amongst the student element in our congregation. He was particularly gifted at getting alongside them and making them feel welcome whenever they arrived. We had a church notice board which advertised student accommodation and part-time jobs. People would drift in at different times during the week to see what was available and a friendly chat and a cup of coffee were sometimes a student's first introduction to the life of the church. Every autumn, or rentrée as it was called, saw the arrival of a fresh intake of students for their year out from a British university. There also tended to be an influx of new au pairs at this time of the year.

As far as the services were concerned, we tended to share the load but were helped particularly in leading worship by a team of lay assistants and several lay readers. The worship in the morning usually followed the Alternative Service Book patterns. Crèche and Sunday School operated upstairs whilst a small Pathfinder group met in our flat. There was also a monthly all-age family worship service. Coffee was always served afterwards. We were fortunate in having some good musicians. Connie Gleisner was our organist and choir mistress and the choir added considerably to the worship and also attracted those who liked choral singing. There was also a very well stocked bookstall in a room at the back of the church which did a good trade under the efficient direction of Jim Colley, a long-term resident of Paris working with O.E.C.D. He took a keen interest in the student work and for many years sent out a circular newsletter to former St Michael's members. Jim dedicated himself and much of his resources to the life and work of St Michael's for many years. He went on to retire to a flat in Cambridge, until one Sunday he collapsed and died on his way home from a church service.

Meals played an important part in the life of this church community. Many lived a long way from the church building and out in the suburbs, so if they were making a long journey into church for a service or a meeting, it was helpful if they could also obtain a meal. A lunch upstairs in the church room always followed the Sunday morning service and around forty on average would stay on for a simple two-course meal cooked by a team of volunteers. The charge in those days was the equivalent of about three euros, and volunteers were called for at the end of the meal to do the washing up! In the afternoons, groups of young people would head off on a sight-seeing trip and perhaps come back to tea. There was one old lady in the church who was not far short of ninety. She would come into church every Sunday bringing with her a large home-made cake which was eagerly devoured by those who came in during the afternoon for tea. Periodically a church catering team would organise a welcome supper. Every newcomer who had been to church with us over the past two or three months and who had signed one of our welcome cards giving us contact details was invited to attend. At the end of the meal there would be a short presentation about life at St Michael's and what was on offer and the talk was usually illustrated with some slides.

The evening service was often the high point in the lives of many students and au pairs who poured into the church building. It was by far our largest Sunday service. A music group composed of different instrumentalists accompanied the singing and many of the modern songs were in evidence. There was no great sense of hurry and the service tended to last for an hour and a half or more. The preaching ministry was especially important as many in our congregation had very little Christian background. Sometimes after the service, a group would go off together for a light supper in one of the cheaper restaurants, perhaps for a hamburger, and at other times pizzas would be ordered and yet another meal would be consumed upstairs. Over the years many young people have testified to the fact that their faith came to life for the first time through the worship and teaching that they received at St Michael's. Sunday worship was supplemented by mid-week Bible study and discussion groups for older members of the congregation in their homes, as well as for the younger people. There was a rapid turnover among the younger element. Students would arrive at the end of September and leave the following June. Sometimes a lay pastoral assistant worker would be employed by the church to work as part of the team, particularly with the students and the au pairs. Two of these who worked with Peter Sertin, my predecessor, went on to be ordained. Peter himself and his wife Marilyn had done much to build up this student side of the work.

Soon after our arrival we were faced with the need to get down to some language study. Gill had O-level French from school and I had obtained an A-level, but we were both exceedingly rusty and our study of the language had been in the days when you could pass examinations with minimal ability to actually communicate verbally. We were fortunate in Paris to find that St Michael's were already running French courses, so we had only to walk down the stairs to get to our French classes and there was no excuse for being late for lessons! Both of our teachers were church members and they were good at the job. There was Astrid who came from the Alsace region of France and Julia who was married to a Frenchman and completely fluent. There were classes for different levels of French and plenty of opportunity for conversational practice. We managed to pick up a working knowledge of French and in 1989 we went on a month's intensive course at the Institute of Tourraine in Tours. That course helped to move us on a step in our ability to use the language. Most of our work was with English-speaking people, so opportunities for practice were limited. But Parisians are very impatient – rightly so, I believe – with foreigners who don't take the trouble to learn French. It would be very difficult to live in the French capital without some knowledge of the language. Our regular services were all in English but at weddings and funerals parts of the service were sometimes in French. So if one of the partners to a marriage was French, I would put the questions and the vows to the French partner in French, whilst I addressed the other partner in English.

On our arrival at St Michael's, we discovered that a Billy Graham mission to Paris was planned for the following autumn. Although the main thrust of this mission was to the French churches in the Paris area, we were keen to support this mission outreach in our area in any way we could. Blair Carlson was Billy Graham's personal assistant at the time and he was resident in Paris for about a year leading up to the mission. He was responsible for encouraging the French churches to pull together in support of the mission, which was not an easy task. He also had to reassure the French authorities that what was planned was not some wild sectarian movement which would damage the country, but rather an enterprise involving French churches of all descriptions with a view to strengthening them. Blair worshipped with us during his time in France and on one occasion he preached for us. It has been good to meet up again with Blair and his family in Sussex, where he has been serving a curacy in an Anglican parish. As a church we helped with the training of counsellors who would be on hand during the mission to assist those seeking to commit themselves to the way of Christ. Some of our members helped as stewards during the mission meetings, which were held in a huge arena at Bercy to the east of Paris. The Billy Graham organisation also encourages the formation of what are called "prayer triplets" prior to a mission. These consist of groups of three people who meet to pray, perhaps once a week, for the forthcoming event. They pray, too, for individual friends who they hope will discover a new faith through the preaching of the gospel. Quite a number of our church members joined these prayer triplets. The American ambassador, Joe Rogers, and his wife Honey, were great supporters of the mission. Joe Rogers had been a keen supporter of President Reagan in the American Presidential election campaign at that time and the President wanted an ambassador in Paris who would be happy to back the Graham mission.

Billy Graham had clearly done his home work before he arrived in Paris. His sermons were, as usual, clear and challenging as he preached the good news of Christ and spoke of all that his death and resurrection can mean to us. But he managed to earth his message in French cultural soil with references and illustrations drawn from French life and literature. I was told after the mission that lots of local churches had welcomed many new enquirers who had come forward for counselling at Bercy. I have to confess that not many were sent to us at St Michael's and those people whom we were asked to contact seemed very hard to find. But we were pleased to be a part of an evangelistic enterprise which was benefiting the French churches around us. Joe and Honey Rogers worshipped at the American Presbyterian Church in Paris but occasionally would drop in on our evening service.

They kindly invited us to a dinner given in honour of the Grahams, and Gill became good friends with Honey.

One of the joys of a city centre church is the huge mix of different nationalities which it attracts. Such a mixture of varied cultural as well as Christian backgrounds is very invigorating and sometimes amusing. There was, for example, the young German who took a fancy to an attractive air hostess of Indian extraction. The young man obviously believed in an honest and direct approach when it came to chat-up lines. One day he opened a conversation with her by saying: "Since I last saw you, you have grown thicker round the waist (which he pronounced 'vaist')". This one remark brought any hopes of a developing relationship to an abrupt halt. A German lady, who I think must have been watching *Allo Allo*, used sometimes to creep up behind me and tap me on the shoulder and whisper in my ear: "We have ways of making you talk!"

The ministry at St Michael's was very much a team effort. When Steve Wookey left us to join the staff at All Souls', Langham Place, his place was taken by Percy Esser who had just completed a curacy in Islington. Percy's original home was in Mauritius, so French was his mother tongue, which was a huge advantage. His arrival helped to boost our work among African people living and working in Paris. Percy was an accomplished guitarist and he had a good singing voice to go with it, which was an asset to our worship, particularly at the evening service or with the children. But not everyone appreciated this gift of Percy's. We were out to lunch one day in the home of an elderly English lady who had been a pillar of the church for many years; she turned to Gill and remarked: "Need Mr. Esser play his banjo in church?" To which Gill replied, "but we like Mr. Esser playing his guitar in church!" We still remained good friends with the lady in question in spite of this difference of opinion! When Percy left us after a three-year stay, Robert and Marian Lovatt joined us with their two little girls, Rebecca and Katie. The accommodation that we had hitherto rented in the centre of Paris had been for a bachelor and was totally inadequate for the needs of a family. A long standing couple, who were members of St Michael's, bought and lent to the church, rent free, an apartment in the suburbs and it was into this brand new flat that the Lovatts moved in 1992. They both proved excellent and hard-working colleagues to work with and Robert stayed on to look after the interregnum after our return to England in early 1994.

The church was blessed not only with clergy but with a number of lay staff workers. There was always a full-time secretary working in the church office throughout my time and with many visitors to the centre during the day, as well as telephone calls, this proved essential. They each brought their own particular gifts to the job in hand and we could not have done without them. We also had a number of short-term lay pastoral assistants whose particular task was to help with the young people's side of the work. Soon after we arrived, John Newton, who was in Paris for his gap year and needed a bit of extra money, took on the job of being the church cleaner. He, and all the staff who happened to be free, used to come up to our flat for a staff lunch once a week which Gill prepared for us. I recently met John again in Eastbourne. He had spent some years as housemaster of a boarding house at Eastbourne College, but moved on to be headmaster of a very large school in Taunton. He is married and has four lovely children. In retirement it is such an encouragement to come across people like John who have kept the faith that was nurtured at St Michael's and have gone on to serve our Lord, sometimes in positions of considerable responsibility.

When anyone on the staff had a birthday, it was a cause for celebration. Someone would pop round the corner to a local patisserie and purchase a selection of miniature cakes and we would meet up in the church office, perhaps later in the afternoon, and open a bottle of champagne. Occasionally we would go out as a group and have a meal together at some restaurant on the left bank of the Seine.

From time to time visitors in trouble came into the centre seeking help. There was the case of the young man who in a rash moment had joined the foreign legion and was living to regret it. Whilst on the run, he dropped in on us seeking help. We tried hard not to hand out money to such travellers but we would always provide a bed for the night within our premises and some food. In the days before it was possible to take as much wine or beer as you liked across the Channel, lorry drivers would be prepared to offer lifts to stranded tourists from Paris to Calais and then across the channel, provided they had passports. This enabled the driver to take with him a double allowance of alcohol. All we needed to provide was a metro ticket to the departure point for lorries leaving Paris at Porte de la Villette and then our visitors would be on their way. Some, however, would come in with elaborate stories asking for an air ticket for another European capital or perhaps one in Africa. Some of these requests were coming from practised con artists and it was not always easy to detect the genuine case from the false. Sometimes we were "taken for a ride" but whenever air fares were mentioned it was not too difficult to turn the request down.

From time to time asylum seekers came to our church, often in some distress and need, seeking help. Bernard, for example, was stateless, having parents who came from two different West African countries. He had no passport or papers. He came to an evening service and sat in a chair afterwards and it was obvious that he was ill. We arranged for him to be treated in a hospital and after his recovery, he slept on the church premises and acted as a sort of night watchman, doing odd jobs around the place during the day. We obtained advice from an advisory service and found that he should apply for French citizenship. We tried hard to persuade him to follow this route so that his presence in France could be legalised. But Bernard was afraid that his application might be turned down. We felt that we could not indefinitely accommodate him if he was not willing to obtain a legal right to remain in the country so there came a time when we felt we must ask him to leave. There must be so many Bernards in all the main cities of Western Europe, with no papers and no home and very little hope for the future. Our church tried to help wherever it could.

Obviously we were keen to see the thriving work amongst students and young people maintained, but Gill and I were also eager to build up the family side of the church. There was always the danger, if we were simply known as a student church, that all people of other age groups would go elsewhere. We needed a good balance within our membership if we were to sustain the student work. So, when a new family arrived we would try and invite them home for a meal to get to know them. We also encouraged mid-week group activity which catered for older singles and married people. When parents contacted us about the baptism of a baby, we invited them to work through with us the three-part preparation course that we had used in Hove. But in Paris we were short of mature and experienced leaders. Most of those who fell into this category were already engaged in leading home groups, of which there were a good number scattered around Paris. So Gill and I took on this baptism preparation ministry and we took the course to families in and around Paris. The course took place around a meal, either in our flat or in the homes of the parents concerned. This often involved us in a difficult journey into the suburbs, either by car or metro, searching for a new address in the dark. Our hosts would always lay on a lavish meal, so it was frequently quite late before we got down to the business in hand. But these visits and the meals we gave to young parents in our home did much to break the ice and help build a relationship with these young couples. This made it much easier for us to discuss the issues of belief surrounding the baptism service and to put across some of the basic truths of our Christian faith. For some the course made little impact, as far as we could tell, but for others it proved to be a significant step forward in their spiritual journey. One such mother whom we visited is now in training for the Christian ministry and is about to be ordained.

The church Christmas sale at St Michael's was a terrific affair. The whole building was taken over either for stalls or for refreshments. There were three sittings for lunch catering for up to sixty at a time and there was also a refreshments bar in the basement. Local firms often donated generously items for different stalls. The most famous of these was Louis Feraud, whose fashion house was near by in the Faubourg St Honoré. Caroline Herbert, who became one of our church-wardens towards the end of our time in Paris, was one of his chief designers. Gifts from Louis Feraud were a great attraction. There was a holiday souvenir stall run by the chaplain, with much help from assistants, which specialised in Christmas gifts. The cake stall was a feast for the eyes of anyone with a sweet tooth, with its elaborate array of cakes including Christmas cakes and Christmas puddings all of which were home-made. At its high point the sale produced around £16,000. But in later years, soon after we left, the flow of gifts from local firms began to decline and the income from the sale fell. Eventually it was felt that all the concentrated effort and time that went into the sale could be better spent elsewhere, but in its day it made a substantial contribution to church funds. It also brought the church in touch with many people outside our regular membership, some of whom were glad to help run a stall. A few of these went on to become active in the worshipping life of the church. This, perhaps, was the major point in its favour.

Although most of our congregation were on the young side, there were a few older members, many of whom had led extremely interesting lives. Many of these came to a monthly afternoon tea at the centre organised by teams from different English-speaking churches in the Paris area. The teas came under the direction of Toc-H, a Christian foundation originally set up during the first world war. Doris Leck a member of our congregation, was their leader. It was from this tea that Sheba, our dog, eventually had to be banned as her figure was beginning to expand dangerously.

One of our church members who was a regular participant at these teas was Madame Klein. She was, as her name suggests, small of stature. She had sharp twinkling eyes in a face that was a mass of wrinkles. Her husband had been French, and she had lived in Paris throughout the war years during the occupation. She had successfully hidden her two sons in the attic of the building where she lived to save them from being deported. As rumours of an imminent invasion grew louder in 1944 she would say to others standing in a shopping queue, "The allies are coming; they'll soon be here. Churchill said they would come. They won't be long now." People warned her to keep quiet, telling her that such talk was dangerous. Nevertheless, she was nicknamed "the pocket Churchill". When Paris was finally liberated, later that year, she was round at the church the following day with dusters and a broom to clean it up and prepare it for a service of thanksgiving. The building had been closed and out of use since the fall of France in 1940. Towards the end of her life, I used to take communion to her in her flat. It was like walking backwards into a 1930s time warp with the ancient furnishings and faded photographs of relations long since dead scattered around the room. Her deafness became so severe that I had to communicate with her through written notes. She knew the old prayer book service so well that she simply followed in her book even though she couldn't hear. One day in desperation I suggested that we prayed for healing for her hearing. I have to confess that I prayed with little faith. Later the following week she telephoned me in great excitement to tell me that she had picked up a hearing aid from a drawer and taken it to be repaired. She could now hear me talking to her over the phone. It was hardly a miracle but it just goes to show that God does move in mysterious ways his wonders to perform.

CHAPTER FOURTEEN

ADAM'S RIB

For Adam no suitable helper was found. So the Lord God caused the man to fall into a deep sleep; and while he was sleeping, he took one of the man's ribs and closed up the place with flesh. Then the Lord God made a woman from the rib he had taken out of the man, and he brought her to the man. The man said: "this is now bone of my bones and flesh of my flesh". (Genesis 2:20–23 NIV)

This part of the creation story presents for us in picture language the mutual inter-dependence of husband and wife and the fact that they are made to complement one another. They belong together. They make or mar each other's lives. They are one flesh.

Gill and I have always looked upon our Christian ministry as a partnership. Gill has never had any sense of calling to be ordained, but she has definitely felt herself to be a partner in the ministry to which I have been called.

In some church circles these days, this is an unfashionable view of ministry. The separateness of the vocations of husband and wife is stressed. For the majority of clergy wives (or hus-

bands), I realise that this emphasis is often in the best interests of the marriage partnership and the family. But where one
partner is ordained, the other partner should at the very least
be in sympathy with the work of Christian ministry and offer
support in so far as time and family commitments allow.

The role of a chaplain's wife in overseas chaplaincies is
particularly crucial since the couple often provide a focal
point for the life of a whole community. If a spouse is
unhappy or homesick living in a foreign country, or if her
personality is such that she actually undermines the work that
her partner is doing, the results can be disastrous. I know of
one instance where the husband accepted a church post
abroad and the wife chose to stay at home. This led on to
the shipwreck of a marriage and an unhappy church. Fortunately the Intercontinental Church Society, with which we
have had close connections for many years, always sees couples together during the course of the interviews. It is
emphasised that the one partner is being interviewed for the
job, but it is also necessary to ensure that the spouse would
be happy to live abroad and be supportive of the ministry. I
remember well that before we went to Barcelona Bishop John
Satterthwaite saw us both together.

We have been very fortunate in being able to serve in our
churches together and we found this pattern to be richly
rewarding. In Paris with so much church life revolving
around the centre throughout the week, Gill had an especially
important part to play.

With many people coming in to St Michael's for meals, it
was important that the catering side of our life was co-ordi-
nated. Gill undertook to be responsible for seeing that there
was always something in the food cupboards. Church Council members tended to work very long hours and they would

arrive for a meeting hungry. Gill would organise a meal so that we could begin our council meetings by eating together. Catering for large numbers entailed the occasional trip to a large cash-and-carry depot on the outskirts of Paris to stock up with large tins and packs of provisions. A pastoral assistant would usually accompany her to provide help with moving heavy loads in and out of the car and then up in the lift from the underground car park. Gill would often find herself offering gentle supervision and guidance to teams of young and inexperienced cooks who were preparing quantities of food for a Sunday lunch or some other church social event. Jim King, an Ulster man living in Paris, was for many years a great help with the cooking of special meals. There were times when Gill found all this cooking and catering quite a burden with which she struggled. From time to time she used to escape for a day of peace and reflection to the flat of a friend who was out at work. On one such day, everything she read and thought about seemed to confirm the important aspect of feeding and entertaining within this Christian community. She realised afresh the joy of sharing food together and she was able to thank God for her part in this ongoing ministry.

With many au pairs, who in some cases were away from home for the first time, it was an asset to have a home to which they could turn and a person with the gift of listening upon whom they could pour out all their troubles. The presence of Sheba in our flat was sometimes enough to cause an au pair to burst into tears. Our dog was sometimes a reminder of a dog she had left behind at home. A few of the au pairs found themselves in real difficulties due to a husband who made amorous advances or a wife who overworked them and gave them little or no time off. In some cases it was necessary to encourage the girl to leave a post and seek alternative employment. Steve, and Percy who followed him, were both bachelors and they were sometimes happy to direct girls in distress upstairs to Gill, knowing that she would offer them a shoulder to cry on.

During the Billy Graham mission to Paris, Gill knew that one way in which she could contribute to the preparations was through prayer. Her prayer partnership with Honey Rogers and Nancy Painter, whose husband was also on the staff of the U.S. embassy, proved to be a great spiritual stimulus. Our home and church was just round the corner from the American Embassy residence, so it was easy to nip across the road and into this very imposing building for a time of prayer. The three of them met about once every ten days over a period of about three years continuing a prayer friendship long after the mission was over. Gill feels that she learnt a lot from these two prayerful American ladies.

One of the mission events was a ladies' tea party which Honey organised in one of the magnificent Embassy reception rooms, at which Ruth Graham was the guest speaker. Some two hundred guests were present for this meeting. It was obviously something that could well be repeated in the future and Honey, who was motivated by a deep Christian faith, generously offered to make provision for such a gathering on a monthly basis provided that a small team drawn from the different English-speaking churches in and around Paris would be prepared to host the meetings and provide good speakers. This initiative saw the start of the English-Speaking Women's Fellowship, which for a period of some nine years drew together an international and interdenominational group of women from within the city and suburbs of Paris. This proved to be a very happy and constructive fellowship of women, which in the latter years met in different church premises. It was a real eye-opener to see how well Anglicans, Baptists, Roman Catholics, Presbyterians and members of a Filipino church community could get on so well together as they shared in this monthly fellowship meeting. Such working and sharing together across denominational and party divisions is surely a practice to which Christians in cities everywhere should be aspiring.

Gill with a 'Family Focus' group, enjoying a light lunch

Gill felt a particular responsibility to strengthen our work among the young families who came to live in Paris, usually on short-term contracts. Working alongside Elspeth Burrell and later Marian Lovatt with various other helpers, she established a group called "Family Focus" which met once a fortnight in the church lounge. They met for a light lunch and this was followed by a varied programme, which sometimes included an invited speaker. At other times talks recorded on cassette tapes were used to stimulate debate Some aspect of faith or family life was looked at and then discussed by the group. A separate crèche was provided for the small children so that mothers could enjoy some adult space together. This became a vital part in our overall church life and outreach to the community and it attracted some twenty to twenty-five members whenever they met.

Our neighbours at the American Presbyterian Church ran a programme each autumn which was designed to help new-comers to "bloom where they were planted." This was the title that they gave to their programme which helped new-comers to settle down to their new life in Paris. The Family Focus group shared this same vision in so far as it set out to help newcomers to make the most of their years in Paris, so that it became a time when they grew and matured as people alongside the deepening of their faith in God. To this end, for example, the group paid a visit to L'Arche, the Christian community to the north of Paris founded by Jean Vanier to cater for the needs of people suffering from severe physical or mental disabilities. A day was spent there seeing something of this important shared, loving Christian community life. A session that was entitled: "A needy world – learning to give and receive" led to the sponsoring of a child from Haiti, called Rosa Bertha. She became the collective responsibility of the group and one of the members corresponded regularly with her family. The very existence of such a group helped a number of wives to settle happily into their new life in Paris and to make friends with others who shared their interests.

Gill played an active part in what was known as the Prayer Ministry Team. On two Sundays a month, at one of the main services prayer for healing was offered towards the end of a communion service. People were invited to come forward to the communion rail where a team consisting of about four pairs would be ready and waiting to pray with them for any particular need that they might have. Sometimes it was a physical problem and at other times, possibly an emotional hurt or a damaged relationship for which prayer was requested. We remember our newly consecrated Suffragan Bishop Edward Holland coming forward and kneeling for prayer and asking us to pray for a renewal of God's grace at the outset of his new episcopal ministry in Europe. Many of the younger members of the congregation found their way up to the front of the church for prayer. They were perhaps on the whole less inhibited than the older generation.

The team would prepare for this work of prayer by studying and praying together beforehand on a regular basis. A course entitled: "Saints for Healing" proved very helpful at one stage. Often team members sensed that they themselves needed first to be prayed for before they could take on the task of praying for others. We were all very conscious of the need to rely upon the Holy Spirit to apply our Lord's healing touch wherever it was needed. We knew that without him we could do nothing.

In my own mind there are a number of unanswered questions that relate to such a ministry. I am convinced of its value and I believe that since our Lord went about healing the sick, Christians today should be praying to the Lord to continue his work of healing and making people whole in every sense of that word. But it also seems clear that miracles are by their very nature rare occurrences. It is also very obvious that for every human being there is a time to die. Sometimes, when there has been long and earnest prayer for a very sick person, it becomes clear that prayers for physical healing are not being answered in the way that we would wish. The Christian is surely guided both by our Lord's wonderful example of bringing healing to the sick, and by the hope of resurrection life that God our Father has given us through the death and resurrection of his Son. So there often comes a point in a sick person's journey when the right course of Christian action is not to pray for physical healing, but to pray that the dying person will know the peace of Christ in his heart and will be prepared to meet his Lord. The pastoral difficulty is to know when it is right to move from one type of prayer to the other.

I look back to one case of a lady suffering from terminal cancer. She and her husband were devout Christians and she was convinced that God was going to heal her. She was encouraged in this conviction by the knowledge that many individuals and church groups were praying for her healing. One group, I recall, telephoned her to say that they were holding a day of prayer and fasting for her healing. By this stage she was already in a clinic. The day after this call she actually felt worse. The poor lady was oppressed by hard questions. Whose fault was it that her condition was worse? Was it her lack of faith? Had the people praying for her been deficient in their faith? Was it God's fault? I couldn't help feeling that well-meaning Christians were putting her under unnecessary pressure at a time when her illness was manifestly getting worse. I longed to be able to help her to come to terms with the fact of death and to help her to focus on our Lord's promises of eternal resurrection life, but this was something she didn't want to hear. She clung to the hope of physical healing in spite of all the growing medical evidence to the contrary. Her eventual death was not, in my opinion, nearly as peaceful as it should have been and this is one of the regrets of my ministry.

But, lest I come across as a total sceptic in this area, let me recount two stories which encourage us to pray in faith that our Lord can, and does, work in answer to prayer, often and usually in conjunction with the work of the medical services. I have always believed that prayer and pills go hand in hand!

One Sunday evening a Sri Lankan lady came forward for prayer. She was suffering from a gynaecological problem which reminded me very much of the woman with the issue of blood, whose healing by Jesus is recorded in the New Testament. As she knelt at the rail with her husband by her side, we duly prayed that the Lord would heal her from this depressing disability. One evening the following month we saw her coming forward again. I have to confess that my heart sank with a kind of "here we go again" feeling. The lady knelt down in front of us with a face wreathed in smiles to tell us that she was completely well again. She had come forward so that together we could offer thanks and praise to God for her healing. We duly prayed in a spirit of great thankfulness to God and I went on to say: "You know what we must pray for now, don't you?". She smiled back a little sheepishly. Before long she was up at the rail again to give thanks for the fact that she was expecting a baby! She is now the proud mother of at least two children.

It was a Sunday afternoon when the telephone rang. It was a call from one of our former church members who had now returned to England. She and her husband had been trying to start a family for a while and now she was pregnant, But during the course of a regular check-up the scan of the foetus had revealed a shadow over the brain of the child in the womb. This could be serious and the expectant parents were naturally very concerned. They asked our church to pray for them. That evening the Old Testament reading was about how the prophet Elisha prayed over the dead child of the Shunammite woman and restored him to life. This seemed to me to be an enormous encouragement to us as a church to pray for the unborn child of our friends who had moved back to Britain. I shared my thoughts and the prayer request with the evening congregation after the reading of the lesson, and we then had a time of prayer for the family concerned. A month later there was another scan and the mother-to-be was soon on the telephone to tell us the great news that there was now no sign of that shadow on the brain of the child that she was carrying. Some time later I was asked to be a godfather to the little girl that was born.

One year Gill suggested to me that it would be a good idea to hold an Easter Sunday morning sunrise service just as dawn was breaking. This would mean arranging for participants to meet at St Michael's soon after 6 a.m. I remember telling her that I thought it was a lovely idea provided that someone else put it all together and carried it through! There were already at least three Sunday services on Easter day which demanded plenty of attention and I didn't feel able to take on anything more, especially at 6.00 a.m!

So, nothing daunted, Gill undertook to make all the arrangements. An informal open-air service in the Tuilleries Gardens was duly advertised. The actual starting out time depended on whether Easter was early or late in the spring that year. It was between 6 and 7 a.m. that a somewhat sleepy group of about fifty, mainly young people, gathered in St Michael's front entrance. and headed off together towards the gardens. If the weather was fine, they settled down on rugs. One year when it was wet, they found a large marquee in the grounds of the Tuilleries full of stacked chairs, all ready to be used later in the day. There was no one around so the group made themselves at home and the service was held under cover and in the dry. A few people brought musical instruments to accompany Easter hymns and songs. The Easter story was read from the scriptures and different people in the party spoke briefly of what the Easter message meant to them. After some prayer, everyone walked back to the church for a breakfast of hot chocolate, coffee and croissants, grateful for the Easter celebration in which they had already shared.

As in Barcelona our Christmas night dinners presented Gill with a major culinary challenge. We catered for about thirty, including whichever members of our own family happened to be with us. It was again a wonderfully international party and at the end of the meal we would drink toasts to each of the countries represented in the room. But before each toast, we would ask one of their representatives what their wish would be for their home country during the coming year. Sometimes there were a few party games after the meal such as charades and on other occasions we just sat around and chatted. We usually wound up the evening with a few carols. One year a Canadian couple, who were only loosely connected with the church but were good friends of ours, offered to come and help us with serving the meal and washing the dishes so that we could enjoy simply being with our guests. They had had their own Christmas dinner around midday. Afterwards they told us this was the most enjoyable Christmas during their time in Paris.

Life was certainly never dull in Paris and we were kept very busy, though we also had our moments of relaxation. It was a joy to live in such a beautiful city and to have so many places to visit and explore. We lived very close to the Elysée Palace, home of the President, who was François Mitterand at that time. Behind this palace and bordering the river Seine were some public gardens ideally situated for taking Sheba for a walk. Gill joined the British and Commonwealth Women's Association and went on some of their guided tours of places of interest. Such trips usually ended up with a meal in a recommended restaurant.

Our most visited museum was the Musée D'Orsay, which contained the famous collection of French impressionist paintings. We had our own favourite restaurant on the left bank of the Seine in the Latin quarter to which we tended to take guests who wanted a meal out in Paris. The Champs Elysées was within walking distance of home and on both sides of this famous avenue lay a whole string of cinemas showing the latest films to be released. During the Christmas season this beautiful avenue would be lit up by a host of tiny sparkling lights festooning the trees on either side of the road. The effect was magical.

Nevertheless life in our church centre was very demanding, especially with our home being so close to all the action. So eventually, following a legacy, we were able to purchase a mobile home on a French camp site north of Paris and not very far from Chantilly. We had a small garden surrounding this home in the country and we were thus able to escape from the bustle of the city for a twenty-four hour period each week. Sometimes we would arrive around midnight on a Tuesday night having just concluded a baptism visit the same evening. We would collapse into bed knowing that there was no hurry to get up in the morning and that no telephone would ring. It was bliss! We needed that regular weekly break in our schedule so that we could draw breath and be refreshed before returning to the fray in Paris.

CHAPTER FIFTEEN

THEY CAME FOR A VISIT

If you enjoy entertaining visitors and feel that you would like to catch up with people you haven't seen for years, then we can recommend taking up residence in Paris! Our flat was right in the centre of the city, just off the Faubourg St Honoré and within walking distance of the Place de la Concorde. We could not have been better situated for those who wanted a few days' holiday and a bit of sightseeing in what has to be one of the world's most beautiful capitals. Our visitors' book, which covers our eight years in Paris, records the fact that we had 480 guests staying with us during that period. We kept no record of the number of meals that Gill prepared. We mention this not to complain because we love having visitors and keeping in touch with old friends, and in the course of those years we were in contact with a huge variety of delightful and interesting people.

Quite early on, Madame Demogé (she who baked the cake for Sunday teas) noticed that Gill was carrying a heavy burden with so much entertaining and offered to provide us with an au pair. The plan was that the au pair should have bed and breakfast with Madame Demogé in her apartment while working with us during the day. Each month she handed to us a cheque for £150 which we passed on to the succession of girls who came to assist us. They helped with changing sheets and preparing for the next visitors and they also gave Gill a hand with cooking and serving meals in the church centre. The only problem was that Madame Demogé decided that these girls all needed building up and was inclined to cook for them a hearty breakfast of bacon, egg and fried bread. Most of the girls, however, preferred a diet which would leave them with a slender sylph-like figure. The breakfasts that Madame Demogé was so eager to serve up had a tendency to make them indeed "thicker round the waist".

A crisis point was reached when one of the girls came home to Madame Demogé's one evening and said that she was tired. Since the following day was her day off, she asked if she could have a lie-in and not be disturbed in the morning. Madame Demogé began to worry about this girl in her charge and convinced herself that she must be ill. So early the following morning, she burst into the girl's bedroom, brandishing a thermometer and calling out: "Stick it up your bottom; stick it up your bottom." This aspect of French medical culture was something for which the poor girl had not bargained. She leapt out of bed in tears and was soon round at our apartment to tell us that she couldn't stand it any longer. It was not very long before she was on her way back to England. Madame Demogé was an astute lady and she soon realised as we talked things over, that it was difficult for her and young girls in their late teens or early twenties to adjust to sharing a home together. She very generously agreed to allow the girls to come and live in our home and to continue to pay their monthly allowance. We were enormously grateful for all the help we received from a variety of au pairs. Gail Nichol was the daughter of our missionary friends in the Sudan and she came to us from the United States. Kirsty Barlow came for a year and later returned to the church to work as a pastoral assistant, and then there was Marianthe, the daughter of the Archdeacon of Chichester. Michael and his wife Daphne sometimes gave us breakfast in Chichester when we came off the ferry at Portsmouth, and for two ceremonial occasions that we attended Michael lent me his clerical morning coat. Each of the girls who came threw themselves into the life of the church community and they made all the difference to the hospitality side of our ministry.

We seem to have collected a considerable number of godchildren over the years and feel that we have not been the best of godparents. Living in different parts of the world, it has not been easy to keep in touch but we found that once we were living in Paris, many of our now grown-up godchildren came to stay for a few days and it was a delight for us to be in touch with them again. We obviously hadn't time to show visitors around Paris so we gave them bed, breakfast and an evening meal, along with a map of Paris, and left them to entertain themselves.

The Charbonnier church weekends were an important feature of life at St Michael's These were held twice a year in the early summer and again in the autumn. The first was designed to serve the needs of the whole church family and so a programme was arranged that would cater for all age groups. The autumn house party was planned mainly with students and au pairs in mind. We rented a conference centre, which had at one time been a private chateau, in a tiny village set in glorious countryside. The grounds of the chateau were superb with a huge lake surrounded by trees and pasture land. This place of great natural beauty had so

*Marion Lovatt with daughters Rebecca and Katie and two
young friends, in front of the Charbonniers Chateau*

much to offer us after the noise and bustle of the city. We
never seemed to have too much difficulty in finding distinguished speakers to come and lead such weekends. These
included Gilbert Kirby, Julian Charley, David Prior, Michael
Sanders and the evangelist J. John. They would sometimes
stay with us for a few days in Paris, either before or after the
weekend, so that they could also enjoy something of a holiday break. We found that with such a rapid turnover of
congregations, such weekends were a great help in binding
us all together and enabling people to integrate with the life
of the church. And many found that the Holy Spirit touched
their lives during these times apart and drew them closer to
Christ our Lord.

Sometimes we found ourselves offering shelter to someone in trouble. Nora had fallen in love with a young man in the congregation and they were planning on getting married. The difficulty arose from the fact that they came not only from different tribes but from different African countries. Nora had been living with her father but when he discovered that she was planning to marry someone from a different country, he was furious and started to threaten her. When she came to us in a very anxious state seeking help, we offered her a room in our flat for a while. The father came looking for her but we managed to conceal her whereabouts from him. In the end the couple were able to get married and they continued together as members of the church for a number of years.

And then there was Peggy. She telephoned us early one morning in a dreadful state. The police had just called at the flat where she and her husband were staying and had arrested him on a murder charge. What was she to do? Gill took the call and invited her to come and stay with us for a while. In the end she stayed for a fortnight. It transpired that her husband, Bob, had been married before but his wife had suffered from a long illness and finally died. The problem lay in the fact that no one seemed to know where she was buried. "Poor Bob. He wouldn't hurt a fly," insisted Peggy. We gently enquired as to whether she had asked her husband about the burial place of his first wife and she replied saying that he had forgotten. At that point I felt that things were not quite right. It occurred to me that if I had lost my keys, I might well not know where I had put them; but if I had lost Gill, I would certainly remember where I had last seen her. Meanwhile Bob languished in a Paris prison and some of our people went to visit him until eventually he was extradited to Switzerland, where he stood trial and was convicted of manslaughter. He spent a relatively short time in prison there and was later reunited with his wife Peggy.

Other visitors included Garth and Gill Hewitt, with some of their family, who came to us for a harvest celebration weekend when the accent was on the work of Tearfund. Garth gave a concert which focused our attention on the work of that Christian relief organisation. Pat Travis was with us for another training weekend for Sunday School teachers which we opened up for other children's workers in the Paris area. When we were away in Tours for our month's French study course, Alan and Catherine Lindsay, who had formerly been in chaplaincy work at Maisons Lafitte and subsequently in the Hague, came to provide cover for us for a month in the summer. We felt for them as they had to endure a Paris heatwave and there were no through-drafts in our flat, so that by the time we arrived back at the end of our month away they were nearly cooked to a cinder!

One day a rather odd letter landed on my desk from a man writing to say that he had a great burden to come and evangelise Paris. His letter included the phrase: "difficult to do in the natural". I think I knew what he actually meant but I couldn't help thinking of another interpretation. It occurred to me that to attempt to evangelise Paris "in the natural" could well lead to the arrest of a naked evangelist! His letter concluded with a postscript: "P.S. I don't speak any French." Thinking that a little research was necessary, I telephoned a church leader in his home town. The message I received back was: "Don't touch him with a barge pole!" I hardly need add that I wrote back declining to offer hospitality to this potential visitor.

As archdeacon as well as chaplain, I quite often received

telephone calls from the Diocesan office in London. One day a member of the Diocesan staff phoned to say that the Archbishop of Canterbury was planning to organise a party of young people from all the dioceses in the Church of England to accompany him on a pilgrimage to Taizé near Cluny in France, which is a popular ecumenical spiritual centre that attracts many people from across the world. Each diocese had been asked to send a representative to a planning meeting at Lambeth Palace. Could I suggest anyone who might go on our behalf? The meeting was due to take place within a week or so which meant that there was not much time to find someone. In the end I offered to go myself and to be responsible for seeing that our diocese collected together a party of young people to take part in this youth initiative. I duly flew over to London for a planning day at Lambeth. Stephen Platten, one of the Archbishop's chaplains, was in charge of the day's programme but the Archbishop addressed us all and outlined his thinking concerning the forthcoming pilgrimage. Many of those attending were clergy responsible for diocesan youth initiatives. It seemed strange to me that in a few cases some of these clergy, instead of welcoming this proposal from the leader of our church and seeing it as an encouragement, appeared rather to resent it. It was as if they didn't want someone else muscling-in on their patch. It was over lunch that George Carey mentioned to me that he and Eileen were going to be in Paris later that summer for a conference and after the conference was over, they would have about ten days to spare before their main summer holiday began with family members somewhere in the south west of France. Could I look into any holiday possibilities for them both during that ten day space? I promised to do what I could to help.

After exploring various possibilities, we finally suggested

an apartment in Paris that John and Doreen Cox, our lay readers, were happy to make available to the Careys. The Cox's were due to be on leave in Wales over that summer period. We also mentioned the fact that our mobile home would be free should they wish to spend some of their time outside Paris. In the end they decided to divide their ten days between these two options. The only problem with the mobile home was that we had no telephone connection there and it was necessary for the Archbishop to be within easy reach of Lambeth should an emergency arise. We approached a French couple who lived opposite and asked if some guests of ours could use their telephone in an emergency. We also asked if we could let his London office have their number should they need to be in touch. This was easily arranged and so the plans for this very unofficial visit went ahead. After lunch in our flat, we drove the Careys over to the apartment where they were to stay and once they were installed, we went home with a view to getting ourselves together before going up to our mobile home to prepare it for visitors the following week. We were just about to leave when the telephone rang. The Careys were on the line. They were locked into the flat and couldn't get the door open. We had deliberately kept quiet about the visit so they could enjoy a few precious days together undisturbed and as far as possible incognito. What would the tabloids make of it if our Archbishop and his wife had to be rescued from a Paris flat by the fire brigade? I then remembered that a couple of close friends of the Cox's might have a key and be able to help. So I rang up Ray Leck and was relieved to hear that he had a key to the apartment; but it was fortunate that I had not rung much later as they were going away on holiday the following day. I told Ray that some friends were staying in the flat but that they were locked in. Could he possibly go over and try and get them out? He was only too willing to oblige. It didn't take him long to make the journey and he had the door open in next to no time. He tells me that he eyed George Carey up and down and felt sure that he recognised him. Ray is a north countryman who doesn't believe in beating about the bush so he turned to the Archbishop and said, "Excuse me, but, are you the Archbishop of Canterbury, or are you not?" To which question, of course, only one reply was possible!

The next stop for our visitors was our mobile home. We collected Mark and Penny Carey at the Gare du Nord on the way up to the village near Creil where the mobile home was sited. We stayed there long enough to hear and watch Linford Christie win the one hundred metres gold medal at the Olympics, and to share a barbecue with our guests. The beauty of this particular mobile home site was that it was occupied entirely by French families, apart from ourselves, and they were nearly all permanent residents. None of our neighbours had the slightest idea who our guests were, which meant that they could relax knowing that they would not be disturbed. Thankfully no member of the Royal Family died, and so there were no calls from Lambeth.

CHAPTER SIXTEEN

A CHAPTER OF ACCIDENTS

The first accident was entirely my own fault. Even as I start to tell the tale, I feel a sense of shame. I forgot a funeral. I had visited the family the previous week and made the arrangements for the service to be held the following week around mid-morning at Père Lachaise crematorium to the East of Paris and a good hour's journey from where we lived. I was upstairs in my study when I remembered the service, which was due to start in about three quarters of an hour. I quickly telephoned the office downstairs and asked them to summon a taxi. There followed a mad rush as I collected robes and books and headed for the entrance. It was Jo Stoddart's first morning in her new job as secretary at St Michael's. "Is he always like this?" she asked Gill. "Not always," Gill replied. As the taxi crawled through the Paris traffic, there was a sense of doom hanging over the journey. I just knew that I wasn't going to make it on time and at Père Lachaise, the crematorium ovens wait for no man. I felt a bit like the character in the John Cleese film *Clockwise*, where he is travelling to make a speech at a headmasters' conference and everything seems to go wrong. The taxi driver's identity added a bizarre note to the unfolding drama: I don't know to this day whether I was being driven by a male or a female. I directed the driver towards the crematorium but got out of the taxi at the wrong entrance. Clutching robes and books, I hurried as fast as I could through alleyways of tombs and past bemused gardeners as I asked them in broken French, "Where do they burn the bodies?" At last I reached my destination puffing and panting, only to be informed by the undertakers that the coffin had already gone into the ovens and that the family had departed for Nanterre. They told me that once the cremation procedure was completed, the ashes would be taken in an urn to a Nanterre cemetery to the west of Paris where they would be interred in a family vault. They agreed to give me a lift with them to Nanterre; and about half an hour later, I was cruising round the périférique (a circular road round Paris) in a hearse containing undertakers and an urn. On arrival at the next cemetery, I poured out my heartfelt apologies to the family of the deceased and suggested that we hold the funeral service standing round the family vault before committing the mortal remains of the deceased to the ground. They kindly accepted this suggestion and the service took place there and then in bright sunshine. Looking back, I am amazed by the gracious and forgiving nature of the bereaved family, who were already distressed by the loss of a loved one. They were far kinder to me than I ever deserved, having let them down so badly. They even invited me back to their home for refreshments after the service and the interment.

During our eight years in Paris I was involved in two car accidents. For one of these I was certainly to blame. I was hurrying one Sunday morning to take a service at Chantilly and was cutting it a bit fine when I managed to bump the rear of a car in front of me. Fortunately no one was hurt and the damage to both cars was relatively slight. The second occasion occurred on the main motorway into Paris quite close to St Denis. There was one of those sudden pile-ups as cars had to slow down suddenly. We stopped in plenty of time but the car behind ran into the back of us and our car was almost a write-off. By the mercy of God neither of us was hurt but it was impossible to drive the car and it had to be lifted off the road and taken to a garage where it remained for several months.

A further crisis arose in connection with a Christmas sale lunch. Gill had prepared vast quantities of chicken in a creamy sauce the day before the sale. A large cauldron of this mixture had then been deposited overnight in the church refrigerator. Early the next morning as I came down the stairs a rather ghastly smell began to penetrate my nostrils. I traced this stench to the pot of cooked chicken which was by now heaving and bubbling. It was clearly totally inedible! I alerted Gill. What were we to do? Around 150 people were due to sit down to chicken supreme later that day. Our chicken was anything but supreme. It was positively disgusting! We telephoned David and Joan Williams, who are marvellous people to have around in a crisis. They promised us that they would find some meat in a supermarket to replace the rotting chicken. But the smell was still appalling and we had to get rid of the chicken so we poured the revolting mixture into large black sacks which we took down to our underground car park and loaded into the boot of the car. It was still quite early when we drove out into a Paris that was just waking up. We first espied the British embassy rubbish bins standing invitingly close to the main entrance to the Ambassador's residence. We were sorely tempted to deposit our evil-smelling burdens into one of these. But we didn't want to fall out with our distinguished neighbours so we pressed on. The rubbish disposal lorries were in the process of doing their early morning rounds and before long, we caught up with one of these. We drew up alongside and hurled our sacks into the back of one of them with a profound sense of relief. Back at St Michael's we were encouraged by the sight of David and Joan entering the building carrying large packs of mince. The cooks were soon busy turning this into "beef supreme" instead of chicken supreme and the multitudes were duly fed.

For the following account I am grateful for an article written for our *St Michael's News* by Elizabeth Manson. The Manson family had lived in Paris for several years, brought there by Graham's job. In 1990 he was posted to Norway, which meant a further family upheaval, a common experience for so many of our church members. But their two older children were at a critical stage in their education with important examinations ahead of them, so it was decided that they should stay on in Paris to complete their secondary education at the British School. The following June the whole family were gathering again in Paris for the final days of the school year. It was in the early hours of June 27th that there was a telephone call informing the parents that there had been an accident. Elizabeth writes:

By the time we arrived at the scene, it was an hour after the crash and Jonathan had only just been removed from the car which had skidded sideways into a brick wall bordering the British school. It was remarkable that it was one of Jonathan's own teachers who had found him; he knew we were in Paris and was able to contact us!

When we arrived, the doctors were working on him in an ambulance and continued to do so for another hour before they

drove him very, very, slowly, to the hospital. During that ago-
nising time by the roadside, we weren't allowed near him. We
could do nothing to help him. We simply cried out to God in
our utter helplessness. At the hospital they did a brain scan,
which revealed that he had suffered severe brain damage. The
next few days would be critical and we would need to be very
patient. Despite the horror, somehow I felt thankful to God for
the gift of Jonathan's life which we had had the privilege to share
and offered all six-foot-two of him, body, mind and spirit, back
into God's hands. We were very conscious of the fact that his
injuries were internal and needed no surgical intervention. Only
God could heal him.

Our helpless cries to God were soon joined by the prayers of
our families and friends. Within a short time, people were praying in Norway, Scotland, England and Switzerland as were our
friends at St Michael's and the prayer group at the British School
of Paris. For two weeks Jonathan was in a coma and during that
time there were many "lows", for example, when permission was
asked for his head to be shaved to enable the doctors to attach
a monitor. Also the sight was unforgettable of his body lying
motionless with innumerable machines and tubes doing his living for him.

But each day brought something to be thankful for – the
squeeze of a hand, the opening of an eye, the time he survived
pulling out his own breathing tube, and the slow realisation that
he would make a full recovery! Very gradually he was unplugged
and detached from all the machines and just three weeks after
the accident, Jonathan was able to walk from the hospital and
travel back to the U.K. where he spent the remainder of the summer convalescing. Just before we left hospital, one of the doctors
who had worked on Jonathan in the reanimation unit on the
night of the accident told us that he hadn't thought that Jonathan
was going to pull through. Ten weeks later the consultant neu-

rologist told us that he had made the most remarkable recovery and was fit enough to start college in a few days time!

This experience has left us with a deep feeling of gratitude to God for his powerful, yet gentle and loving touch on all our lives; the wonderful skill and dedication of doctors and nurses and emergency services; the genuine love, care and concern of Christian friends and the support of "the body of Christ". How much we appreciated the letters and phone calls. And then there was the shake up of our priorities. Suddenly A-level results seemed unimportant!

I remember visiting Jonathan in hospital when he had regained consciousness and was on the road to recovery and, together with family members, we were able to offer prayers of thanksgiving for his progress thus far and to pray for continued healing. Some years later on a visit back to St Michael's, we had the joy of meeting with Jonathan and discovering that he was a regular worshipper at the church.

The B.B.C. Radio 4 *Today* programme helped keep us in touch with what was going on the world around us. One morning we woke up to hear on the news that there had been a coach accident involving a party of English people on their way to a nudist holiday-camp somewhere in the south of France. The coach had come off the road and turned over onto its side against a steep bank. The accident had occurred some hundred kilometres or so to the south east of Paris. The news report spoke of a number of the passengers now in hospital being treated for injuries, some of them serious. It so happened that we were booked that day to take a baptism service in a village almost due south of Paris somewhere near Fontainebleau. We studied the map and reckoned that it would be possible to do a round trip which would take in the hospital where some of the British injured were being treated. There were no other chaplains at the time covering that area to the south so we felt that, if at all possible, we ought to make the journey. We duly set off south and took the baptism service in an ancient Roman Catholic chapel lent to us for the purpose. After a family lunch we were able to slip away and drive further to the south east in the direction of the hospital. On arrival there we were stopped by a tabloid newspaper reporter who wanted to interview us after we had visited the patients. The hospital authorities had very wisely refused to let him in. We were able to see most of the patients, with the exception of two who were in intensive care. They seemed really delighted to be visited by an English clergyman. Some were truly grateful that their injuries were not more serious and said that they would be going to their local parish church when they got home to give thanks for their deliverance. Some of them had only limited French and were finding communication difficult. Here and there we were able to help with translation and one mother was able to obtain a baby's feeding bottle as a result of enquiries we made on her behalf. We prayed with some of the patients and felt glad that we had been able to visit some of our fellow countrymen at their time of need when they were stranded and injured and so far from home. We reckoned that the very considerable mileage that we had had to cover that day had been well worth the effort. When it came to leaving the hospital, we asked one of the nurses to show us a side exit so that we could avoid meeting the newspaper reporter. When we reached the hospital court-yard, Gill walked slowly over to where the car was parked, turned it round and drove slowly towards the gates where she had to stop and pick me up. As she was doing this, she was spotted and recognised by the reporter, who started running after the car and yelled for her to stop. I jumped in and we beat a hasty retreat. I felt that any conversations I had had with patients in a hospital were not for sharing with the public, especially as any reporting would have been coloured by the fact that they were on their way to a nudist camp. Nor did I particularly want to see the headline: "Archdeacon visits nudists" splashed across the top of one of our daily newspapers. This incident is fairly typical of the experience of many chaplains in Europe who suddenly find themselves faced with some local tragedy; it is up to them with God's help to do what they can to be of use.

The final accident was much closer to home. Percy Esser rushed into my office one morning to tell me that Gill had been knocked down by a motorcycle in a road just round the corner. I hurried round, to find Gill lying in the middle of the Rue d'Anjou bleeding from her head. She was conscious but incoherent. Some people from an apartment at the side of the road were passing out blankets. The emergency services were there within minutes and were marvellously efficient. They encased Gill's head in some form of netting and slid an inflatable mattress under her. Very gently she was lifted into the back of an ambulance and I was able to travel with her to the emergency hospital to the north, just inside the ring road. All the way to the hospital, Gill never stopped talking. The trouble was that she kept repeating the same question: "Will I have to wear a wig?" I told her that I didn't think she would, but she repeated the question yet again: "Will I have to wear a wig?" At one point I tried changing tack and suggested that she would look very good in a blonde wig, but it made no difference. The same question kept on coming: "Will I have to wear a wig." It certainly gave me insight into the strains that anyone with a relative suffering from Alzheimer's disease must go through. We duly arrived at the hospital and had to wait for a while as other more urgent cases were seen to. X-rays revealed that there was no fracture of the skull and eventually Gill was wheeled into a very brightly lit emergency operating theatre. I stood anxiously by as the doctors got to work and started sewing her up. There was a painful gash on one of her arms and this needed attention in addition to her head injuries. It was during these procedures that Gill resumed normal consciousness. She gazed around her and looked up at all the bright lights and then she saw me standing there. Her first words were: "For a moment or two I thought I must be in heaven, but I can't be because you are here!" That was a remark that certainly put me in my place! I had to return to the church to collect a few of Gill's necessities and was able to tell those who had been anxiously praying for her that she was doing well and getting back to her old self. She sensed during this whole ordeal that there were people praying for her. They kept her in hospital overnight to keep an eye on her and then she was able to come home. On looking back we realised that her injuries could have been far worse, if not fatal, and we were thankful to God that she was spared to continue serving him within the St Michael's church family.

CHAPTER SEVENTEEN

SOME TESTING TIMES

The life of any church has its darker side, as well as its moments of light and joy. St Michael's was no exception. We certainly all had our difficult moments.

Much of the assistant chaplain's time was taken up with listening to students pouring out their problems. Sometimes they chose to come and see either Gill or me in our flat. One student professed to be under attack from a local Satanist group and many hours were spent trying to sort out her problems. In the end it all turned out to be an illusion: there was no substance to the evils she had been describing. The exact reasons behind this strange saga remain something of a mystery to us to this day. There was one student who was suffering from severe anorexia nervosa. We telephoned the parents in England, who came out and took her home, and she went on to make a full recovery. One young man went into a serious depression; he locked himself inside his student accommodation for several days and we had to ask the police to break in so that he could be properly looked after. He, too, had to return to the U.K.

With such a young congregation, it wasn't only in spring

time that romance was in the air. All the year round people seemed to be falling in, and sometimes out of, love! There were moments of great joy and celebration when some of these couples came together to get married at St Michael's.

Daniel and Soyola celebrate their marriage at St. Michael's

As happens throughout mainland Europe, the civil side of a marriage in France takes place at the local town hall. If the couple want a religious ceremony to mark their marriage, they then proceed to a church or some other place of worship. We had quite a number of such marriage ceremonies at St Michael's. The liturgy remained much the same for all of them, but most couples managed to insert their own individual style and flavour into their marriage service, which is just as it should be. One couple, who were both professional dancers, entered the church in step to some dance music followed by their close family, who also managed to keep in step. There were some interesting cross-cultural marriages. The majority of these were between French and English partners but there was also Daniel from Cameroon who married Soyola from Kenya. This was a lovely African wedding between two committed Christian people. I assisted at one Ghanaian wedding which was a rousing affair and the music from the band that accompanied the singing must have been audible down the street. Some marriages took place in one of the Roman Catholic churches and I was often asked to take part, usually reading a passage of Scripture and giving an address.

We did our best to prepare couples for their marriage. They would come to us for a meal and my method of preparation was to take them step by step through the marriage service and we would then discuss issues as they arose. So in the introduction to the service, we would look at the reasons given for marriage. I would ask them, for example, if they had an agreed approach to the question of children. Had they ever discussed this together? I once came across a couple, whom I had not prepared, who went into their marriage not having agreed on the question of children: she wanted children and he did not. This was one of the reasons why the marriage ended on the rocks.

It is hardly surprising that among those who got married and who stayed on as members of the church, there were some couples who had their teething problems. Sometimes they came back to us for another meal and a further chat. In some cases we soon felt out of our depth. Gill had had some training in counselling when she was preparing to be a probation officer but I had had none. We were fortunate in having as a friend, Myra Chave-Jones who is a psychotherapist. She was living in England but loved coming to Paris and was quite prepared to do a bit of work whilst she was with us. So if we were faced with any problems that were beyond us, we would suggest a session or two with Myra. In a few cases someone might then be referred to a French counselling service, provided their knowledge of the language was up to it. There was no equivalent to Relate available to us. I suspect that this is often the case for English-speaking congregations in European countries and this can impose quite a burden on Anglican clergy abroad. We were always very grateful for Myra's visits. From time to time she gave talks to church groups on subjects such as, Coping with Anger and Understanding Depression.

Money was something we could not take for granted at St Michael's. Many of our members were very new to the Christian faith and they had to learn to give; so from time to time there was teaching on Christian stewardship. The cost of sustaining the work at St Michael's was enormous. There was a large full-time staff to support and all the money had to be found locally. There were no grants forthcoming from central church funds. In addition to the usual running costs of a church and community centre, we were based in a building that was very costly to repair and sustain. There was always something that needed attention. One year we had to re-lay the church floor, taking up some old linoleum that was curling at the edges and beginning to prove dangerous. This was replaced by a parquet floor which should survive many generations of worshippers. In addition to all our local commitments, the church council took the decision to devote a tenth of our income to the support of overseas mission work. There was the occasional financial crisis when we looked like finishing a year with a large deficit. This was a serious matter as we had very little in the way of investment reserves to cover a shortfall. Somehow, with the grace of God helping us, we managed to end most years in the black. We could, however, never afford to become complacent, which was perhaps a healthy state of affairs. It taught us to trust more fully in God and His goodness.

The young nature of our congregation meant that most of those in leadership had not been around in Christian circles for very long. We should not have been surprised, therefore, if occasionally people were drawn away into some strange sect. This happened to us two years before the end of our time in Paris, when a South African preacher with some Jewish connections came into town. As is usually the way with sectarian preachers, a main plank in their message majored on the denunciation of all other main-line Christian denominations. Such criticism is hard to refute because we know ourselves only too well and we realise that we have a long way to go if we are to be truly pleasing to our Lord. I remember one middle-aged lady with dyed blonde hair arriving at our church. After the service she fixed me with a steely stare and informed me that she had left her last church because there was sin in the church. I cannot remember now how I replied to this comment, but I felt like saying: "Madam, please do not scratch around too hard here, as I dread to think what you might unearth!"

Our travelling preacher from South Africa, however, not only wrote-off all the other churches in Paris but taught, amongst other things, that the second coming of Christ was imminent and would definitely take place within the next year or so. "There is no time to lose", he said, "you must sell everything and join my fellowship and engage in preaching the gospel until the great day arrives." One couple who were about to get married took him at his word. The wife-to-be had been at the very heart of our church life and was a dedicated Christian. The direct and simple nature of this preacher's appeal was very attractive to her and one can understand why. Consequently the religious side of their marriage ceremony took place in the preacher's flat. The couple

broke off all their links with St Michael's. They got rid of
their possessions and left Paris to go on a preaching tour of
Eastern Europe. It was all very distressing for their friends
in our church with whom all contact was broken. About two
years later they were back in Paris and more or less destitute.
They slept rough and had no permanent home. Gradually, as
support for them had diminished from the group they had
joined, the truth dawned on them that they had been taken
for a ride and that the preacher was an extremely manipula-
tive man who had taken advantage of them. Eventually they
returned to St Michael's full of apologies and were reconciled
to us as a church before we left to go back to England. During their period of wandering, they had become the parents
of a child. Members of St Michael's helped them to get back
on their feet again. They eventually moved to a new home
on the coast in the west of France where they are now happily settled. When we were back in Paris on a visit to St
Michael's a few years ago, the church laid on a special lunch
for all who had known us. About sixty came to that lunch
and amongst them were this couple and their two children.
We are still in touch with them, thanks to e-mail.

There were times when we felt at St Michael's that we
could organise ourselves more efficiently. I believe that the
staff team was always a happy team and that we got on well
together. But I, along with most clergy, had had no proper
training in church administration and so we came to feel that
it would be helpful to bring in an outside consultant who
would take a good objective look at our ways of operating and
running the church. To illustrate our problems, let me quote
from a contribution to a farewell album that was put together
for us as we were on the point of leaving Paris. This was written by our good friend Alison Jones (now Alison Haddock)

and here she is describing her work in the office when she first took on the post of secretary. "Little did I know what a hive of activity the office could be! It could take up to one hour to type a letter by the time you had answered five telephone calls, chatted to someone looking at the notice board, paid the Picard man, made the mistake of asking who would like a cup of tea and making ten cups instead of one, etc."

I had already come across some of the publications put out by Administry, a Christian firm that sets out to help churches with their administration. They send out consultant advisers to churches and also run training courses for church administrators. Their publications cover a whole range of subjects such as, Managing Change and Church Finance. Their organisation was led by John Truscott when we first approached them and we invited John to come out and spend a few days taking us apart and putting us together again. He worked very long hours over a period of several days, interviewing all the members of staff as well as members of our church council. Gill and I both had sessions with him so we, as well as everyone else that he interviewed, were free to express our opinions as to the strengths and weaknesses of our church organisation. It was a bracing experience, not unlike taking a cold shower! John came to us as a practising Christian who was convinced that good and efficient administration was all part of the stewardship of our gifts as Christians. He was always gracious in the way he dealt with people. After returning home, John put together a lengthy and detailed report, the contents of which were sent to me and were considered by the members of the Church Council at one of our meetings.

John was rightly critical of the way our church office operated. It could not function efficiently and do all the things that it was attempting to do within a small enclosed space. He recommended that we install a new welcome desk at the front entrance of the church. This was to be staffed, for as much of the working day as possible, by volunteers. This would become the first port of call for visitors who dropped in asking the time of services next Sunday or how they could find the British consulate, along with a host of other quite mundane questions. The notice boards containing advertisements for jobs, accommodation and items for sale were all moved downstairs, away from the office, and placed on the walls around the front entrance. This meant that the person at the welcome desk could direct enquirers to these notices without interrupting the office work upstairs. A new telephone was installed by the welcome desk so that calls could be directed to the chaplain, the assistant chaplain, or some other lay member of staff without in most cases disturbing the church secretary at her work. If someone called in real need, it was always possible to refer such a person to one of the staff upstairs.

At the same time it was felt that Connie Gleisner, who had been working in the office both as church administrator as well as being in overall charge of all the music, should concentrate entirely on the music side of church life. This meant that she also had to build up her music student clientele to supplement the income that she would be receiving from the church as Director of Music. As can be imagined, such changes create quite an upheaval and there is always an element of pain involved. Here and there John put his finger on some difficult relationship problems, not all of which could be solved overnight; but even here he proved very helpful. He gave me two useful bits of advice which have stayed with me.

1. When you are faced with criticism, even when it is delivered in a rude, angry and totally unacceptable manner, ask

yourself: "when you strip away the invective and the unpleasant manner in which the message was delivered to you, what core truth is there within that criticism of which you ought to take notice?"

2. If you are ever faced with an intractable relationship problem with a parishioner and the two of you simply cannot work it out together, find a wise third party who will look at your problem impartially and then meet together as a threesome. Sometimes a facilitator can help two people who are at odds with each other to resolve a difficulty.

Since John's visit, I have tried on occasions to act on both these pieces of wise advice. Administry are a business organisation and have to charge reasonable consultancy rates, so an exercise of this kind does not come cheap. But I believe that any expenditure that we incurred was well worth it and we certainly acted on many of the recommendations that John made.

CHAPTER EIGHTEEN

SOME SPECIAL EVENTS

Frèsnes prison was situated a few kilometres to the south of the centre of Paris. It was a gaunt and daunting place to visit, surrounded by forbidding grey walls, and its interior was scarcely more inviting, with its stone floors and seemingly endless corridors interrupted only by wire mesh and firmly locked doors. One of our members, Heda Böhnish, was a regular visitor to this institution. Every week she would catch a bus and make her way to a reception area where she would meet with just a handful of the prisoners. And on a few occasions in the year at festival times, she would arrange for a team from St Michael's to go in and take a service for any who wished to come. The service was quite short and simple as the team and prisoners sat around in a circle and worshipped together. After the service there was time when we could intermingle and chat together. Most of those whom we met were in prison for drug offences. Some were still awaiting trial. The room where we met was drab and depressing, but at least our visit was a sign to those who came to the service that they were not forgotten and that there were some Christian people out there who cared about them. So for those few who were able to come to those services, it was like a chink of light breaking into their otherwise dark world and that made it special.

Back on the home front, we held the occasional mission weekends which we called guest weekends. We invited guest speakers to come and address us at our main Sunday services and they also spoke and took questions at evening supper parties on Friday and Saturday evenings. Keith de Berry came one weekend, bringing a team with him from All Souls', Langham Place which included Kim Swithinbank. Kim spoke at an early evening drinks party held in a home venue. Sadly some of the team had to drop out at the last minute and not all of those who came were up to chairing the cut-and-thrust debate and discussion sessions on issues of unbelief as well as faith, but Keith himself (though by now getting on in years) was as sharp as ever in the pulpit. Paul Weston and Roger Simpson were two other very gifted preachers who came for weekends of a similar nature and usually afterwards we were able to encourage some of those who attended to join a Christian basics study group to look at some of the most basic tenets of Christian belief. It is now, sadly, often the case that those who hear the Christian message for the first time have practically no background knowledge of the Christian story. Girls will wear crucifixes round their necks as jewellery with no idea of the historic background behind the object that they are wearing. So most of those who hear the challenge of the Christian message have not enough knowledge of who Jesus Christ is to make them ready to become his committed followers. Hence the need for some kind of Christian Basics course to be on offer in any church that is taking its mission seriously. For many churches these days, the Alpha course is filling this gap, but other courses such as the Emmaus course can equally well serve the purpose.

In order to reach businessmen in the city, we laid on the occasional businessmen's luncheon. These were high quality three course lunches served with a good wine, at a cost for each participant in the region of £13, as they would be used to spending this amount, if not more, on a business lunch. Gill usually organised the cooking and the catering with a team of helpers. The charge we made for the lunch enabled us to pay for a return airfare for a speaker from the U.K. and usually there was a small surplus which we were either able to retain as a starter fund for the next lunch, or in some cases to donate something to a charity. The speaker was given a subject the purpose of which was to encourage us to think in a Christian way about matters of everyday life. So a leading banker was asked to speak on a Christian approach to money. Professor Sam Berry of London University gave a talk on issues relating to science and faith. The lunches were organised on an inter-church basis so men were invited to attend from right across Paris and the suburbs. One year the luncheon was held at our sister church in the centre of Paris, St George's, and their ladies cooked and prepared the meal. I had invited Lord Cheshire, the founder of the Cheshire Homes, to be our guest speaker on this occasion. There was some confusion over who was to collect him from his hotel and bring him to St George's. It ended up with my racing through the streets of Paris to collect him, only to find him sitting calm and quite unruffled in the foyer. I rushed in late and rather flustered, full of apologies. He told me that he had not been worried and felt sure that someone would turn up to fetch him before long! At the luncheon he spoke on the importance of prayer in his life. You could have heard a pin drop as he spoke. His audience were riveted and I am sure that his testimony made a profound impression on all who heard him. I believe that it was toward the end of his career in the R.A.F. that he was converted to Christ and became a devout Roman Catholic. It was during this visit to Paris that a member of our embassy staff told me of an incident that had taken place during the second world war. Leonard Cheshire led a bombing raid which was targeting an aircraft factory at Limoges in central France, which was fully staffed by French workers. Cheshire flew three times over that factory, thus warning workers inside the building of the need to escape to safety; it was on the third run-in over the target that the bombs were dropped. Only one factory worker was killed. A few days before our luncheon, Leonard Cheshire visited Limoges and there had been a highly emotional reunion with survivors of that wartime raid. A few days later he read the lesson at our annual Battle of Britain memorial service and afterwards he wrote a very kind and warm letter encouraging me in my ministry.

The annual Battle of Britain memorial service in mid-September was another important point of contact with many who were outside our church family but who wanted a service that would commemorate that particular significant victory and also give to veterans the chance to pause and remember those who had lost their lives in that conflict. On the Friday of that weekend there was a memorial ceremony at the Arc de Triomphe when the normally low-burning memorial flame is turned up. At our Sunday service the British Ambassador read the lesson and many embassy representatives from other Commonwealth countries, as well as members of the French veteran associations, were in attendance. The local R.A.F. association was heavily involved in all the arrangements as well as our embassy Defence Attaché. One year, Branse Burbridge, a former second world war pilot, was our guest preacher. At my final service of this kind, Lady Mary Soames, the youngest and only surviving daughter of Sir Winston Churchill, was in the congregation with other members of the Soames family. Her husband, Sir Christopher Soames, had been the British Ambassador in Paris some years previously. I had prepared my sermon containing a reference to Winston Churchill before I knew that she was coming. When I saw her sitting in the front row, I saw no reason to leave this reference out! Each year after the service we hosted a drinks party in our apartment upstairs. All those who had come as guests to the service were invited to attend. A team from the church prepared delicious canapés and the Defence Attaché provided the champagne!

As in Britain, November 11th is a red letter day in France, if not more so. For the French observe the day as a public holiday. The British Legion organised a service in Notre Dame Cathedral and all the English-speaking churches took part. For most of our time in Paris, the chaplain to the British Legion was Bruce Robertson, the minister at the Scots Kirk in Paris. We were good friends with Bruce and his wife Edie and I sometimes stood in for him when they went on holiday, as he had no assistant. In our last year in Paris, the Robertsons had retired and I took over as British Legion Chaplain, which meant that for one year, I had the privilege of preaching in Notre Dame. The St Michael's choir joined forces with the St George's choir and the direction of the music was shared by our two choir directors. Their joint contribution always added something special to the service.

Carol services are always a tremendous draw in all overseas chaplaincies and St Michael's was no exception. The crowds at our first carol service were so great that we had to consider alternative arrangements for the following year. Eventually we settled into a pattern of having a more family-orientated service, to which younger children could come, late on the Saturday afternoon. Our Sunday carol service was then held round the corner in the massive church building which was the home of the French Presbyterian congregation. In all, around a thousand people must have attended one or other of these services most years. Connie Gleisner did splendid work with the choir, which was usually augmented for the Christmas season. One year we gave away copies of J. John's booklet *What's the point of Christmas?* to any who wished to receive one. A month or so before these services, Gill was usually over in England for a visit, sometimes to see one of the family at university, and she would not fail to pay a visit to one of our major supermarket stores and come away with about six hundred mince pies. These, together with glasses of mulled wine, were offered to all our worshippers at the end of the services. I always gave what I called an introduction to the service after the first hymn. This was in fact a short talk, which sought to explore the meaning of Christ's coming to earth amongst us and this was followed by the Bidding Prayer. It is my belief that those who come to carol services are not in the mood to take-in a sermon towards the end of such a service, but that they are more inclined to listen to a short and pithy address that comes in near the beginning. My hope and prayer was that an appropriate word would get them thinking about the Christian message which would subsequently be contained in the readings and the carols.

From time to time royal visitors would arrive in Paris. One year Prince Charles and Princess Diana came together and a ball was given in their honour at the British Embassy to which we were invited. Gill's initial reaction was: "What on earth shall I wear?" It was Caroline Spellman (then a member of our congregation and now the Conservative Member of Parliament for Meriden) who came to the rescue: she lent Gill the most fabulous ball gown and when we were all dressed up, my wife looked stunning! Her second great fear was that she might suddenly find herself confronted by the Prince of Wales and be required to dance with him. As it turned out, she had no grounds for fear on this account. The British Embassy residence in Paris is one of the most beautiful of all our ambassadors' homes across the world. I only hope that for the sake of economy it will never be disposed of. The building was once owned and occupied by a sister of Napoleon. I was told that It was bought by the Duke of Wellington for the sum of £25,000. The ladies at this ball were all dressed in splendid evening dresses, many of which were specially made for the occasion by one of the fashion houses in the adjacent Faubourg St Honoré. I was standing next to a friend towards the end of the party and his wife was just a few yards away. He looked at her and said "Ah, my very dear wife"; and then added as an afterthought: "very dear dress!"

The summer of 1992 was the occasion for a state visit to France by her Majesty the Queen. It was a difficult time for our Queen with royal marriage problems hitting the headlines of the newspapers at home. The French newspaper *Figaro* published a cartoon which depicted our Queen standing at the top of a stairway and about to descend from the aircraft which had brought her to Paris. President Mitterand was to be seen waiting at the bottom of the stairs. From the Queen's head came a bubble containing her thoughts as she was about to meet the President of the Republic: "If he asks me how the family are, I shall hit him with my handbag!" I am sure that such a thought never entered the Queen's head, but it was nevertheless a clever and amusing cartoon. The Queen and Prince Philip received a warm welcome from the people of Paris and her mastery of the French language was much appreciated. At one reception where there was a demonstration by some Scots Guards of a sword dance, she was overheard explaining the intricacies of the dance in French to President Mitterand. There were visits to Versailles and to other city centres in France and a host of receptions. The President of the Republic gave a dinner for the Queen in the Elysée palace, which I attended. I confess that for me a moment of great excitement came when I met the one-time great French tennis champion, Jean Borotra, who was in his heyday in the 1920s. I found myself next to him in the entrance hall to the Palace, though sadly conversation was difficult as he was then about ninety years of age and almost stone deaf. Needless to say, the banquet was a sumptuous occasion. The Queen in turn gave a dinner at the British Embassy residence to which we were both invited. Gill again had the problem of what to wear! This time it was Caroline Herbert from Louis Feraud who turned up trumps and lent her a dress from their fashion house. It was a dark blue sequinned number which I thought made Gill look a bit like a dowager duchess! The downstairs rooms at the residence all became dining-rooms for the occasion, with large circular tables. They were even bold enough to serve an English white wine with the fish. The ambassador at the time was Sir Euan Ferguson, who was shortly due to retire, so this royal visit meant that he went out in something of a blaze of glory. The Queen's state visit was deemed to have been a great success. The last state visit that we had witnessed was in Khartoum in the 1960s when Her Majesty was driven from the airport to the centre of the city standing upright in an open car. On that occasion she was dressed entirely in white and looked magnificent. What a reign it has been and long may it continue!

When our time came to leave St Michael's, we were given the most wonderful farewell party and were showered with some very generous gifts. Sheba had by now expired, partly through old age and partly due to a surfeit of over-rich French food. It had become known that after our return to Sussex we were going to look for a West Highland White terrier puppy. Part of our gift from St Michael's was a cheque to enable us to buy such a puppy along with all sorts of accoutrements to help us look after her. On receiving this wonderful gift, I told everyone that our new dog would have to be called Michelle. There was a further large cheque and various people sang songs about us which were funny as well as serious and there were a number of farewell speeches. The one danger of such an occasion is that it is a bit like eavesdropping on your obituary notice or a funeral oration. The speakers forget all your faults and mistakes and say all sorts of nice things about you. The great temptation is to believe them! And the further danger is that it can lead to a swelling of the head. Whether that is what happened to me, I cannot be sure; but it is a danger to beware of. There was one more splendid drinks party which the Ambassador gave for us at the British Embassy and we then departed for England on the crest of a wave. Very soon, however, we were to be brought down to earth with a bump.

CHAPTER NINETEEN

AN ARCHDEACON AT LARGE

Some time after the bishop had invited me to become archdeacon in northern France, I was having lunch with a senior diocesan official in London. I had really no idea what might be involved in this new aspect of the job that awaited me in Paris. When I asked him: " What exactly does an archdeacon do?" His face took on a rather puzzled expression and then suddenly lit up. He leant across the table and said: "The linen; the Bishop is very worried about the communion linen in some of the chaplaincies." I was slightly nonplussed by this reply. Was I going to spend much of my time during the coming years poking about in vestry drawers in European chaplaincies inspecting their linen? I sincerely hoped that there would be more to the job than checking up on ecclesiastical laundry. I never have been much good at ironing!

One of my first duties as archdeacon was to preside over an Archdeaconry Synod. This was held once a year in France and on this occasion the meetings took place at the American Cathedral in Paris. I invited Bishop Stanley Betts, a former Bishop of Maidstone, to come and take Bible readings which would be inserted into the worship side of our programme.

It was not, however, a happy synod. There was a poor spirit amongst the clergy and a lot of simmering anger. In the debates speakers were at times quite rude to each other. Part of the problem lay in the fact that Bishop John Satterthwaite had divided the diocese into spheres of responsibility between him and his suffragan bishop. The latter was to cover the Archdeaconry of Northern France which covered all of France except for the Riviera, while Stuttgart in Germany was thrown in for good measure! He also covered certain other parts of the Diocese. This on the face of it seemed a good arrangement, but in practice it meant that if you asked the assistant bishop for advice and perhaps a decision about something, the reply would often be: "I don't know about that. I shall have to ask the Bishop." It was this sort of response that lay behind much of the anger and frustration that the clergy were exhibiting since Bishop John was not in the habit of visiting our part of France very often. One positive outcome of that rather fraught synod was that it was decided to invite Bishop John to come over and meet us all with a view to better mutual understanding. With Bishop John's consent, we went on to organise a residential meeting at a retreat house to the south of Paris. The Bishop and all the clergy from the Archdeaconry stayed overnight in an atmosphere of prayer and worship. I arranged for each chaplain to have a twenty-minute session in private with the Bishop during which they could have as frank and as open a discussion as was felt to be necessary. This pattern seemed to work very well and our time together at Vanves retreat centre was time well spent. A period of much easier relationships ensued.

Not long after the retreat, Bishop Edward Holland was appointed assistant bishop in the Diocese of Europe. He had already had experience as a chaplain in Naples and, before that, in Gibraltar so he understood the nature of the churches that he was visiting. He was a wise and understanding pastor and a good friend to the clergy who were serving as chaplains. When in the Paris area, he often stayed with us and I can remember when we shared a day off and we all went to see a Woody Allen film together. He knew how to relax as well how to work. I believe that during his period in Europe, he did much to make the Diocese mean something to churches that were a very long way from the diocesan office in London.

After our first synod, we established the practice of holding a twenty-four hour retreat leading up to the synod meetings with a retreat leader from England as leader. Our retreat leaders over the years included Brian de Saram, Andrew Knowles (an old college friend and now a Canon of Chelmsford Cathedral), Bishop Edward and Bishop Peter Ball who was then Bishop of Lewes. By no means all of the synod members made it to the retreats. But with quite a number of retired people serving as synod representatives, there was always a fairly good turnout and I believe that this period of prayerful preparation before a synod made for a positive and constructive spirit when it came to the business meetings. We alternated these annual affairs between Paris and another chaplaincy in some other area of France. Synods away from Paris were always residential: the very fact of eating together helps to build up relationships. As friendships developed amongst the members, I believe that people began to look forward to these annual events and they were certainly a reminder to us all that the church is far more than simply a local congregation. We all belong together in the Body of Christ. A key member of the Synod in those days was Alec Russell. Not everyone found Alec easy to get on with, but I found him an enormous help and support. I have never been too strong on the details of church rules and procedures. So when in doubt I would turn to Alec and get his opinion. He had the sort of brain that could store away detailed information and he usually could come up with the correct answer. He was an accountant who knew his way around matters of finance. This expertise also proved invaluable to us. A small standing committee of the synod, whose membership had to be drawn from the Paris area, met in between the synods to plan the programme for the following year. This took place in a most convivial atmosphere around our dining room table!

The Archdeaconry covered a huge area and, since my first responsibility was to St Michael's, it was impossible to be away often at weekends visiting other chaplaincies. I felt that the most useful aspect of my role was to keep in touch by telephone with brother clergy (there were not yet any sister clergy when I started on the job, though that was soon to change). In the Paris area there was a clergy fraternal that met from time to time whilst at St Michael's we were part of a team, so there was no need to feel lonely. But in many of the chaplaincies such as in Lyon and Bordeaux, there were no other clergy for miles around and it must have been easy to feel very isolated. A telephone call at least gave out a message that someone was thinking about them and concerned for their well-being.

Having an assistant chaplain at St Michael's, I could be away for a Sunday morning, visiting and preaching in one of the Paris churches such as Chantilly or Maisons Lafitte and then be back in the centre of Paris in time for the evening service. In this way it did not feel as if I had been away for a weekend and St Michael's did not feel neglected. Occasionally we would go further afield and spend a weekend in one of the chaplaincies. I enjoyed visits to Strasbourg where our friends Barney and Evie Milligan were living and working. Barney combined his duties as chaplain in Strasbourg with the job of representing the churches – particularly but not exclusively the Anglicans – at the European institutions, that is the Council of Europe and the Parliament of the European Community (as the E.U. was then known). This brought him into contact not only with parliamentarians and civil servants, but also with ecumenical partners. So visits to Strasbourg were full of interest. I especially remember one weekend when Archbishop Robert Runcie was staying there and he took a lively question-and-answer session for school children in the huge "hemicycle" (the name given to the assembly hall where the parliament met and many other gatherings took place). I also heard how in that same room, Ian Paisley had tried to shout down the Archbishop and that his interruption had ended with surprising geniality!

From Strasbourg, it was only a short distance further east to Stuttgart so we were able to visit the Revd Michael Naidu an Indian priest who was living in Stuttgart and working part time in the chaplaincy as well as with the Bible Society.

Sometimes I was involved in a period of pain for a particular church. There was the time when I had to drive up to Rouen to preside at a service of deconsecration of a church building which was about to be sold. The church community there had shrunk and it was no longer possible to sustain the church property. The small congregation subsequently moved to another place of worship, owned by a different church community, and they were looked after by the Missions to Seaman chaplain resident in Rouen. But it was a sad moment for those few worshippers as they gathered in a building they had known and loved for many years.

And then there was the church building in Bordeaux, where Brian Eaves was the chaplain. I.C.S., with Brian's full support, took the decision to sell the church building and to invest the capital realised, thus providing some income for the maintenance of the ministry in the south west region of France. There was fierce opposition to this move from a section of the Bordeaux congregation and it was a difficult time for all concerned. I went down to attend a meeting of the Bordeaux church when the reasons for the decision and the plans for the future were presented. I was there to see fair play and I certainly wanted to support Brian Eaves through a difficult and painful period. I.C.S. had been pouring large sums of money each year into this chaplaincy. The level of giving within the church at the time was lamentably low and drastic action had to be taken. I am quite sure the right decision was reached but there was no avoiding the sense of pain and loss. Some years later the money from the sale of the church building was reinvested in a property that became the chaplain's residence, thus avoiding the need to pay rent. The church congregation in Bordeaux meet in a chapel lent to them by the Roman Catholic Church and this still serves them very well. Meanwhile the chaplain covers a number of other congregations which meet for worship in the Aquitaine region. The chaplaincy is thriving and, with greatly increased giving, it has become financially viable.

In 1986 the chaplain covering Lyon and Grenoble was Gerald Hovenden. They lived in a small three bedroomed house in Lyon and made the journey most Sunday afternoons to an evening service in Grenoble. Sometimes they stayed over in Grenoble for an extra night or two to enable them to do a bit of visiting and to keep in touch with church members; but it was difficult to give adequate cover, living as they did at such a considerable distance from Grenoble.

Gerald and his wife Pat were expecting a child. Rachel was born in hospital but it was a difficult birth and for a while Pat and the baby were very ill. We were able to take the T.G.V. from Paris, which took us in a matter of two hours into Lyon, and over a weekend we aimed to be of some support to Gerald and to help out with the services. Thankfully, Pat and baby Rachel were soon on the mend. We were glad to be able to be of help to one of our clergy at a time of crisis. I began to feel that this was what my role as archdeacon was all about.

Later from St Michael's we were able to take a team down to Lyon for a guest weekend as an encouragement to the church. I was also invited by Gerald to speak at one of their church weekends away for the Lyon and Grenoble congregations which was held at a beautiful centre in the hills overlooking Grenoble.

Gerald eventually moved back into an English parish and his place was taken by Peter May. We went down to be with them over one weekend when they were celebrating with a harvest thanksgiving. During the course of a chat in their home, Peter told me that he was predicting the closure of the Grenoble church by the following April. That was in about six months' time. I remember telling Peter that we couldn't just let that happen. If for any reason Grenoble was proving a bit too much for him, then we must find someone else who could come out and keep the work going there. When I got home, I was in touch with Patti Schmiegelow, the General Secretary of I.C.S. and also with Bishop Edward. A retired chaplain who had had a very fruitful ministry at Cannes, was asked to go and hold the fort at Grenoble. So Ian Watts, whom we had known through a visit to us in the Sudan, once again came out of retirement and moved with his wife, Dorothy, to a flat in Grenoble. With a clergyman living on the spot, the church immediately began to grow. Since that time, the churches have both grown, initially with significant financial support from I.C.S., to the point where they both have their own full-time paid chaplains. They are now both financially self-supporting.

Fontainebleau is about sixty kilometres south of Paris. There is a very well known business school there (known as INSEAD) and a number of young British high-fliers in the business world go there for intensive study courses. One of our St Michael's members, Deigan Morris, was a professor at this college. He and his wife Barbara, used to come up to St Michael's about once a fortnight and there were others, too, who came to us from that area from time to time. We thought that it would be worth trying to hold services in Fontainebleau around Easter and Christmas. The results of these initial experiments proved quite encouraging so we then moved to a monthly service in a church lent to us by the Église Réformée. The next step was to explore the possibility of finding someone who would come and work in Fontainebleau as a non-stipendiary minister with accommodation and expenses provided. It was at about this time that Gill and I went on holiday to Egypt just after Christmas to visit our son Andrew, who was teaching English at the American University of Cairo. Whilst we were there, we met John and Pat Benwell who had just had to leave Somalia where John had been working for an aid agency, but was also acting as a non-stipendiary minister looking after expatriates in Mogadishu. The political situation had become so dire in Somalia that all expatriates had been obliged to leave. John and Pat had no idea what their next step was to be. When I spoke to them about the opening at Fontainebleau they seemed interested. An added bonus was that John spoke French. It was finally arranged that the Benwells would go and work in Fontainebleau for a period of six to nine months. A weekly service would be established and we would see then how viable such a development would be. A modest apartment was rented for them and they both threw themselves into the planting and establishment of a new church. When the time came for the Benwells to leave, there was a regular congregation and, thanks to the sterling efforts of Pat, a Sunday School was up and running. Clearly this work had to go on. The next appointment was Bill Wilson. He was a bachelor and it was agreed with him that he would earn a third of his stipend through teaching English. The rest of his stipend and expenses were to be found partly by the Fontainebleau community and partly by grants from I.C.S. and some help from St Michael's. Bill began his ministry there shortly before I left to return to the U.K. He did excellent work and the church continued to grow under his leadership, moving to the place where it was financially able to stand on its own feet. Bill was later succeeded by Dominic Newstead who currently lives on the outskirts of the town with his wife Annie and their four children. Some eighteen months ago we covered for them for a few weeks whilst they went away for a family holiday. It was such a delight to see how the church had grown, from those small beginnings just over ten years earlier.

Most of our chaplaincies had only a few teenagers attached to them and that was certainly our situation in Paris. No one church had a strong enough youth work to support a Christian holiday youth venture on its own. But if we were to act together, that would be a different matter. We made contact with other churches in the Archdeaconry and set about organising a week's summer youth holiday at Houlgate on the Normandy coast. David Frost, who had been a youth leader during our time in Hove, was invited to come out to lead this new initiative. We had quite a number at St Michael's of student age who were willing to take part as assistant leaders and for the first of these house parties we had about thirty teenagers drawn from many of the chaplaincies. This pattern was repeated over several years and it proved a great means of strengthening our work amongst young people at an age when the church, generally speaking, seems very good at losing them. It was just one more example of what can happen when a group of churches pull together and work as a team instead of trying to go it alone.

As an archdeacon I was automatically a member of the Diocesan Synod which met every summer for about four days from Monday to Friday at a Roman Catholic centre in London Colney, near St Albans. The fact that this Synod was residential was very much in its favour. When work was done for the day, delegates would gather round the bar for a drink before proceeding to dinner. The atmosphere of the place and the fact that we all worshipped in the chapel helped us to relax together. People grew to trust each other across churchmanship lines and it was an opportunity to build friendships with people from other parts of the Diocese. It gave us all a greater sense of belonging to the wider church and it was often encouraging to hear news of church developments and growth in other parts of Europe.

In 1992 the Diocese was celebrating the 150th anniversary of the founding of the Diocese of Gibraltar. The area covered by the Diocese is very extensive and Gibraltar can hardly claim to be at the centre of Europe. So although there was a weekend of celebration in Gibraltar itself which many of us enjoyed, it was decided that each Archdeaconry should organise its own celebration. Ours was fixed to take place from January 23rd to the 26th which in the life of most churches is a quiet period after Christmas. A full programme was arranged to cover these four days and we were able to obtain special rates at Frantours Hotel for delegates to the weekend as the manager and family were linked with our church following a family baptism. The Riding Lights Theatre Company put on a revue entitled *Rolling in the Aisles* which provided us with an entirely new and fresh way of looking at some of the well-known Bible stories. There were performances on the Thursday, Friday and Saturday evenings and also a matinée on Saturday. The arrangements surrounding these performances were very demanding upon us in terms of time and money, but it all proved worth it in the end. I enrolled our friend Ian Cawood to head the organising committee for this production and Tiffany Beves also joined the team. Within a week she had telephoned a host of companies with British connections working in Paris and got them to contribute sponsorship for this production, which went a long way towards covering our costs. This subcommittee did sterling work organising ticket production and sales, sorting out accommodation for the actors and arranging for stewards on each night, as well as refreshments at every interval. Having invited church members from all over France to come to Paris for a church weekend of celebration, it was important that we had a programme that would make the journey worthwhile. The Riding Lights production added a lighter touch to the weekend's events and proved a great draw. After the weekend was over, I had lunch out with Ian

A childrens' event with Ishmael at the American Cathedral in Paris during the Diocesan 150th anniversary celebrations in 1992

Cawood and he told me in passing that he had asked Tiffany to come and work with him in his fund management firm. I remember asking him whether he thought there might be any romantic possibilities in this relationship. He smiled and assured me that he never mixed his business life with his social life. Ian and Tiffany are now married, with three lovely children!

Other activities over the weekend included a Saturday morning lecture on, The Christian Faith and the Future of Europe, given by David (now Lord) Alton; a special children's programme on the Saturday afternoon was organised by someone whom we described quite aptly as a kind of Christian Pied Piper, called Ishmael. Andrew Knowles led a twenty-four hour retreat for those who preferred a bit of peace and quiet. Riding Lights also set up a drama workshop for all those interested in learning how drama can be used to put across Christian truth, and Andrew Knowles also led a workshop on Evangelism in the Local Church. We managed to persuade all our churches (with one exception) to cancel their regular Sunday services, which meant that all the clergy and plenty of lay people came into Paris for the celebrations. We all gathered in a massive dining room at the Frantours Hotel for a buffet lunch on the Sunday and in the afternoon the whole company attended St Sulpice Church for a celebration Eucharist at which our Bishop John presided and preached. Connie had got together an *ad hoc* choir from all the churches and, after one good practice, they led us in the singing. A number of instrumentalists added an extra musical touch and it was a particular delight for Gill and me to have David Bubbers, my former vicar, and his wife Evelyn with us for the weekend. David was part of the small orchestra and he accompanied the singing on his trombone. Each church had been asked to prepare a banner appropriate to their region of France and so it was no surprise when the Bordeaux church came in bearing a banner covered in grapes and with the inscription "I am the true vine"; Chantilly excelled themselves with a horse on their banner and an inscription which read: "Run the race that is set before you looking unto Jesus." It was a great service and it was wonderful to see so many Anglican church groups gathered together from all over France for a celebration as we rejoiced in all God's goodness to us over past years.

Some time earlier in the day we heard that a young man that we had visited had just died from Aids. So from the "high" of that amazing service, we both drove to the apartment where the young man had died, to seek to comfort a grieving mother who was certainly at a "low" point. It was strange to move in one afternoon from a place of exuberant rejoicing to a place of great sadness. Such is sometimes the lot of the clergy. From there we moved on to a reception given by the British Ambassador in honour of our Bishop, who was staying at the residence as his guest. There was a further diocesan celebration at Westminster Abbey to which all the eight Archdeacons in Europe were invited, the preacher being Archbishop George Carey.

As we entered 1993, I was beginning my eighth year in Paris and the work of being chaplain of St Michael's as well as archdeacon was a heavy load. I had at least another five years to go until retirement and I felt that I should move to a slightly less stressful job for that last stretch. So I began to explore possibilities of alternative employment back in the U.K. Having worked in Hove for seven years, the Diocese of Chichester seemed a good place to start looking. Eventually we were offered the living of East Hoathly and Chiddingly, and we moved to our new Sussex home in January 1994. We were soon to discover that the tranquil appearance of rural England can be somewhat deceptive!

CHAPTER TWENTY

PASSING THROUGH THE FIRE

When we arrived in East Hoathly in January 1994, I was about to turn sixty. An old friend and parishioner from Hove days had been busy painting some of the rooms in our new home. We soon set to work unpacking in an attractive rectory which was surrounded by a large expanse of garden. After eight years of living in a city centre, the garden was a real bonus for us. Soon after we arrived I was up early one morning in my boots and a very old anorak, digging up the vegetable patch. We had employed a firm to come and erect some fencing and one local man, who lived just across the road from us, was working on the job. Drifting over in my direction, he pointed up at the house and said: "When does he get up then?" I replied, "He is up. And he's standing here talking to you." There was a brief moment of embarrassment, but since I could not help myself from laughing, it soon passed. We enjoyed a good relationship during our time in the village. He was a mine of information on the history of the place.

It is fair to say that we suffered from a degree of culture shock as we settled in to village life after Paris. The day after

I arrived, I wandered up into the village and bought four sausages at the butcher's shop. Later that day one of the church wardens dropped in on us. "I hear you bought some sausages at the butcher's", he remarked. "Who on earth told you that?" I asked. "News spreads fast in these parts," said Eric. I was frankly amazed that my purchase of sausages could in any way be described as news. I could have bought sacks of sausages in Paris without causing a ripple of comment. I began to realise that we were moving into a goldfish bowl existence where every move would be noticed.

Some time later a friend called Christine, who came originally from Vietnam and who now lives in Paris, came to stay for a few days. As we were going out for a walk, Christine turned to me and said: "Brian, if I were to stay here, would I be an oddity in this village?" I was somewhat at a loss for words but thought that a mildly facetious answer would suit the situation best. "Yes, I suppose you would," I replied. "I could wheel you around in a barrow and we could make a collection for a charity." She roared with laughter and we moved on. But this little exchange highlighted the fact that we were going to miss the broad international flavour of our former church with its twenty or more nationalities. It is certainly not the fault of any English village if it so happens that all its inhabitants are of one race and one colour. But our new situation was fundamentally different; and of course we were the ones who would have to adjust.

Our two village churches were about two miles apart and set in the midst of the most beautiful countryside. There were, however, only rather poor bus services so we decided to run two small second-hand cars. I drove a bright turquoise little Fiat Panda car, ideal for negotiating the narrow country lanes of what was quite an extensive united benefice. There were three Sunday morning services at 8.00, 9.45 and 11.00 a.m. so it was quite a race to get from one church to the other. If I was taking the 8.00 a.m. service at Chiddingly, a kind couple would give me breakfast so that I could be on hand for the 9.45 a.m. service in the same village. There were evening services on about three evenings a month and our three layreaders were very helpful both in leading and preaching at these services in particular. There was a mixture of old and new in the pattern of services and I managed to get the two church councils to agree to having the same sort of morning service on a given Sunday so that I could use the same sermon in both villages.

At the time of taking on this living, I thought that I understood something of village life. I had spent many of my formative years growing up in villages in Worcestershire and later Warwickshire; but for much of that period I was away at boarding school or at university and was therefore totally ignorant of village politics. I had to learn that the height of a hedge between two properties or the use of the village hall could become matters of supreme importance. In a church where there are many students, you can express disagreement with another person's view on some issue and still remain good friends with them. In a village, however, there is a tendency to take sides when opinions differ over a matter of village politics. A contrary expression of opinion may well be taken personally. You are liable to become "one of us" or "one of them!" I realise that these are generalisations which don't apply to every rural community, but I can speak only from personal experience.

A big plus for me was that there was a thriving tennis club within easy walking distance of our new home. I soon joined and before long was enjoying a regular game of men's doubles. There was a church-aided village school on our doorstep which was doing well under the excellent leadership of Paula Duff. There was a close relationship between school and church and I took regular assemblies there, alternating with another very good school at Chiddingly. Both schools brought children to church for special occasions such as for their nativity plays. I agreed in the summer to teach tennis to children at the East Hoathly primary school. One child asked Paula: "Do all vicars teach tennis?"

Most clergy are given what is commonly known as "a honeymoon period" when they take a new living. There is a feeling of thankfulness that the interregnum is over and everyone wants to make the new vicar feel welcome. I have to confess that my honeymoon at East Hoathly did not last for very long. Both villages had their own Parochial Church Councils. At Chiddingly the meetings proceeded very smoothly. Business was dealt with without fuss and there was a good atmosphere. At East Hoathly tensions and undercurrents within the P.C.C. soon began to emerge. The two churchwardens had done an excellent job during the interregnum but they both found it difficult to adjust to a new rector with his own style of leadership which, as events unfolded, didn't seem to suit them.

Things began to go awry when one of the wardens came to see me about the monthly family service. She told me that during the previous rector's time, she had run this service herself. She made it clear that she was not very happy with my handling of the service so far and she added that she wished to take it over again. I tried to explain that I felt a personal responsibility for conducting all sorts of worship service in the church. I would be happy to share ideas with her and to work with her, but I would wish to remain in overall control of the family worship. She told me later that she felt that I had replied to her request in a very patronising way. I have always felt sorry that this was how my response came across to her and I am sure that I could have handled that interview better. But the root of the issue was, I believe, one of control. I still believe that whilst a parish priest should delegate parts of the service to other lay people and especially to layreaders, he should retain the overall leadership of the church's worship. From that interview onwards things began to unravel like a piece of knitting that is falling apart. The churchwarden who had visited me resigned from her post and a small support group gathered around her. It was a bit like a P.C.C. subcommittee, though in this case they were planning and acting quite apart from the rector.

It was in October of that first year that Gill had a very graphic dream. She dreamt that she was caught up in a fire. She was running away from the conflagration but her coat was alight and in flames. She acted quickly and threw off her coat and found that she was completely unscathed by the experience. She woke up with a scream and I came to with a start. She told me the contents of this dream, which explained that sudden scream. A few days later in her daily Bible reading, Gill came across the verse in Isaiah chapter 43 verse 2 which contains the words: "when you walk through the fire you will not be burned . . . the flames will not set you ablaze" and then in verse 5, "Do not be afraid, for I am with you." These verses of Scripture became an important landmark and encouragement to us in all that we were encountering. We felt reassured that all would be well in the end.

In November there was due to be a visit to East Hoathly of a party of French people from a town in northern France with which we had just been twinned. This visit was to coincide with the Remembrance Sunday weekend, which was always a major event for the village. There were parades with flaming torches, bonfires, and fireworks. But for us that year there were to be fireworks of a different kind.

One Saturday evening about a fortnight before the French party was due to arrive, I had a visit from the remaining church warden. He told me that what I have chosen to call the "support group" were calling for a special meeting of the P. C. C. the following morning after the service of Holy Communion. They had certain complaints to make and they wanted to confront me about the way in which I was leading the church. I had had no prior warning of this proposed meeting so the news came to me as a considerable shock. I immediately telephoned the Archdeacon, Hugh Glaisyer, and asked for his advice. He informed me that a P. C. C. meeting arranged in such a manner with virtually no prior notice was illegal. Nevertheless, I felt that there were obviously issues that had to be confronted so agreed that the meeting should go ahead but it was not to be treated as an official meeting and no minutes were to be taken. I contacted a number of other members of the P. C. C. who had not been invited to attend this meeting, so that they could also be present. For me that Holy communion service was a nightmare and the meeting that followed was not much better. We felt that it was better that Gill stayed away from our village church that morning and we were both invited over to lunch by some friends in Chiddingly afterwards.

A few days later, remembering John Truscott's advice about a facilitator in times of dispute, I suggested to the couple around whom our difficulties had begun that we call in a third party to help us sort things out with a view to reconciliation for the good of the whole church. This was agreed and Hugh Glaisyer came over and the five of us sat down together in their house. Sadly, this produced little that was positive. I felt that, since reconciliation lies at the very heart of our faith, it had been worth the try.

It was in that same month that Gill went for a routine breast scan. A letter soon followed telling her that she needed to report to the oncology centre in Brighton as things were not quite right. She had an appointment with Brian Hogbin, an old friend of ours from our days in Hove, who told her that she was suffering from breast cancer and would need an operation as soon as it could be arranged. Gill took this news far better than I did. She explained to me that she had found our recent difficulties in the village church far more difficult to handle than the cancer.

Amidst all this gloom there had been some brighter moments and one of them was the founding of a village choir which drew in singers from both the villages to lead the singing at the forthcoming carol services. Mike Fairhurst, a school music teacher, led the choir and taught us with enormous patience and skill. I reckon that Mike could almost get music out of a stone! Even the formation of this group was not without its traumas but when it came to the carol service, the singing was led by a choir of about thirty, the church was packed and we had mulled wine and mince pies afterwards. Gill was able to sing in the choir. She had prepared food in our home for all the choir members so that we could have a party after the service. But she herself was driven off to hospital by a friend immediately the service was over so that she could be prepared for surgery the following morning. Brian Hogbin performed the operation and Gill made a speedy recovery. It was soon time to go back to see Brian about the results. He told us that he had removed a very small lump but that there were also some cancerous cells in the lymph glands. Radiotherapy was prescribed though not chemotherapy, and this lasted for about six weeks. Many people in the village were very kind in offering Gill lifts to and from the hospital but for most of the time until near the end of the treatment, she preferred to drive herself.

1994 had certainly been a testing year. We felt that we had passed through the fiery trial about which Gill had dreamt. My brother Richard died following a prolonged illness. David Cooke, our son-in-law, was taken seriously ill and had to return from Africa with Carolyn to the U.K. for medical treatment. They had been serving in Nigeria with the Leprosy Mission. Our daughter Susanna's marriage broke up in Paris. Our son Andrew had had a very difficult year on the personal front. Our experience of parish life had proved painful. And to top it all, Gill had been operated on for cancer. We had indeed passed through the fire but the fire had not destroyed us and we had that promise that God would be with us through our tests and trials. Perhaps 1995 would prove to be different.

There were many aspects of village life that were good and enjoyable. We did our best to become involved in clubs and village activities. We joined the gardening club and entered flowers and vegetables at the annual shows. We attended events in the halls and supported the annual Chiddingly Arts Festival sponsoring a concert in the church, at which Garth Hewitt sang. We attended jumble sales and wine-tasting evenings and the annual East Hoathly church fete was held in our garden and everyone reckoned that it was a success. We bought a volleyball net which provided a bit of extra sporting activity for the church youth group on the rectory lawn. So not all was gloom and doom during the two years we lived in East Hoathly and the vast majority of people in both villages were extremely kind and supportive of us. We were greatly helped by Linda Allen who worked part-time giving me secretarial help. The expenses that the two parishes together provided were generous and were sufficient to cover this work. Geoffrey Barlow took over as churchwarden and he, too, was a source of great encouragement.

At Chiddingly, and later at Framfield, there was a dramatic play-reading of T.S. Eliot's *Murder in the Cathedral*. It was directed by Jim Forest and the chief part of Becket was played by David Burrough, who for many years had been a professional actor. I played the parts of the Fourth Tempter and the Fourth Knight and greatly enjoyed the whole production, which brought together many people, young and old, from both the villages.

The churchwarden who had resigned was very gifted in working with children and young people and amazingly, in spite of our mutual problems, we were able to put together and run a service specially designed for youth once a month. We had a keyboard and two middle-aged guitar players who accompanied the singing. Some twenty to thirty parents and children used to attend. It was a bit of a struggle but worth all the effort.

However, the turning-point for me came quite early in 1995 when I discovered, quite by chance, that the leaders of the Sunday School children's work had cancelled the Sunday School for the whole of Lent. They had contacted all the parents and told them this news but they omitted to inform me of what they were doing. I felt that such behaviour and lack of communication was making my position untenable. Wherever I had been before, I had been able to work as part of a team with all sorts of different people, but in my present parish this was proving to be impossible. So I rang up Bishop John Hind, who was then the Bishop in the Diocese of Europe. I told him that things had not been working out well for us in our rural parishes and that if he thought that we could be of use somewhere in his diocese, then we were prepared to consider moving yet again. His response was very encouraging. I also passed on a similar message to Patti Schmiegelow, who was at that time the General Secretary of I.C.S. I was then serving as Chairman of the I.C.S. council, whose offices were in London near to Tower Bridge.

Around midsummer there was a vacancy at the church of St John and St Philip, the chaplaincy in the Hague, and Patti urged me to apply. I telephoned Bishop John and asked whether he thought I should put in an application. He said that he had told Patti that he would like to see me go to the Hague. To cut a long story short, when the post was advertised in the press we applied for the job and in due course I was nominated to be the new chaplain. We went out to the Hague and met the wardens and members of the church council. Many probing questions were asked. My age by now was telling against another move. I would be sixty-two by the time we reached the Hague, but I offered to give them five years if they agreed to the appointment. We were very happy to hear that the Council in the Hague were unanimous in wanting to proceed with the appointment. So the die was cast and we accepted. Through all our difficulties in Sussex, we received considerable support and encouragement from both the Bishop of Lewes, Ian Cundy, and the Archdeacon, Hugh Glaisyer. It is at times such as these that the Anglican system comes into its own with its support systems so that when churches or clergy are in trouble, they are not left to sort it all out on their own.

Bishop Ian warned me that we would not have an easy ride once the news of our forthcoming move was announced and he was right. Our last few months leading up to the final services at Christmas time were indeed difficult. In the blame culture so prevalent today, everyone wanted to know who was or what was the cause of our departure after a stay of only two years duration. When I was asked why we were leaving so soon, I replied that it had not been plain-sailing within the East Hoathly Church and at the same time we felt that our gifts would be better used in a European chaplaincy church than in rural Sussex. Much of our past experience had been in chaplaincy work, which we knew and understood, while we were still quite green when it came to village church ministry. But the questions and recriminations continued.

We were not idle during those final four months in the benefice and were able to run an Alpha course in our home which drew in about twenty people. Those who took part seemed very appreciative. Mike continued with his valiant work leading the choir and once again the carol services drew in the crowds.

Looking back, I still feel that the two parishes needed someone else to come in and pour oil on troubled waters. Peter Clarke, who eventually succeeded me, had had previous experience of rural ministry. He stayed in the post for ten years and was much appreciated by many for his care and pastoral concern.

On the personal front, I am reminded of Andy Wheeler's title for the history of the Anglican Church in the Sudan which he edited, *But God is not defeated*. No matter what the ups and downs of our church life, our sins and our failures and our all-too-human weaknesses, God is not defeated. The gates of hell will not prevail against His church for which

Christ laid down his life. If my head did swell a bit as a result of the Paris send-off, then East Hoathly did me a service in shrinking it down to size again! I learnt during those two years that there were aspects of life and situations with which I simply could not cope. My human weakness was shown up and that was no bad thing for my long term spiritual health. I regret the fact that other people got hurt in the process including some who were in that support group. I still try to make a point of praying each week on a Friday morning for all those who I felt caused me hurt. We cannot undo the past or take back words that we wish we had not said. But prayer remains the one positive thing that I can do on behalf of those I left behind. And in the meanwhile we still keep in touch with a number of very good friends that we made in both East Hoathly and Chiddingly.

CHAPTER TWENTY-ONE

A GEZELLIG PLACE TO LIVE

"Gezellig" is a favourite Dutch word that describes something that is pleasant or congenial and that was certainly true of the Hague, with its cheap public transport system of trams and its bicycle lanes on many of the roads. Our new vicarage was near to some woods which were ideal for walking the dog and many of the roads were lined with trees. There was much less traffic congestion that in most major cities and it was easy to get to the shops on foot. A short tram ride from the church brings you to the North Sea resort of Scheveningen. It can be bitterly cold in winter, with blocks of ice forming on the beach. But in the summer it is a popular holiday destination for tourists. The Dutch are not famous for their cuisine but they do make a very good cup of coffee! The Hague was well supplied with restaurants that were managed by a host of different nationalities, Indonesian ones being particularly popular. The Mauritshuis Museum hosted a Vermeer exhibition in 1996 and art enthusiasts came from all over Europe to see this famous collection of paintings. Our lot had indeed fallen to us in a pleasant place. Amsterdam – not the Hague – is the capital of The Netherlands but the Hague is the centre of government and the home of Queen Beatrix and her family. Consequently all the foreign embassies are based in the Hague. It also plays host to the International Court and the War Crimes Tribunal. The Organisation for the Abolition of Chemical Weapons also has its headquarters in the Hague. The Shell Company have their main offices within walking distance of the Anglican Church and a number of our congregation work for the Patent Office.

The Church of St John and St Philip, The Hague

The church building, vicarage and hall were all built quite soon after the end of the second world war. There has been an English church in the Hague for over four hundred years, sited in various different buildings. The previous church, however, which had been built in Victorian times quite close to the heart of the city, was destroyed by R.A.F. bombs during a raid in 1944 when an attempt was made to destroy some rocket sites concealed in the woods. I am full of admiration for the post-war generation which built the present complex of buildings. The church itself was constructed to a very high standard, as was the vicarage. And this all happened during a time of national reconstruction after the devastation caused by bombing and armed conflict during the war years. The hall itself was a poorer quality building but it served its purpose well for several decades.

We were once again blessed with a vicarage garden, much of which was relatively wild with tall trees and shrubs and bulbs at ground level which provided a feast of colour in the spring.

The church congregation was once again very international in its composition but the difference this time was that forty percent of the worshippers were Dutch. It was customary for one of the churchwardens to be Dutch and during my spell in the Hague the treasurer was also a Dutchman (who was later succeeded by Astrid, a Dutch lady). There was an amusing moment at one of our council meetings when he left the room to relieve himself. A few moments later we heard angry barking from the hall. Someone in the meeting suggested that we ought to pause and pray for Hans! One of us went out and found him pinned against a wall with Michelle barking angrily at his ankles. I think she must have thought that he was an intruder. Hans escaped unscathed.

The church had had an interregnum lasting about six months. For a number of reasons the previous year had not been an easy one. The church at Voorschoten, which was about ten miles from the Hague Church, was in the process of becoming an independent chaplaincy under the leadership of Philip Bourne. The service marking this great turning point was held the day after my Induction in the Hague. It was a move that was certainly to be welcomed but the operation to sever the twins in order to give to each its own separate life was not achieved without a certain amount of pain all round. One of the reasons for this was that the finances and assets of the two churches had all been lumped together. It is not hard to imagine that there was a certain amount of tension when it came to sharing out the cake. Fortunately for me, all the necessary steps had been taken before I arrived and the two churches were on their way to starting their own separate lives. Philip and I had no problem in getting along with each other and we both felt that the two churches needed to settle down for a while so that each could discover its own individual identity. For quite a while, therefore, we didn't arrange many joint activities. After two or three years there were a number of joint ventures and there were many church members who had friends across the divide.

Our treasurer at that time took a particularly gloomy view of our future prospects. The church was very short of money and he predicted that within a matter of months we would be bankrupt unless drastic action were taken. A provisional budget had been drawn up for consideration by the Church Council, which allowed for a a massive deficit at the end of the year. Some of us found this to be totally unacceptable so we began to look for ways to ease the pressure. We had to serve notice on a paid cleaner for the church, and a team of volunteers from the congregation was found to cover this area of work. The monthly magazine, which had been professionally produced, had also been making a substantial loss for some time, and this was replaced by a home-produced magazine using a computer and a church printer. We made it a rule that for the time being only essential repairs would be attended to. At the same time the needs of the church were put to the congregation and we held a Stewardship Sunday. The level of giving began to rise gradually and our needs were met. That summer we held a church fête which involved many in the local community in different ways and that, too, helped us to balance the books by the end of the year.

On a personal level, Gill and I had to decide what to do about language study. The Dutch living in the Hague seemed to have an excellent grasp of English. Even the lady who sold flowers in the shopping centre up the road would respond to us in English. In the Sudan, Spain and France Gill had made valiant efforts to learn the language and, although she had learnt enough to get by, it had always been a struggle. We came to the conclusion in the Hague that it simply wasn't going to be worth her while to invest a lot of time and effort studying Dutch, so she contented herself with learning a few greetings. There were times, however, when it was important for one of us to speak a little, especially when answering the telephone, so I decided to have a go. Each week I cycled to a Dutch class taken by Mevrouw Brown who gave Dutch lessons to a number of different students. I slogged away at these studies for several years and spent one week of intensive study at a residential language centre. I made some progress but at my age it was painfully slow. With all our congregation speaking such good English, there was little opportunity to practise. But it did mean that I could cope with telephone calls about times of services and other church events. And sometimes, when there was a Dutch/English wedding or funeral, it was useful to be able to utter some words of greeting in Dutch and to put the questions and vows to the Dutch partner in their own tongue.

In the Hague I was not only the chaplain of the Church

of St John and St Philip but also the honorary chaplain to the British Embassy. I always enjoyed very friendly relationships with the embassy staff in Paris but it was only in the Hague that these were put onto an official footing. Soon after our arrival, Paul Dimond, who was Deputy Head of Mission at the Embassy, along with his wife Carolyn, took us out to lunch. I asked his advice as how I could best serve the needs of the embassy staff. He suggested that I would do well to drop in on the embassy bar on a Monday evening and simply get to know people. This was a piece of advice that I did not find it too difficult to accept! Paul and his wife were regular members of our church congregation. It was not long after our arrival that Miss Rosemary Spencer was appointed to the post of Ambassador. She was a committed Anglican and came as often as she could to our 8.30 a.m. communion service. With all the pressures of dealing with people during the week, a quiet service with only a handful of worshippers plus an absence of noise and bustle was what suited her best. Rosemary was very hospitable and we enjoyed many a social gathering at the embassy residence. Her Christmas staff parties were occasions to remember, with good food, good company and an informal atmosphere. Some years there were a few songs and skits. One year I donned a wig and one of Gill's ponchos, plus a string of beads, and performed the Joyce Grenfell nursery school skit. I asked the audience to imagine they were back in their infant nursery school and I used the names of embassy staff members in place of Joyce Grenfell's children's names. I remember turning to the Defence Attaché and saying: "Roger. Use your hanky . . . and again . . . and again . . . and now wipe!" Fortunately for me, Roger was of a very forgiving nature. Rosemary was also very supportive when we later set up a Jubilee Development Fund for the church and a number of events to publicise the fund were held at the Embassy.

Ian Whittle had already been serving in the Hague as an associate chaplain for about three years when we began working there. He was gifted linguistically and had a good grasp of Dutch. He made a good number of friends within the Dutch community during his time in the Hague. Many valued his friendship and his pastoral care as well as his preaching. When he left us in 1998 and moved back to Norfolk to take up a ministry in a number of rural parishes, his place was taken by Oliver Harrison, who came to us as a deacon straight from his theological college. Ollie kept everyone on their toes. He was a totally unpredictable character and was never dull. His most significant area of work was amongst the young families. He and his wife Jessica produced Daisy after they had been with us for a while, which resulted in a natural rapport with other young families who were coming to our less formal worship service at 9.45 a.m. Ollie was given responsibility for this service and under his leadership it grew considerably. He also took a group of nine of our young people on a trip to London to take part in the Archbishop of Canterbury's youth initiative entitled, The Time of your Life. They were joined by a number of other young people from our North West Europe Archdeaconry. They camped together in a crypt under one of the London churches. They attended a variety of seminars on the Saturday which ranged over a wide choice of issues from Third World Debt, to Understanding the Bible. There was also a session on vocation led by Ollie himself. The evening was given over to a variety of entertainments and the Sunday saw different styles of worship services in Westminster Abbey, Southwark Cathedral and St Paul's Cathedral. I gather that Ollie and most of our group were at St Paul's, where the singing was led by Matt Redman and a group called Soul Survivor. The climax of the weekend was a service of Holy Communion at which the Archbishop presided. Ollie, with the aid of Eurostar, managed to steer all of our party safely back to their families in the Hague. It was an excellent initiative.

Another colleague was the Revd Dr Robert de Muralt. He was a Dutch non-stipendiary priest who had previously served overseas in the Dutch diplomatic service. He trained for the ministry at Chichester Theological College and was of a higher churchmanship than me. But I came to value Robert's friendship and support: I appreciated having a colleague from a different church tradition to my own and found this stimulating. As it turned out, we agreed on all the basic tenets of the faith. With Robert and Ollie around, discussions at staff meetings on a Monday morning could be lively occasions. It was enormously helpful to me, when I was so new to the Netherlands, to have the benefit of Robert's wisdom when it came to legal matters or local customs. He was also very familiar with the local church scene and this could at times be very useful. A Dutch congregation of a church known as The Catholic Apostolics worshipped in our church once a month and Robert used to preside for them at a Book of Common Prayer Communion service in Dutch.

Roland Price was another non-stipendiary priest who joined us soon after our arrival in the Netherlands. He and his wife Thea became good friends and their younger children settled well into a local international school. Roland was Professor of Hydroinformatics at Delft University which was within commuting distance of their home in the Hague. Both Roland and Thea were, and still are, great assets to the church in the Hague. Thea supported Gill with a Monday morning fellowship group, Mainly for Mothers. There were many in our congregation who have appreciated their pastoral care and concern.

When Ollie's three years were up, he returned to the U.K. and served a second curacy in the Midlands. His place as curate was taken by Wendy Zandstra-Hough. But we were to be with Wendy for only about six months. She carried on the good work that Ollie had built up with the family worship service. She was also good with the older members of our congregation, of whom there were a considerable number. Wendy also pioneered an annual retreat for women in our Archdeaconry.

We were fortunate to have also within our staff team an excellent lay reader. Rosemary Van Wengen was a Professor of English in the University at Leiden. She had a great gift both for preaching and leading worship. It was no surprise to many of us when she sensed that God was calling her into the ordained ministry. After a period of study at theological college, she became a non-stipendiary curate at Benenden, not far from the home to which she and her husband Onno retired.

We were indeed fortunate to move into a church which was so well staffed. Chris Farr looked after the music and directed the choir and there was some secretarial help available in the church office. Chris's wife, Alex, was very supportive and each week produced first-class detailed orders of service. With a growing congregation drawn from all around the Hague, there was never any excuse for any of us to be idle. Amongst our number there were always a few who were refugees or asylum seekers. One couple in particular used to visit regularly a centre for asylum seekers in the Hague: Kees and Sarah Tanis later went on to run an orphanage for fifty boys in Mozambique. This is a venture which still receives considerable financial support from the members of St John and St Philip.

One of my duties that came just outside my remit at St John and St Philip was to join the Board of Management of a Christian Hostel for students from overseas who were taking postgraduate courses at the Institute of Social Studies, which was within cycling distance of our home. The Dovecote Hostel, as it was called, was founded by Patti Schmiegelow, at one time a member of staff at St John and St Philip. The hostel wardens, Russ and Corrie Herald, were ideally suited for the task of providing a homely Christian setting for students studying a long way from their own homes and families. The hostel welcomed Christian students particularly but by no means exclusively, and the atmosphere in the home was always warm and welcoming. The students cooked for themselves but about once a week they would all have a shared meal together with Russ and Corrie and there would also be an informal time of worship and Bible study for those interested. The Board were responsible for supporting the work that the Heralds were doing and for ensuring that there was adequate financial backing. We also had to make sure that necessary repairs to the building were carried out. We met about once a quarter and Russ presented us with a progress report on the life in the Hostel. There came a time, however, when the Institute opened new student accommodation much nearer to the lecture halls and the demand for rooms at the Dovecote dwindled to the point where it was uneconomic to continue. Nevertheless for a number of years it served several generations of students and did a very useful work. We owed much to the dedication of Russ and Corrie, as well as to their daughter Miriam, who together made a home-from-home for so many students from abroad.

CHAPTER TWENTY-TWO

A TIME TO WORSHIP

One of the great assets that awaited us in our new church setting was the wide range of worship services that were on offer. Being the Anglican Church in the Hague, we needed to provide for the needs of Christians of varying shades of churchmanship as well as for those from a non-Anglican background. The varying range of services helped us to do this. There was the weekly 8.30 a.m. Holy communion service (once a month using the 1662 Prayer Book) which appealed to those who wanted a quiet service. The 9.45 a.m. family worship was ideal for parents with small children. It didn't matter if a baby needed its nappy changing or a child was restless and began to cry. It was a safe and unthreatening environment for parents coming to this service in the church hall. We always encouraged the parents of newly baptised children to come to this service. It only lasted for three quarters of an hour and was followed by coffee. The coffee served after all our services was the genuine article! The Dutch wouldn't have tolerated the watery mixture which goes by the name of coffee at many English church events! Numbers at this service varied enormously but on a good

Sunday one could expect sixty or seventy.

The 11.00 a.m. service was the main Sunday service. and there was a touch of formality about it. A robed choir processed into church singing the opening hymn. Communion services alternated with services of the Word. The level of choral singing was high. The choir sang an anthem most Sunday mornings and, once whilst we were there, they produced a C.D. of their work. The congregational singing was also strong. There was a definite emphasis on preaching in this, as in each of our chaplaincies. One sensed an air of expectancy as one stood up to preach which was certainly an encouragement for the preacher. It was not unusual for someone to take me up on a point made in the sermon, which went way beyond the "nice sermon vicar" comment! The opening part of the service was attended by the whole congregation, after which the children went out to their separate classes. Sometimes they returned to go up to the communion rail for a blessing. There was the full range of children's groups starting from the crèche and going through to Pathfinders for the teenage group. Around one hundred and fifty attended this service each week. One Sunday a month, however, it was a family service which was often followed by a lunch in the hall.

Evening worship alternated between communion and what was called Prayer and Praise. Numbers were usually in the thirties but somehow this service never quite seemed to get going. A music group led the worship for the most part but they found it difficult to attract new members. Nevertheless, this service met a need for those who were used to a less formal style of worship. About once a quarter there was a full 1662 service of sung evensong with the choir in attendance singing certain parts of the service. We were reminded of what a beautiful service this can be with some good choral singing. Quite a number of Dutch from other churches would join us for this service.

At the end of both morning and evening services a prayer ministry team was on hand to offer prayer to any individual who had come to church that day with some specific need. From time to time a period of prayer for healing was inserted into the main service, both in the mornings and in the evenings. Once a month there was a 1662 service of matins at 9.45 a.m, to which around thirty to forty would come and that included the choir. There were just a few who looked forward to this service in particular, and it was important that their needs be met.

It was during Ollie's time that we held a number of youth services in partnership with the Church at Voorschoten and the American Presbyterian Church in the Hague. The Voorschoten church held their services in the British School and they also had a youth worker, Ben Mizzen, on the staff, so they attracted quite a large group of teenagers under Ben's leadership. Ollie and Ben worked together to put these services together. I used to attend but left the arrangements to them. There was one particular Sunday evening when I had something of an altercation with one elderly lady who was interrogating a young man from the American Church. She wanted to know why he was wearing a baseball cap back to front. An intervention from me brought this conversation to an abrupt halt! Next week, our head sideman pointed to this lady coming into church and gave me a nudge in the ribs. "There she goes," he said, "She's waiting for another five rounds with you!"

When it came to our first Easter, we discovered that, apart from the 8.30 a.m. communion, there was only one morning service, at 11.00 a.m. The team that usually led the 9.45

a.m. service, together with all the Sunday School teachers, were taking a break. Having been told that not many families with children came at Easter, we were concerned that if any families with young children did come on that key day in the Church's year, then there was nothing specifically for the children. So we arranged to show a video of the Easter story to children in the vicarage lounge and to have an Easter egg hunt for them in the church grounds when the service was over. We made it clear in all the publicity that children were welcome and in the event about thirty turned up and crowded into our living-room to watch the video and then stuffed themselves with Easter eggs later that morning. The main service was absolutely packed out so the following year we had two services in church. One was a family worship service, while the other was the usual common worship communion service. The Easter egg hunt also found its regular place in the morning programme. Both services were very well attended each year. It proved yet again the very simple truth that if a church makes no provision for children in its programme, then they certainly won't come. But once parents get the message that it is safe to bring their children and that they won't be the object of icy stares if a child has an off day, then they may well give church a try. It is also true that some parents are quite content to let their children run wild in a service and sit back as if they didn't belong to them. That too is unacceptable!

A very popular service at St John and St Philip took place on Christmas Eve at 4 p.m. It was designed for parents with small children and they came in their droves. By the time we arrived It was something of a tradition. Some years it was a disaster and some years it was a great success. There is a high risk factor in holding a service at such a time, as all children are reaching a fever pitch of excitement and are not easy to control. On some occasions the person leading the service was simply not on the children's wavelength. The address was way above their heads. There was nothing visual for them to look at and no participation from them was asked for. The result at such times was that if they were well behaved they sat still and looked bored to death; and if they weren't well behaved they ran berserk around the church. One year there was near pandemonium by the end of the service. After such an experience it is hardly surprising if the parents who have come for the first time bringing their children with them never darken the door of the church again. But there were two years that I particularly remember when this service went really well and in both cases it was school-teachers, Gill's sister, Jane and another year our daughter, Carolyn, who were running the programme. Children arriving at church were immediately told that they were going to be shepherds, sheep or angels and as the service progressed they were all drawn into the wonder of the Christmas story and into taking a part in it. Such informal services need much preparation, as anyone who has had a hand in them will testify.

One year as we approached Lent, the question of the Imposition of Ashes on Ash Wednesday was raised. This was not part of my tradition but I realised that it was the practice in many Anglican churches and I had come across it in Barcelona. I asked myself the basic question: Is it biblical? One reads of people repenting in sackcloth and ashes but there is also the emphasis on repentance being a matter of the heart and not one of outward show. I have come to the conclusion that all symbolism can be healthy and helpful provided people understand what the symbol signifies. Repentance is certainly a very basic Biblical concept and one which the modern church is perhaps in danger of forgetting. So a symbol which lays emphasis on the need to turn from sin and to turn more fully to God could very well prove helpful to the worshipper or so it seemed to me! So we duly went ahead on the following Ash Wednesday and offered the Imposition of Ashes to any who wished to receive it. There was no sense of compulsion. Its symbolism was briefly explained. Most seemed to welcome it and those who were unsure or reluctant stayed in their seats during this part of the service.

Occasionally I was asked to perform some sort of a service in a private home. I was once approached by a lady who was not a member of our church but who wanted me to come to her home and offer prayer in one particular room. She told me that different members of the family who slept in that room felt particularly uncomfortable about its atmosphere. They could not put their finger on exactly what it was, but there was a sense of extreme coldness and sadness about that room – a feeling of desolation. It seemed to me that the fact that different people had quite independently made the same sort of remarks about this room was significant. So I agreed to visit the house and pray in it. Robert de Muralt was very helpful in lending me a book of prayers for use on such occasions. When I arrived at the house, I suggested that it might be a good idea to pray in every room to which the owner of the house agreed. When I arrived at the offending room, I prayed that any evil spirit or presence that pervaded that room would be banished from it in the Name of Jesus Christ our Lord. In conversation with the lady of the house, she told me that it was thought that the room in question had been used by a previous owner, who was a doctor, for conducting abortions. When I met her some months later, she told me that there had been no further problems with that particular room.

There were other more joyful services in homes to which I was asked to come and pray for God's blessing on the dwelling and all who made their home there. This happened twice when I was in the Hague. The Ghanaian Ambassador had recently had her residence refurbished and she had not been living there for very long. As she made a new start in this home, she asked me to offer prayers there and to seek God's blessing on all who came and went from that house. I was very happy to oblige and again, Robert's book of prayers proved very helpful. We moved around the house praying for different areas within it. We prayed for bedrooms on the upper landing (without going into each one!). We prayed in the kitchen for all who worked to prepare the meals. We prayed in the dining room for all who would eat there in the future and in the living room for all who would relax there. The Ambassador had invited a number of friends and colleagues to be there so we all moved round the house as I led the prayers. After this dedication and prayer for a new home, we enjoyed a buffet meal together.

The other home where we went to pray was Robert de Muralt's. His wife, Hanna, had very tragically died as the result of a road accident and after a period of several months Robert sold up the family home, which was in a residential area at some distance from our vicarage and moved into a flat in a newly built block that was only a few hundred yards from the church. I went there one evening and again we prayed in each of the rooms, dedicating this new home to God and seeking his blessing upon it. Afterwards we stayed and had supper with Robert.

There were two annual Remembrance services which I had

to lead. One was organised by the Australian Embassy and was held on Anzac day at the end of April. It was the occasion when the many Australians who died in the ill-fated Galipoli campaign during the first world war were remembered. This took place in a chapel at the far end of the Hague and was followed by a reception in the Australian embassy. Other Commonwealth representatives were invited to attend the service and the reception that followed. And then there was the November 11th Remembrance Day service at Kijkduin cemetery to the south of the city. This service was held in the open air with a large crowd gathered round a memorial and row upon row of gravestones marking the burial plots, mostly of very young airmen who had died whilst serving with the R.A.F. After the service was over, we all made our way to another set of memorials erected in memory of Dutch people who had died whilst serving in the resistance movement which was active in opposition to the occupying power. Young girl guides laid small bouquets of flowers at each memorial as we remembered those Dutch who died for the sake of the longed-for freedom of their country. I always found these ceremonies deeply moving. The various Commonwealth ambassadors took it in turns to host a reception for us all after the service was over.

CHAPTER TWENTY-THREE

A TIME TO BUILD

When the time came for Ian Whittle to leave us, something had to be done about the assistant chaplain's accommodation. Ian's house was delightful; situated in a quiet cul-de-sac, it was surrounded by a small garden which was Ian's pride and joy. Its greatest asset was that it was in the centre of the Hague and an easy cycle ride to the church, but it was not quite large enough to house a family and it was also expensive to rent.

The Church Council decided to take the plunge and look for a property to buy. It was difficult to find anywhere suitable within our price range. In the end we were able to buy a three-bedroomed apartment in a suburb of the city. It was about half an hour's cycle ride from the church but there was a reasonably good tram service. Distance from the church was a problem but, at the time, it seemed to be the best option. The flat had previously been occupied by a couple working for Shell who had been members of our church. The bank took quite a deal of persuading to grant us a loan. There was a moment when it looked as if they would turn us down. At that point Erik de Graaf, whom I had got to know on the

Dovecote Board, took charge of the negotiations with the bank and a loan was soon agreed. With the help of a legacy and some generous gifts that were donated in connection with a special gift day, we were able to put down a substantial part of the purchase price as a deposit. The regular mortgage payments each month then worked out at less than the rent we had been paying on Ian's flat. There was to come a time, after we had left the Hague, when the tram services were altered and travel from this apartment to the church became much more of a problem. So this flat was duly sold and a replacement was purchased very close to the church. Rosie Dymond, the present assistant chaplain, can now cycle to work in a matter of minutes.

Our church hall was used by a large number of different organisations as well as for church functions. There were ballet classes in the afternoons. Mums and toddlers met there in the mornings and it was often hired out for children's parties and concert rehearsals. But as a building it was showing signs of wear and tear and it really needed upgrading if it was going to meet the demands of a new millennium. One of its chief disadvantages was that no entrance way into the hall was visible from the two approach roads. So anyone new to the area trying to get inside for some activity often spent quite some time trying to gain an entrance. Often they ended up knocking on the vicarage door in desperation. This hardly seemed to be sending out a message to the community that all were welcome here. I sometimes remarked that the way into our church life during the week was one of the best kept secrets in the Hague.

The Council spent many an hour debating the hall question. We agreed to invite an architect to draw up plans for a new entrance at one end of the hall which would include a welcome area that would be open during the week. The initial set of plans was examined at an annual general meeting and referred back to the Council for further study. Members of the Council were uneasy about this plan so it was a case of going back to the drawing-board. At one point when we seemed somewhat bogged down in our discussions, Rosemary Van Wengen suggested half way through the meeting that we have a pause for prayer. We took her advice and, after prayer, it was amazing the way the discussions progressed. The architect drew up a further set of plans which would involve a complete refurbishment of the hall with French windows leading outside on to a terrace. It was much more ambitious and far more expensive than the original plan but the church members, with a few exceptions, backed the project, which was then agreed at a special general meeting of the church membership. A jubilee development fund was set up and a subcommittee of three, under the leadership of Tony May (a senior partner in a multinational company with offices in the Hague), was appointed by the Church Council to liaise with the architect and to oversee the project. There were a few hiccups along the way. The plans were turned down by the Hague City Council and this in turn led to a change of architect. The old plans had to be considerably altered before agreement was reached with the local authorities. I had moved on into retirement by the time these setbacks occurred and it was my successor, Michael Sanders, who had to carry the load during the final two and a half years of the development. The funding came in mainly through direct giving but there were also a number of special fund-raising initiatives. These included church concerts and a number of summer fetes. Some former members of St John and St Philip also gave generously. Once the builders started work, the hall was out of use for quite a considerable time. The "three wise men", as they were called, who were members of the sub-committee overseeing the work were Tony May, a business man; Eke Statema, an engineer; and Renee Schmall, a lawyer; they all had their parts to play and Tony was especially involved in overseeing progress. Gill and I were invited back to the Netherlands in June 2003 to attend the thanksgiving celebration service and the official opening of the new premises by Queen Beatrix of the Netherlands. The Queen attended the service and unveiled a plaque commemorating the completion of the Jubilee Development Project. Bishop Geoffrey Rowell, Bishop in the Diocese of Europe, preached at this service. We were both absolutely delighted with the final results of all the work that had gone into this project. It far exceeded my wildest dreams. The hall with its new flooring and high-beamed ceilings and long, deep blue curtains (which improved sound quality) was stunning. The old, very cramped and tatty, coffee area was greatly enlarged and the kitchen was completely renovated. The new entrance is broad and welcoming and clearly visible from the road. The building now includes a new church office, a church lounge and a choir vestry, plus a splendid staircase. The paved area outside the main hall makes for a wonderful extra reception area during the summer months. The new premises are a major asset for the present generation of church members and provide a great centre for serving the wider community.

But of course the real business of the church is to build up the people in the Christian faith. That process was going on long before we reached the Hague and it continued through our time there and onwards, right up to the present day. In our first year there we attempted to hold a church weekend away. Such weekends had been held in the past in partnership with the congregation at Voorschoten, but St John and St Philip were not yet ready to go it alone in support of such a weekend. About thirty of us went away to a retreat centre and it was a useful time for those who took part, but clearly this was not the way forward for the immediate future. In each successive year we set aside a day, either for a retreat or for some kind of training. Bishop John Taylor (formerly of St Albans) came and took a training day on a Christian approach to the Old Testament. One year Paul and Diana Hunt (Gill's brother and sister-in-law) came and led a day-long retreat with addresses interspersed with periods of quiet, Oliver Ross led a similar day for us another year. Tom Smail, who had recently retired from parish ministry, led another weekend for us.

During the winter months we encouraged those members who were prepared to get down to some serious study to enrol for parts of the St John's College, Nottingham Extensions Studies courses. Groups were formed to tackle a unit of the course. We were guided in our choice of courses by Ambrose Mason, the Diocesan Director of Education within the Diocese of Europe. We began with the New Testament unit. We met together as a group about once in three weeks, reviewed progress and considered together some of the discussion questions that were set for us within the course material. I enjoyed leading this particular study group and found that my old brain was being stretched and stimulated by the exchanges that took place and the reading material that was set for us. Those taking the courses were obliged to produce written assignments, mostly in essay form, which were sent away to outside examiners, appointed by St John's, who graded the work that was sent to them. One of the units studied came from the London Bible College. After the New

Testament course, I led a group which worked through the Old Testament unit. It was good to have Jean Swift with us on this course: she was the wife of the Irish Ambassador to the Hague and a practising Roman Catholic. She brought an extra, ecumenical dimension to our study group. Some years after we had left, it was good to hear that two of those who had embarked on this study programme during our time had gone on to finish the course and were now licensed lay readers and active in assisting in the worship of the church. Another lady went on to complete a degree in theology.

We sensed the need to increase the amount of pastoral care that we were able to extend to people by building up a pastoral care team which would include lay visitors who had received some basic training. Our friends at Voorschoten had recently worked through a course in pastoral care which had been produced by Scripture Union. With their help, we were able to obtain the study material and arrange for a series of training sessions led by Camille Maddox and Helen May. We invited several congregation members to enrol and we met together about once a fortnight over the course of a winter period, exploring listening skills and seeking to understand the process of bereavement. Some who completed the course were appointed as pastoral visitors and given two or three parishioners, who were housebound and lonely, to visit on a regular basis. Each of those who visited was accountable to the chaplain and would meet with him from time to time to assess how things were going. This was just one further aspect of seeking to build up the church and its ministry.

With many young families linked to the church, issues of parenting were very topical. We were fortunate in having within our membership Katherine Fortier, a child psychotherapist. She ran a course entitled Help, I'm a Parent which was open, not just to church members, but to any in the community who felt they could do with improved skills in rearing a young family. Such courses continued well after we had left.

There was steady growth in children's and youth work during this period and towards the end of our time the Pathfinder group in particular began to grow significantly. New lay leaders were appointed to help with this side of the work. Jeremy and Mary Bentham took over the work amongst the older teenagers and they begin to meet in their home on Sundays around lunch-time. This was the only time that they could collect together a group of young people, many of whom lived a considerable distance from the centre of the Hague. It was only after we had left St John and St Philip's that funding was found to appoint a full-time paid youth worker to help take the work amongst children and young people a stage further.

There were the usual confirmation preparation classes for young people as well as for adults. We held three Alpha courses during our years in the Hague. Course members would come to the vicarage for a meal in our dining room and we then moved into the next room for the talk and the discussions that followed. We found this course to be a fruitful way of taking people forward in faith and commitment, while for some of those who attended, confirmation was another step along the way. On one of these courses we had three octogenarians. They usually sat at the same table over supper. Two were already firm believers but the third was not so sure. The latter seemed to come into a real faith during the course and then died very suddenly later that year.

As in most chaplaincies, St John and St Philip was keen to take its share in building up the world wide church through the spread of the gospel. When we arrived, there was a member of the church council, Henk Aben, who was responsible for keeping in touch with all of our mission partners overseas. He did an excellent job writing letters to them and keeping us all informed of their needs. When the time came for Henk to give up this role, we set up a missions subcommittee which was answerable to the Church Council. Each member of the committee had an interest in one mission partner and took responsibility for being their contact person. The group would meet every now and again to exchange news and to pray for our partners overseas and one of them would report back to the Council. They would also recommend support levels for different mission projects and individuals for the Council's consideration. There was substantial support given to Derek and Trich Dodd, former church members, who were working with Youth With A Mission in Amsterdam. Another mission partner was Yvonne Paap, who worked for some time in Korea and later in the Philippines. She subsequently returned to the Netherlands to work part-time with the L'Arche community, which was founded by Jean Vanier. Mention has already been made of Kees and Sarah Tanis and their work with orphans in Mozambique. Our Archdeaconry synod decided to set up a twinning link with the Diocese of Luweero in Uganda – a part of the country I had visited during my spell in East Africa in 1985. As money was collected through gift days for our Jubilee Development fund, cash was also set aside to donate to a church building in Uganda and it was not long before enough had been collected to complete the roofing of a new parish church in the Diocese of Luweero. Quite a few of our members visited Luweero to help strengthen our links with that diocese. Whilst not all our members were well off and some were living on modest pensions, most of the expatriate community were earning handsome salaries and it was good for us all to be reminded through these mission partnerships of our responsibility to share what we had received with brothers and sisters in poorer parts of the world.

CHAPTER TWENTY-FOUR

A TIME TO MOURN

I was up early that Sunday morning, as I was due to take our 8.30 a.m. Holy communion service. I switched on the radio to get the Radio 4 news from London and could hardly believe my ears. Princess Diana and her friend Dodi had been killed in a late-night Paris car crash in an underpass close to the river Seine. We had driven along that route and could picture the scene.

This dreadful news dominated the thoughts of everyone as they gathered for worship later that morning. A few arrived weeping. Television cameras were positioned near the church entrance to glean reactions of the British community in particular to this sudden tragedy. I remember giving a brief interview which was later shown on Dutch T.V. news channels. I expressed the profound sense of shock that all of us were experiencing.

In the Hague we were fortunate to have cable T.V. with some thirty different channels, so we were able to observe the reactions of the British public and the emotions expressed as ever increasing floral tributes spread out around the gates of Kensington Palace. Later we watched the Royal family, clothed in black, as they examined the bouquets and the attached written labels with messages of grief and sympathy. And then there was the sad funeral procession through the streets of London followed by that moving service in Westminster Abbey with the crowds in the streets outside taking part as best they could. All this was visible to viewers like us across many countries in mainland Europe.

Even in the Hague the floral tributes piled up along the railings outside the British Embassy offices in the Lange Voorhout in the city centre. A silent and respectful queue of well wishers filed into the embassy building to sign one of the three books of condolence which were laid out on a reception room table. The queues were at times so long that people waited for two to three hours to sign their names. When the British Ambassador, Rosemary Spencer, spoke to some of those who were waiting and said that she was sorry it was all taking so long, they replied that the waiting was all part of their desire to express how they felt towards the Princess. I met with Ambassador Rosemary Spencer to discuss the possibility of a service of remembrance in the Hague. Together with a small group, we drew up a service plan and were particularly grateful to the minister at the Kloosterkerk for lending us his church for this important occasion. This church is very close to our embassy buildings and is the chief place of worship for Queen Beatrix of the Netherlands. Bishop John Taylor had been booked to preach at a similar service of remembrance at the Madeleine Church in Paris and he agreed to come and repeat his sermon at our service in the Hague on September 17th. As High Almoner to Queen Elizabeth for the Royal Maundy occasions, he had had some dealings with the Royal family and was therefore ideally suited to speak at such a service.

It was eventually held a month or so after the accident and by then the intense public outpouring of emotion was beginning to wane. But some three hundred came to the Kloosterkerk for the service and they were not just from the Hague. Archdeacon Geoffrey Allen and almost all of the neighbouring chaplains attended. The clergy processed with our church choir in the lead. The first lesson was read in English by the Defence Attaché and again in Dutch by the Revd Ter Linden, who had recently retired from being the chief minister at the Kloosterkerk. Our Ambassador read the second lesson. The choir sang an anthem based on words from Psalm 25. Representatives of different churches present led us in the prayers, and special mention was made in prayer for the two young princes who had been bereaved of their mother. The Bishop preached an eloquent sermon which drew attention to the positive contributions that the Princess had made to our public life.

It is not often that one is called upon to share in such a very public expression of mourning; but every clergyman has the experience of being alongside parishioners at times of grief and bereavement. The process can, of course, be long and drawn out. It often begins some time before the loved one has breathed their last breath and can continue for several years after the funeral. It is a privilege to be with someone, or perhaps with a couple, while they are passing through such a painful stage in their life journey. One seeks to offer support and understanding and to hold out before them the Christian promises of resurrection life in Christ.

This was the case with Peter Ebskamp, who was very happily married to Nellike. Peter was a Dutchman whose career had been in teaching. Over a period of years he suffered from cancer. One operation followed another. He was amazingly courageous and optimistic and must have outlived the expectations of most of the doctors who treated him. I visited him and Nellike frequently during the final stages of his illness, when he could no longer make it to church. The three of us would share a simple service of Holy communion in their living room. As Peter grew weaker, he needed constant attention and the strain on Nellike was intense. I visited them when the end was very close and Nellike came to the door to let me in. She told me that he was very weak and no longer conscious. As I approached the bed, I realised that the real Peter had just left us. He must have stopped breathing as Nellike had opened the door for me.

When it came to the funeral, there was of course the grief; but there was also an expression of confident faith in Christ's triumph over death, a triumph which Christ shares with all who look to him in faith. The way ahead for Nellike was painful and hard, especially as she was soon to face the loss of an elderly parent, as well. But she was helped by the support of her friends and the church to which she belonged and she is now a regular member of the choir at St John and St Philip.

In Paris, with such a young congregation, funerals were few and far between; but in the Hague we had our fair share of older members, so death and bereavement were a definite feature of church life during the course of a year. This is even more the case for English vicars who are often called upon to preside at the funerals of people with no church connection at all. There is, however, a particular sadness when a young husband or wife or child dies leaving behind a grieving family. This happened when Tony Trussler died after a long battle with cancer which included a very major operation in the United States, in a last ditch attempt to save his life. When visiting the Trusslers, we were shown a school photograph of Tony as a boy and were amazed to discover that he had been a pupil at Gill's father's school in Twickenham. Sitting right in the middle of the photograph were Gill's parents. This gave us just one more link with the family. Tony died full of faith in Christ and his funeral was held in our church. We felt very much for his widow, Ali, and his young son, James, who were left behind.

An important contribution towards easing just some of this pain was being provided by our church counselling service in the Hague. This was set up some ten years before we arrived. It was, and still is, a very useful aspect of the church's total ministry. There are of course many other forms of pain and grief that cause people great sadness. For some it is a broken relationship; for others it is the memory of a blighted childhood that was marred by the abuse of a close relative – something the victim has kept secret for many long years, yet the pain is still there. There are so many reasons why people are hurting in today's fractured society.

Those who offer counselling have mostly received training through the St John's College, Nottingham, extension studies programme. This includes at least one week of residential study in Nottingham. The three counsellors work under the supervision of a professional psychotherapist and are directly accountable to her. Not only is she in a position to give advice in respect of a client's therapy; she can also, in certain cases, indicate that the time has come to refer the client on to someone better qualified to handle the case. The counselling room is tastefully decorated and is situated in the church tower. This service is widely used, not only by some of our own church members but also by members of other churches as well as by people with no church connection at all. Prospective clients, for their part, have to make a move by contacting a member of the counselling service before any interview can take place. There are no fixed fees for these sessions. Clients are encouraged to make a contribution towards the costs of running the service. The counsellors serve in a voluntary capacity but their supervision has to be paid for.

I personally found it most helpful in certain circumstances to be able to suggest to a parishioner that they might consider making contact with a member of the counselling service. Once someone began seeing a member of the team, strict confidentiality was always observed unless a client specifically asked for the chaplain to be involved at some point. In any church, where members tend to be rather interested in other people's business, discretion is essential. Complete confidentiality was sometimes difficult to maintain when a client called out across the coffee room on Sunday after church: "See you next Thursday, Helen, at two o'clock". The team, made up of Camille, Helen and Valerie, is still carrying on this important piece of Christian service.

A death that struck right at the heart of our staff team occurred when Hanna de Muralt was knocked down in a road accident whilst loading some shopping into the back of her car. She landed on her head and fractured her skull. After some ten days lying in a coma in a hospital bed, she finally passed away. Robert and Hanna had had a wonderfully close and happy marriage. Understandably, the loss of Hanna was a terrible blow to Robert. I remember coming away from the hospital with him not long after Hanna had died. Gill and I strolled up the road with him from the vicarage and we had a quiet bite of food together in a restaurant. Hanna's funeral was a wonderfully inspiring occasion, with the accent on resurrection faith and hope. The de Muralt family is a large one and the church was full of friends and congregation members who came to pay their respects. We were very pleased when Robert was able to move to a new apartment close by to the church. He himself has not enjoyed good health recently but he continues to serve the church that he loves by taking the occasional service, usually with the help of another member of staff.

Some time later, tragedy struck again. Mark was a young man in his early thirties and a very active member of the embassy staff. He seemed to have a bright future ahead of him and was much admired by all the girls. A week or so before he was due to go on holiday, he organised a staff boating trip on a Saturday along some of the Dutch waterways. Gill and I were able to be a part of what was a very pleasant social outing. Soon afterwards Mark left the Netherlands with a friend for a holiday in Mali in West Africa. And then news came through that he had been tragically drowned in a swimming accident. The friend with whom he had gone on holiday had to arrange for the return of the body via Dakar in Senegal to the Netherlands. His parents flew out from England and we went to meet them in a hotel. They were clearly stunned by this sudden and tragic loss of their son.

It is no exaggeration to say that the whole of the embassy staff were in a state of shock and grief. I met with Ambassador Rosemary and several other embassy members of staff to plan the funeral. Most of those who came to the service were not church people, but they all felt the need to say their own farewells to Mark and to express their grief. Different colleagues took part in the service, either by singing a solo or by reading a lesson or giving a eulogy. I spoke briefly on the gospel reading and pointed to Christ as the Way, the Truth and the Life and our one sure and certain hope in the face of loss and death. It was perhaps especially at such a time as this that I felt that my link with the embassy was so worthwhile. It is so good to know that my successor, Michael Sanders, has been able to maintain and foster this link.

There is indeed a time to mourn. Such occasions occur, of course, in every chaplaincy across Europe. But although there are times when we grieve along with the rest of human kind, we also have a message of life to proclaim through Jesus Christ our Lord.

CHAPTER TWENTY-FIVE

A TIME TO CELEBRATE

When it was time for a celebration in the Hague, it was often the church catering committee which set to and organised a special meal. Gill led this group for a while and was helped by a willing and able team. Kate Knowles, in particular, was a great support and she took over the leadership when it was time for us to leave.

We had wondered whether there would be any need in the Hague for the kind of Christmas night dinner party that we had enjoyed in Paris. It was Loek Caspars who made up our minds for us. She was a retired Dutch doctor who was living alone. In conversation with her, we discovered that Christmas was a particularly difficult time for her. As a young girl she had been active in the Dutch resistance movement during the second world war. She used to cycle from place to place carrying important messages in her shoes. Many of her friends and colleagues lost their lives during those terrible years of conflict and Loek has never forgotten them. She has written a book describing her wartime experiences. So when she spoke of the pain she suffered at times when everyone else was celebrating, we could sympathise with her feelings of loss and bereavement. We asked her if she would like to come and join us for dinner on Christmas night. We then soon discovered that there were a few others who would probably be at a loose end over Christmas and so gradually the party began to grow. Our house, with its large reception rooms and an open log fire, was ideally suited for parties. Fortunately Gill enjoys cooking and entertaining so our Christmas night celebrations with friends drawn from around the world were times of great joy for us. Whichever family members happened to be with us over the holiday period always joined in with the spirit of the evening and were a great help in welcoming and looking after the guests, who usually numbered about twenty. A piano in the corner of the sitting-room made it natural to end such an evening with the singing of a few carols.

One Christmas time was particularly memorable for us as a family as our son, Andrew, married Claire on 20th December 1997. The civil marriage had already taken place back in Cambridge where they were about to make their home together and they came over to the Hague for the church service, which I conducted. Many family members and friends joined us and a considerable number of church members were keen to be present at the service. We entertained all who wished to stay on to a French-style Vin d'Honneur afterwards. This involves a celebratory drink (usually something that sparkles!). Gill organised the catering for the reception which was held later in the hall for invited guests. A member of the congregation who had been a professional chef prepared all the desserts and Gill cooked the main course ahead of time. We employed a team of young people from the church to act as waiters and they were supervised by Richard, who was studying at a local catering college. The Hall was festooned with balloons and illuminated by candles and Christmas tree lights. It was very much a home brewed occasion, which left us happy but somewhat exhausted as the bride and groom departed for the start of their honeymoon in Amsterdam.

We had our fair share of wedding services in church, plus the occasional service of prayer and dedication where one or both of the parties to a marriage had a divorced spouse still living. A special liturgy, recommended for use by the House of Bishops, had been designed and produced in 1985 for such second marriages. It seems to fit the bill admirably and strikes a realistic balance between penitence for past errors and total mutual commitment for the future.

A good proportion of our congregation had come to us from Africa, so it was hardly surprising that we had the occasional African wedding. Frank was in the Hague working with Shell, and Taye was pursuing a course of further study. They were both from Nigeria and had been married in their home country in accordance with local custom, but there had been no service in church. They were keen to seek God's blessing on their union and so a service of blessing was arranged in St John and St Philip. They wanted a small reception after the service and asked if they could use our home for the purpose. The couple went shopping with Gill on the morning of the wedding to purchase provisions for the reception later in the day. Immediate and somewhat hasty preparations were undertaken in our kitchen whilst the bride went upstairs to change into her wedding dress. After the service the congregation, which was made up mainly of Nigerian friends and colleagues, came back to the vicarage for photographs and food. It was a celebration with a very African flavour which delighted us both. We were due to leave for the airport at Schiphol early the following morning at about

4.00 a.m. so we had a rather tight schedule. Fortunately the wedding party finished early!

There was another important Nigerian celebration to mark the fortieth anniversary of Nigerian Independence. The Ambassador, Dr. Odosomu, was a very active Christian and a member of our congregation. She arranged for a service of thanksgiving to be held at Trinity Baptist Church – an enormous building the size of an aircraft hangar. Clergy from every conceivable part of the church spectrum were invited to take part in the service. There was a band to accompany the singing and the music was loud and lively with plenty of percussion and a strong beat. I was asked to read one of the lessons and the sermon was preached by the minister of the International Christian Centre in London, Pastor Matthew Ashimolowo. The taking of the collection was strikingly different from the offertory in most English parishes. As the plate goes round in a British church, worshippers tend to adopt a pious and somewhat solemn appearance. Sometimes they look as if they are about to face a tooth extraction! But in the Nigerian service, everyone processed up the two aisles, many of them swaying rhythmically in time to the lively musical accompaniment. There were lots of bright smiling faces as notes were deposited in buckets placed near the front of the church. They certainly took seriously the words of the apostle Paul, "The Lord loves a cheerful giver."

Dr. Odosomu and family were a great asset to our church community. On one occasion she led us in some rousing singing in church and spoke of how she had come into a living Christian faith. She regularly read a lesson at morning services and her daughter, Wemi, sang in the church choir. Sometimes when we had a church lunch with an African flavour, her cook would be sent round with a selection of spicy and very tasty Nigerian dishes. On Christmas Eve there was usually a party at her residence which began with a short carol service with some vigourous accompaniment followed by festive refreshments. The party ended in time for us to move on to the midnight communion service at church.

*Bishop John Hind visits us for the ordination
service for the Rev. Oliver Harrison*

In June 1997 Oliver Harrison was ordained deacon by our diocesan Bishop, John Hind, and the following year he was ordained priest. Both these services took place at St John and St Philip Church. When I started serving within the diocese, such ordinations were indeed a rarity. Happily, with the growth of chaplaincy work and the planting of new churches within the Diocese of Europe, such services now happen much more frequently. Certainly Ollie's arrival and subsequent ordinations were welcomed with great enthusiasm in the Hague and they were occasions for celebration. They were also an opportunity to meet Ollie's parents, who came out to the Hague to be present with Ollie for both these important services.

In 1998 the Archbishop of Canterbury paid an official visit to the Netherlands, the main purpose of which was to strengthen the ties between the Anglican Church and the Old Catholic Church.

When the dogma of papal infallibility was accepted by the Vatican Council of 1870, many Roman Catholics from Germany, Switzerland and Austria split from the Church of Rome and formed an alliance with certain Dutch Catholics to form the Union of Utrecht under the leadership of the Archbishop of Utrecht. This breakaway section of the Roman Catholic Church became known as the Old Catholic Church. The Church of England entered into full communion with the Old Catholics in 1931. Although there is complete freedom to worship in each other's churches and to give and take communion in either church, the relationships have not always been as close as they might have been. In the Hague the language barrier was one obstacle to a closer working relationship. The priest of the Old Catholic Church in the Hague spoke very little English and my Dutch was severely limited. There was also something of a gulf between us in terms of our worship styles. Nevertheless, whenever we did meet on special occasions, relations between our two churches were always cordial, while in other centres in our Archdeaconry – such as in Utrecht, where the English chaplain spoke good Dutch – there was much closer co-operation. Certainly our church in the Hague looks back with gratitude to the hospitality that was offered to us in the years immediately after the war, before the new church was built on its present site. We were able to use the Old Catholic church building in the centre of the Hague for all our services for a period of about five years up until 1950.

An Archbishop's official visit requires meticulous preparation. One of the Archbishop's chaplains, the Rev. Dr. Herman Browne, came over to the Hague in advance of George Carey's visit to talk over plans with the various interested parties. A very full programme for the weekend was mapped out and it was arranged that the Careys would stay at our embassy residence as guests of Ambassador Rosemary. Their first stop after arrival at Schiphol airport was the British School of the Netherlands in Voorschoten, where the Archbishop met a group of students from the senior school. A great variety of questions were fired at him, ranging from issues of science and religion to the Church's attitude to homosexuality. The next stop was the War Crimes Tribunal, where the Careys were able to meet with two of the judges. The British Ambassador gave a dinner that night in their honour for about thirty guests.

Almost all of the Saturday was devoted to meetings with representatives of the Old Catholic Church. It was agreed that we should look at ways of sharing more fully at the local level. The morning began with a service of sung matins in the Old Catholic Cathedral in Utrecht. In the afternoon the Archbishop and his party, which included the present Bishop of Lichfield, met over a cream tea with Archbishop Simonis, the Roman Catholic Archbishop of the Netherlands. That evening the Old Catholic Archbishop Glazemaker of Utrecht gave a dinner in honour of the Careys.

There was a Sunday morning Sung Eucharist at the Old Catholic Church in the Hague, at which our Archbishop preached. After a reception at a hotel opposite the church, there was a lunch back at the Embassy residence which was followed by a quick private visit to the Mauritshuis to see just a few of the paintings. There was then a somewhat frantic drive through the Hague to the Institute of Social Studies, circumventing a demonstration that was being steered by the police through the city centre. At the I.S.S. the Archbishop gave a short dissertation on Religion and a New World Order. This was followed by a lively period of questions and answers covering a whole range of issues, in which the question of world debt kept recurring. Meanwhile Eileen and Gill went back to our vicarage for a short breather.

Archbishop George Carey at a church reception during his official visit to the Netherlands in 1998

The final event of this whistle-stop day was a service of Holy communion at St John and St Philip held at 4.45 p.m. to fit into a tightly packed programme. A number of clergy from other churches in the Hague joined us for this service and there was a great sense of joy and praise as we welcomed the Archbishop to our church. In my introductory welcome I recalled that for a while he had taught me doctrine at St John's College in Nottingham. I added that if any in the congregation were having problems with my teaching in the church, they would know to whom they must address their anxieties when the service was over. The Archbishop preached on the theme of thanksgiving and presided at the Eucharist. The choir sang an anthem and there was an item of liturgical dance. A reception followed in the hall after the service when gifts were presented to the various members of the Archbishop's entourage. Somehow we managed to keep to schedule and at 6.30 p.m. a large embassy car arrived to transport all our somewhat weary guests back to Schiphol airport.

When it came to celebrating the millennium, we decided to hold a special party at the church about a week before Christmas 1999. We invited two special guests, Adrian and Bridget Plass, to come over for the weekend and on the Saturday evening in church they put on the kind of programme for which they have become famous. It was a mixture of skits and poems illustrating some of the more absurd aspects of church life, whilst at the same time they inserted items of a more serious nature designed to prod and challenge their audience into a more wholehearted approach to Christian discipleship. During the interval a lavish spread of party food awaited everyone in the church hall. On Sunday morning Adrian was our guest preacher. He gave us his own unique telling of the story of the prodigal son, which brought home to us afresh the depths of God's love for all his children, no matter what their age or nationality.

On New Year's Eve itself there was some concern about travel difficulties, with many parties getting under way as the evening wore on. So we arranged for a short service of thanksgiving and dedication at 4.00 p.m. During the service we sang a hymn which Richard Bewes had composed especially for the millennium as well as Cliff Richard's song version of the Lord's Prayer. At the end of the service worshippers were all given a candle to light around midnight, together with a printed prayer for use in their homes as the new millennium was dawning.

A united service to celebrate the new millennium was held in a large Roman Catholic Church with friends from the Roman Catholic English-speaking Church, the Church of our Saviour, led by Father Sjaak, and from the American Protestant Church led by the Revd Mike Bailey. Father Sjaak arranged the first section of the service, which was penitential in character. The three clergy leading the service poured water from three jugs into a common font, symbolising our shared baptism: "One Lord, One Faith, One Baptism". The clergy then moved down the aisle sprinkling people with water from the font as a sign of God's grace and renewal. This was a new experience for most members of our church and for members of the A.P.C. It was agreed that I should put together the Bible reading section of the service which followed. This began with a slow reading of Psalm 23 during which Sylvia Burns performed a music and movement interpretation of the words. Our choir then sang a version of the same psalm to a setting composed by our organist's son-in-law. Two of our church members then took us through a dramatised Scripture reading and I followed this up with a short address.

In the final A.P.C. section of the service, children featured strongly. May 14th happened to be Mothering Sunday in the Netherlands so each child was given Mothering Sunday cards to present to all the mothers present. We then joined together in prayer for children throughout the world. The dominant theme for the service was "Jesus Christ, the Same, Yesterday, Today and for Ever." The congregation numbered around eight hundred as we left the church building with the hymn, "We are one in the Spirit, we are one one in the Lord," ringing in our ears.

Our Ambassador, by now Dame Rosemary, gave us a farewell party at her residence, which doubled as an occasion to make more widely known our Jubilee Development Project amongst the British community. We so appreciated all Rosemary's friendship and support throughout her time in the Hague which came to an end when she, too, retired a few months after our departure. Seeds were sown at that party, which resulted in substantial financial support, from one of the international companies, for the employment of a church youth worker to join the team led by my successor, Michael Sanders.

Our final church party was a splendid affair which was tinged with sadness as it came just a few days before we left the Netherlands after five very happy years serving in this English-speaking church. A great feast was prepared and Gill was kept well away from the kitchens. We were presented with a very generous cheque, which helped us pay for renovation work on our new home in East Dean. There were also a number of individual and more personal gifts from all sorts of very kind people. I remember a slight feeling of panic creeping over me when someone whispered in my ear: "You are about to be given a statue". We were just about to move

At Buckingham Palace, having received the O.B.E.
in October 2000

from a very large house into a much smaller one. "What on earth are we going to do with a statue?" I asked myself, "and where can we possibly put it?" Over the last month or so we had been getting rid of surplus furniture and other household items, and now we were about to receive a statue. I am not very skilled at looking pleased and delighted when receiving something for which I cannot think of a useful purpose. But I need not have worried. My fears proved groundless. The statue turned out to be a beautifully made stone version of a West Highland White terrier that now has an honoured place in our garden in a prominent position where we can see it from our living-room and kitchen windows. Michelle has been known to pose for photographers squatting beside this replica of her breed. So I was able to express genuine delight on unwrapping this gift after all.

CHAPTER TWENTY-SIX

LETTING GO

Nearly all those who live long enough are obliged to retire sooner or later. But for everyone passing through this stage of life, it is an upheaval. For clergy, it certainly turns their lives upside down. At a stroke, they say goodbye to their home, their job, their church, the community amongst whom they have been working, along with their status within that body of people. There is a real sense in which we, like scores of other clergy, had to "let go" when we left the Hague and made a fresh start in the Eastbourne area. Another aspect of letting go for clergy is their loss of any sense of power to influence events within the church. Whilst in the Hague, I was chairman of our Church Council, a member of the Archdeaconry Synod and a member of the Bishop's Council. I was able to speak up when these bodies met. Whether anyone actually listened is another matter! But I had a voice. In retirement clergy do not even have the right to a vote when their parish church holds its annual general meeting. I am reminded of a comment made some time ago by a friend of ours who was headmistress of a large school: "One minute I was the queen bee; the next minute I was nothing!" This is written, I would add, not to

307

bemoan my lot but merely to set down a few facts. After all, we are all called to walk in the steps of one who for our sakes emptied himself and came down to earth as a human being for the sake of humanity. He "let go" of the heights of heaven to descend to our earthy level.

And in so many ways this stripping away of one's former life and role in the church is quite liberating. One no longer has to attend a ceaseless round of meetings. One is free to spend more time with friends and family. There isn't the same pressure to meet deadlines. There is less haste, and more time to stop and listen to what God might want to be telling us to do with such retirement years as may remain to us.

In East Dean, we have indeed come to a pleasant place in which to live. The Dutch would describe it as "gezellig"! It is a jewel of a village nestling in the Sussex Downs. From our garden set into the slopes of a hillside, there is a fabulous view of acres of grassland dotted with sheep. As you gaze across this vista, your eyes are drawn down towards the Birling Gap and the sea beyond. East Dean is a friendly village, with its new Millennium Hall which has generated a host of activities ranging through a keep-fit club, the table tennis club, a weekly market, coffee mornings, lunch clubs as well as the occasional performances of the local amateur dramatic society. Our local church has proved very welcoming to us and we find that we also have a real part to play within that community.

So although retirement inevitably leads to a letting go of what is past, there can also be, in our experience, a taking up of new opportunities for friendship, and for service as well as for recreation. We can heartily recommend it!

Soon after our return to the U.K., Gill was elected to the Council of the Intercontinental Church Society, with whom we have served in our three chaplaincies in Europe. She keeps in touch with a number of chaplains through e-mail and we host a prayer lunch twice a year, when news is exchanged and prayer is offered for different aspects of the Society's work – not only for the permanent chaplaincies but also for the holiday campsite ministry which is a common feature of a number of French and Spanish holiday resorts. Serving on the Council keeps Gill in touch with what is going on and she takes a particular interest in the well-being of clergy wives. From time to time she sits on a panel which interviews candidates for vacant chaplaincy posts.

Our daughter, Carolyn Cooke, after her ordination service in Southwell Cathedral, 2002

We both feel that we owe much to the members of I.C.S. who have prayed for us over the years, aided by the quarterly prayer leaflet that is regularly produced. We also look back with thankfulness to the friendship and support which we received from a succession of chief executives of the Society, who would pay visits to chaplains on the job. Their visits, along with those we received from bishops in the Diocese of Europe, were regular reminders that we were not alone in our ministry but part of a much wider Christian family. Extra stimulus was provided through the annual I.C.S. chaplains' conferences that alternated between a conference centre in the South of England and a retreat or conference centre on the mainland of Europe. We looked forward to these as an opportunity to meet up with old friends and to find refreshment and renewal through worship and learning together. There was a time some years ago now when chaplains gave an annual verbal report to the conference and these tended to take up the majority of conference time (I remember at the very first of such conferences a chaplain giving us a detailed account of a surgical operation which had led to the amputation of his wife's big toe!). For at least ten years, however, such oral reports are, thankfully, a thing of the past and chaplains now present written reports which can be read at leisure. I.C.S. usually manages to include speakers with exceptional teaching gifts, which means that these annual events become opportunities for some in-service training for those who attend. So I am glad to be able to retain some link with the Society as well as with the Diocese of Europe. Bishop John Hind kindly made me an honorary Canon of Gibraltar Cathedral and on retirement I became a Canon Emeritus. It was only after we were relieved of chaplaincy responsibility that we had the opportunity, during the course of a holiday in Spain, to visit the Cathedral in Gibraltar, where I preached at the Sunday morning Eucharist and we enjoyed the hospitality of the Dean, Kenneth Robinson, and his wife.

We have had the pleasure of visiting all three of our former churches in Barcelona, Paris and the Hague and in each case it was a joy to find that the church had grown and developed since our day. In every instance, it has proved the truth of St Paul's words where he writes that one plants the seed, another waters, but it is God who causes the church to grow. We had a fascinating visit to St George's, Barcelona to provide cover whilst Peter Jordan and his family took a few days off after Christmas. It was great to be able to meet up with a few old friends that we had known back in the seventies and it was exciting to see the way the church had grown. Staying with John and Eleanor Copestake for a few nights, we heard of a new church plant that was coming to life in Madremania up the coast from Barcelona.

Another trip took us to the south of France for a few days' stay with Cameron and Moira Walker (he was formerly a chaplain in Ghent, Belgium). They drove us up through winding roads and hairpin bends to Andorra, where we all joined in the celebration of twenty-five years of church life stretching back to those early Christmas services when we were still based in Barcelona. There was a eucharist which was presided over by Bishop Henry Scriven, Suffragan Bishop in Europe, and I had the honour of preaching the sermon. Yet again we saw how God had given the increase.

Early in 2002 Derek Frank, the Chaplain of All Saints, Vevey, went on sabbatical leave from early January until just after Easter. We were invited to travel out to Switzerland to fill the gap. A small one-bedroomed apartment with views of Lake Geneva was put at our disposal by a charming Swiss lady. I drove the car across Europe, loaded up with our personal luggage, a computer, books and Michelle. Gill flew out to Geneva a few days later. It seemed strange at first to be acting chaplain again after a year in retirement but the whole church gave us a very warm welcome and people were most hospitable. We found the whole experience to be spiritually invigorating.

Vevey is a in a beautiful part of the world bordering on to Lake Geneva with awesome views of snow-capped mountains all around. It was a short walk to the church from where we were living and on the way down the hill we passed well tended gardens which, as winter turned to spring, were full of primroses and a variety of bulbs in bloom.

The headquarters of the big international company, Nestlé, is situated in Vevey and many members of the congregation were employed by this one company. Under Derek's leadership, major building works were carried out underneath the church, thus providing ample and attractive meeting rooms for Sunday Schools and church social events. Mums and toddlers groups met there during the week. Children's and youth work were both thriving under competent lay leadership. Home groups met on a regular basis, both in Vevey and in surrounding districts. Church people are prepared to travel considerable distances to find a church where they can feel at home within this Diocese. The Honorary Consul for the area was Sandra Darrah M.B.E. She was very active in the community as well as being a member of the church. Once a month she organised a lunch in the undercroft of the church and this was open to any in the community who wished to attend. In such ways the church became a magnet for expatriates living in the area. Derek moved to another post in Geneva soon after our departure and his place was taken by Clive Atkinson with his wife, Yvonne, and their two small children. Since then, we have heard nothing but good in respect of the continuing life of this chaplaincy.

Linked to All Saints', Vevey is a small church high up in the mountains at Chateau D'Oex. I went up there most Sunday afternoons by train, following what must surely be one of the world's most scenic rail routes. The service usually followed a 1662 prayer book service of Evening Prayer. Hymns were sung with the aid of tapes that were switched on at the appropriate moment. The congregation was normally quite small and mostly elderly, except at certain times of the year when tourists swelled the numbers.

The Easter weekend brought our stay in Vevey to an end. There was a family service on Good Friday morning followed a bit later by a quieter service of prayer and reflection. On Easter day there was a full church for a great service of celebration. Afterwards we were invited to a superb Easter lunch party which we had to leave early in order to catch the train up to Chateau D'Oex where a larger-than-usual congregation awaited our arrival. With a number of young people taking part, we used a common worship order for Holy communion and various musical instruments accompanied the singing of Easter hymns. Older members of the congregation, who were not used to this form of service, seemed pleased with it.

Next day it was time to pack-up and we were soon starting on the long drive for home. In these days of retirement, however, there is no need to rush and our return journey was punctuated by two night-stops on the way.

Other forays into the Diocese of Europe have included a weekend retreat in the Netherlands for the Archdeaconry of North West Europe, a church weekend away for the Chantilly Church and a quiet day for the Fontainebleau church council members. At the latter, we worked through the Growing Healthy Churches course which has been produced as the result of research into certain growing churches in a northern English diocese This apparently proved to be a useful exercise for the members of this council, helping them to think positively about their role as servants of their church. We were also able to provide three Sundays' cover for the chaplain of Fontainebleau and his family when they went away for their summer holiday. It has been heartening to see the enormous growth in the life of this church since those small beginnings when we used to travel down from Paris for the occasional service around one of the festivals. A further visit to this chaplaincy to provide cover when the chaplain is away is planned for the future and we have recently led another church weekend for one of the chaplaincies in the north of France, the theme of which was God on Monday. We certainly do not find retirement boring!

So although, like all vicars, we have had to do some "letting go", a new kind of life and part-time ministry has opened up for us for which we are profoundly grateful to God. We have indeed been richly blessed.

RECOMMENDED FURTHER READING

But God is not defeated by Samuel E. Kwyanga and Andrew C. Wheeler. This is a book which celebrates the first centenary of the Episcopal Church of the Sudan 1899 to 1999. This can be purchased through the Church Mission Society, Partnership House, 157 Waterloo Road, London SE1 8UU.

Don't bother to unpack by Dr Dorothy Lowe. This is an entertaining and absorbing account of five years (from 1959 to 1964) spent mainly in the southern Sudan by the author, her husband the Revd Canon John Lowe and their three children. This book is obtainable from Dorothy Lowe, 228 Cambridge Road, Great Shelford, Cambridge CB2 5JU.

Faith and New Frontiers by Brian Underwood. A story of planting and nurturing churches, 1823–2003. This is the third volume of a trilogy that tells the story of a mission and church planting through the Intercontinental Church Society, particulary during th years 1999 to 2002. It can be obtained through I.C.S., 1 Athena Drive, Tachbrook Park, Warwick, CV34 6NL.